Volunteers for the Gallows

ANATOMY OF A SHOW-TRIAL

BY *Sandor*

Béla Szász

Translated by

KATHLEEN SZÁSZ

1971

CHATTO & WINDUS

LONDON

Published by
Chatto & Windus Ltd
40 William IV Street
London, W.C.2

*

Clarke, Irwin & Co. Ltd
Toronto

Volunteers for the Gallows appeared under the
author's pen-name Vincent Savarius in Hungarian:
Minden kényszer nélkül, Nagy Imre Intézet, Brussels,
1963; in French: *Volontaires pour l'échafaud,* René
Julliard, Paris, 1963; in German: *Freiwillige für den
Galgen,* Verlag Wissenschaft und Politik, Cologne,
1963

ISBN 0 7011 1697 8

Printed in Great Britain by
Ebenezer Baylis & Son Ltd
The Trinity Press, Worcester, and London

*None of the persons mentioned in this book are
invented. All are, or were, alive.*

Contents

I

The T-Shaped Table

THE building housing the Budapest Ministry of Agriculture, erected some two hundred years ago in the days of the Empress Maria Theresa, was originally intended for a barracks. However, few people in Hungary recall this symbolic historical prelude, for, as long ago as our grandfathers' days those concerned with agriculture in Hungary were looking for guidance towards this same shabby and patched-up neo-classical building and it was from here they awaited–for many generations in vain–some solution of the country's agrarian problems.

A generous, even extravagant broad flight of stairs and a wide corridor lead to the rooms of the Minister, the Undersecretaries and department heads which are situated in the front of the building, while the side-wings and the back are criss-crossed with windowless, narrow passages sparingly illuminated by tiny electric bulbs. Even in 1949, the rooms still smelt of dusty bundles of files pushed back and forth for decades, and the ghosts of bureaucrats, dead for a hundred years, haunted the archives.

When at the end of 1948 I was appointed head of the press and information department, my room opened neither on to the elegant principal gallery nor the depressing criss-cross corridors. Journalists visiting me entered from the main staircase into a spacious hall.

On the 24th of May, 1949, about half-past nine in the morning, a few Hungarian and a number of foreign journalists assembled in this hall. We were about to visit a once world-famous Hungarian stud-farm. I had invited B. J. B. Groeneveld, the Dutch agricultural attaché, to join the excursion, for, being the only agricultural attaché in the entire Western diplomatic corps and thus having little opportunity to visit agricultural research centres or discuss matters in his particular field, he must have felt lonely and isolated in Budapest. He used to come and see me almost every week, asking questions with tact and circumspection, for even then he must have been far more keenly aware than I was of the precariousness of my situation.

Groeneveld and I were sitting in my room, in deep leather arm-chairs placed under the window, and he was asking me about the experiments of the Hungarian agronomist, Kurt Sedelmeyer, when the official whose job it was to organize our expedition announced that everything was ready for our departure. Accredited foreign correspondents usually came in their own cars but visiting journalists and Hungarian newspapermen travelled in the automobiles provided by the Ministry. I had accepted Groeneveld's invitation to share his car, although this was already frowned on as a form of fraternization with the West. I had taken my place at his side and the engine was running, when one of the clerks of the press department tapped the window and informed me that Géza Losonczy, the Undersecretary of State, had sent over two Argentinian journalists to see me. No-one apart from myself spoke Spanish in the department and the two journalists were leaving next day.

I had spent seven years in Argentina and was interested in what my Argentinian colleagues could tell me about Buenos Aires. So I went without hesitation. I apologized to Groeneveld for deserting him and promised to arrange for him to see Kurt Sedelmeyer. Then I got out of the car and returned to the building. The promise I gave to Groeneveld remains to this day unfulfilled.

I found the Argentinians standing in the hall, somewhat at a loss. I joined them and we waited for the lift. In Hungary, in office build-ings as well as in blocks of flats, the lift takes passengers up only; they have to descend on foot. This is how it came about that while the obsolete contraption was taking us up to the first floor, three ÁVH* investigators who had been looking for me during my brief absence from my office, were going down the stairs. A few minutes earlier, as Groeneveld and I had walked down to the car, these same three secret police had been crammed in the tiny lift, going up. This fact I reconstructed, in part, five or six hours later from hints dropped by the investigators, in part five or six years later from the recollections of my former secretary.

One of the ÁVH men introduced himself to my secretary as a journalist; she told him that my party and I would be back about

* ÁVH — Államvedelmi Hatóság: State Security Authority, the Hungar-ian political police.

2

three o'clock in the afternoon. She did not mention the matter to me when I returned a few minutes later to my office, as she thought it completely unimportant. She did not, of course, know that in the morning I had had a call asking me to be at Party Headquarters at about two thirty, as there were a few things to discuss before the 3 o'clock meeting. I had a long session with the Argentinians, then, a few minutes before half-past two, I set out towards the nearby Party Headquarters. At the same time, one of the three ÁVH men showed up again at my office, asking for me.

In 1945, the Hungarian Communist Party had appropriated for its offices the building of No. 17, Akadémia Street. Soon, the neighbouring block of flats was requisitioned. And then it swallowed up several more blocks, but its appetite was still unsatisfied; it removed more and more families from their flats and constantly shifted and re-built its offices. Instead of permanent revolution, it lived in a fever of permanent removal. In May, 1949, the Rural Propaganda department occupied a newly-furnished, attractive suite of rooms at Party Headquarters.

The assistant head of the department was called János Kukucska. He had never changed his quaint Slovak peasant name–it means Peeping John–believing, probably, that being the possessor of a name that everyone remembered at first hearing must benefit his career. This farmhand turned Party official emphasized his peasant origin by wearing high boots and a lambskin cap, although neither his urban way of living nor the climate of the capital warranted this outfit. In addition to his peasant background and quick mind, this smiling young man was assured of a vertiginous career by his capacity to agree readily and enthusiastically with the views of his superiors, even when they conflicted with his own experience and the obvious facts.

We sat facing each other across his desk. But no sooner had we begun talking than we were interrupted by the ringing of the telephone. He lifted the receiver and handed it to me:

'Comrade Keresztes's secretary is asking for you.'

Mihály Keresztes, Communist Undersecretary of Agriculture, really ran the Hungarian agricultural administration; István Csala, the Smallholder Party Minister of Agriculture, was a mere figurehead and was regarded as such by all officials in the Ministry. Csala attended receptions, driven in a huge automobile, and articles signed with his name appeared in the newspapers–articles that he had perhaps not even read–but in the Ministry his voice carried no more weight than that of the doorman. Although the multi-party system

3

had not yet been liquidated, the Ministry was already controlled by the Communist Party through Mihály Keresztes.

As Keresztes was leaving that day for the Soviet Union with a peasant delegation, it seemed reasonable that he should have remembered something that had to be taken care of at the last moment. However, his secretary did not connect me with him, but merely informed me that the Peasant Party member of parliament, Szücs, the other leader of the delegation, was in conference in Keresztes's room and wished to see me before his departure. 'All right,' I replied, 'I shall be back at the Ministry immediately the meeting at Party Headquarters is over.'

Two minutes later the telephone rang again.

'It's for you again.' Kukucska was annoyed. 'Tell them,' he added, 'that if it's so urgent, Szücs can come here and call you out of the meeting. We are going to begin in a minute.'

I repeated Kukucska's words to Keresztes's secretary and replaced the receiver. A minute later the telephone rang yet again. This time I answered it myself.

A male voice I had never heard before said, 'This is Szücs,' adding that he absolutely must see me at once to hand over some documents, but as he was waiting for important telephone calls in the Undersecretary's room, he could not leave. He would be obliged if I would come over for a few minutes. If I had no car at my disposal he would send his to fetch me. 'Don't be ridiculous,' I replied, 'I can walk a hundred and fifty yards. I'll come right away.'

'You can start the conference without me,' I told Kukucska, 'I'll be back in about fifteen minutes.'

This was the second promise I made that day and never kept. I was in such a hurry that I left not only my brief-case but also my raincoat in the Party official's room, despite the fact that the mild western wind had brought on a steady drizzle. The first week of May had held out a prospect of early summer but now, at the end of the month, I could have done with an overcoat.

I turned up the collar of my jacket and crossed the road with quick steps. I looked neither to the right nor to the left, even less behind me, and thus did not observe the thin, bespectacled fellow shadowing me. As soon as I reached the gallery leading to Keresztes's room, two men barred my way. One was short, greying, with regular features and a military bearing, the other tall, flabby and overfed with a strikingly brutal face.

4

They asked my name. I told them–Béla Szász. Then the grey-haired man presented his credentials.

'State Security,' he whispered stressing each syllable. 'Come with us, please.'

'What for?' I asked, surprised. 'Why don't you telephone if you want something from me?'

'It is a very urgent matter,' the younger of the two replied, putting his hand in his pocket and keeping it there.

It was obvious that protest would be useless and though I racked my brains in vain for an explanation, I went along with the two detectives, far from guessing that I was no longer even relatively free, for no Communist functionary had been arrested in Hungary since 1945. When old crimes were discovered or some act of corruption came to light, the case was first investigated by the Party's Control Committee, the guilty member was expelled, and only then did police procedure follow.

We started down the stairs. This time the ÁVH men had not missed me. The grey-haired man headed the procession, I followed and behind me, as rear-guard, the brutish-looking young man. Some people we passed smiled at me in greeting; it did not occur to any of them that here was a man who had reached the cross-roads of his life and was on his way towards exploring a hazy landscape that, though he didn't know it, had long been waiting his coming.

We left the building by the main entrance, then turned into a side street where a medium-sized car was waiting. Beside it stood the thin, bespectacled man. He opened the rear door without a word. My two companions made me sit between them; we were rather cramped. The bespectacled one took his place next to the driver.

'Where are we going?' I asked.

'To Headquarters,' the grey-haired detective replied and began a conversation with complete ease, as if we were sitting in a drawing-room. He told me we had once met at a reception where I was talking to someone about mediaeval Spanish plays. Did I remember? I did not. My cool reply did not deter him, he went on talking, smiling, as if we were the best of friends.

The car drew up at the entrance to 60, Andrássy Street. Before 1945, this building had been the headquarters of the Arrow-Cross Party, the fortress of Hungarian fascism. In 1945 it had been occupied by the political police and gradually, just like Party Head-quarters, it had swallowed up the neighbouring buildings, then the entire block and finally all the tenants were evicted from the side-streets. The entrances and street-corners were guarded by uniformed security men with tommy-guns, and at the Andrássy Street entrance to ÁVH Headquarters the citizens of the people's democracy were kept at a distance by heavy iron chains slung between squat, concrete posts. From the tops of the small posts and from the window-sills of the Andrássy Street façade, red geraniums nodded their flaming heads towards the tommy-guns.

The detectives showed their credentials, then took me up on foot to the first floor. From the main corridor we turned into a panelled lobby hung with mirrors and decorated with the sort of carvings that the South-East European *nouveau riche* filled his hall with at the turn of the century.

'We are going to see Comrade Péter,' the bespectacled man said almost kindly, and he opened a door.

Lieutenant-General Gábor Péter was Head of the political police. He and I had met several times, mainly at official receptions. Like most militants of the former underground Communist movement, we used the familiar second person singular when talking to each other. Péter's long, narrow waiting-room was furnished with a desk and two drawing-room suites. The grey-haired investigator pointed to a deep, purple armchair:

'Please sit down . . .'

I sat down.

'I should like to call the Ministry,' I said, 'for I was told that Deputy Szücs is waiting for me in the Undersecretary's room.'

I put no stress on the words 'I was told', for I was not yet convinced that it was the ÁVH-men who had telephoned me in Szücs's name. The three men exchanged glances. 'I'll ring them right away,' the flabby young man offered, 'and tell them you'll be there in about half an hour.'

He opened the double padded door of his chief's room and disappeared behind it. I lit a cigarette but did not offer one to my companions. Besides us there was only an obviously bored, blond youth in the waiting-room. His epaulettes showed him to be a lieutenant. He rested his elbows on his desk and fiddled with the telephone. Five or six minutes went by, then the detective returned.

'Let's go,' he told his colleagues. Then he turned to me, 'I called the Ministry,' he said reassuringly.

We left the building. A powerful American Buick was waiting at the door. Only after we had taken our places in the car did I notice that all the windows, including the back-window and that separating the driver from the passengers, were shrouded from the outside world by black curtains. Again they made me sit between the grey-haired man and the brutal-faced detective and when, with a sudden jerk, the car sprang into motion, the grey-haired one said:

'We shall now blindfold you.'

'Do we have to play cops and robbers?' I asked, vexed.

'You ought to be glad,' the detective replied, reaching for a folded napkin obviously prepared in advance, 'for if we blindfold you, there's at least a chance that you may come back . . .'

This was the first, though still mild and veiled, threat; until now they had treated me with awkward politeness, a clumsy pretence of friendliness, as if it were important to them that I should have no reason to complain of their treatment of me. But even now, the detective's words appeared to me a childishly romantic taunt rather than a prophecy heralding real dangers. I made no reply but lit another cigarette. I deduced from various sounds that the car crossed a bridge over the Danube, then took the steep road up one of the Buda mountains, at such speed that the tyres squealed at every turn and I bumped now against one, now against the other of my neighbours.

We raced on for about half an hour but now none of us spoke. Finally we must have turned into a side-road for the motor slowed down and soon afterwards we stopped. The front door of the car opened and slammed. I heard the grating of a metal gate, then we were rolling over gravel, there was a soft thud, and then the hum of the motor grew louder indicating that we had driven into a garage. Although the driver switched off the engine, neither of my companions made any move to get out. There was a heavy, dull silence. Only my sense of smell found something to report: a pervading odour of petrol and oil. I could see nothing through the bandage but presumably a light-signal must have flashed for not only my two neighbours but also the detective in front sprang simultaneously into action.

They helped me out of the car, one took my right arm, one my left, and we started down a flight of stairs. But as there was not room for the three of us on the narrow stairs, and as the rhythm of our steps did not coincide, we groped, now pushing and pulling, now crowding in on one another in an oblique formation, deeper and deeper down. When we reached the bottom, the men let go of my arm. An iron door banged shut behind me and the bandage was ripped roughly from my eyes.

Five or six savage-looking men surrounded me.

'Traitor!' a short, round-faced man hissed in my face.

'You rat!' another whispered almost inaudibly, baring his teeth.

What surprised me was that the faces of these men appeared not so much angry as gloomy and worried. I felt as if I were surrounded by a bunch of outwardly adult but mentally immature creatures, about to commit a murder from fear.

'Have you searched him?' one of them asked. 'Is he armed?' Then he turned to me with a command:

'Strip to your shirt and pants.'

They explored even the hem of my underclothes, took away all my possessions, my wallet, fountain-pen, cigarettes, lighter, wrist-watch, belt, shoe-laces; I was allowed to keep only my handkerchief. I was standing with my back to the iron door through which we had entered. To the left were three smaller iron doors and, opposite, the passage grew wider. As soon as I was dressed again they unlocked the first small iron door and pushed me in.

I found myself in a cell in which I could not stand upright because of the low, vaulted roof. The cell was approximately six feet long and two and a half feet wide; attached to the right wall by iron brackets was a one and a half inch thick board on which lay a folded horse-blanket. A man of medium height could only have sat hunched up on the bunk, which was fitted waist-high to the wall; even if he pressed his chin to his chest his head would hit the cellar roof.

The walls and the iron door were constantly covered with fat drops of water which every so often swelled into rivulets and set out on their suicidal course along the path laid down by their predecessors. The air was palpably humid and the blanket had absorbed so much of the damp that it felt like a sponge fished out of a bathtub. A naked bulb glowed in a square recess over the iron door but it only irritated the eye without dispelling the darkness of the cell.

While I was taking stock of my surroundings my gaolers peeped in several times through the Judas-hole, but after a brief five or six minutes the key turned in the lock and I found myself once more in the passage. I was searched again. One of the detectives asked his companions whether they were certain I had no weapon hidden on me, then two of them led the way, two placed themselves on my right and left, and one walked behind me jabbing his gun into my backbone and ordering me to put my hands on the nape of my neck. In this way our little group advanced towards the end of the passage. Then we mounted a flight of concrete steps to the ground floor and thence, up wooden stairs, to the first floor.

Here the staircase widened. Again, the windows were hung with black curtains shutting out daylight and the outside world. Above a double door, coloured bulbs glowed. They must have signalled 'pass', for the young detective entered without knocking. A moment later he returned and nodded to the others. The door opened wide to admit me.

I found myself in an enormous room. Its numerous windows were draped in black. Opposite the double door they had pushed together two long narrow refectory tables in the shape of a capital T. The semi-circular, black-curtained window recess behind the upper, horizontal line of the T created a theatrical effect and optically lengthened the stem of the T extending towards the entrance.

My attendants made me stand at the bottom of the T, then withdrew. Far away, behind the top stroke of the T sat five men, some in uniform, some in civilian clothes. In the centre was Gábor Péter, head of the secret political police. Of the other four I knew only one, Colonel Ernö Szücs, Péter's deputy. Péter looked at me grimly and asked:

'Which espionage organization have you been working for?'

'Now really . . .' I replied breaking into laughter, partly because these dignitaries enthroned behind the T-shaped table looked ludicrous enough, partly because it didn't even occur to me to take Péter's question seriously and therefore, I drew the only possible conclusion, namely that I was the victim of some childish prank, that they were playing a game, making a fool of me. I was not concerned that Péter had dropped the familiar second person singular and addressed me as though I were a stranger: perhaps that was part of the joke too. When I replied, I addressed him by his first name.

'Don't make me laugh, Gábor . . .'

'We'll see who has the last laugh,' Gábor Péter shouted jumping up from his chair, 'when we come to your contemptible doings in South America.' Then he sat down again, glaring at me.

'Who is Wagner?' he asked, smiling ironically with the air of one dealing a death blow to his enemy.

'Wagner?' I mused, recalling first the music teacher of my school days, then an old acquaintance, a historian, deported by the Nazis. Neither could be the Wagner in whom Péter seemed interested. Then suddenly it came to me:

'Do you mean the Hungarian consul in Bratislava?' I asked. 'I know him only superficially . . .'

Péter waved his hand and, as if this had been a cue, the others sitting at the head of the table broke into a chorus of synthetic police-laughter.

'No, that isn't the Wagner I am thinking of,' Péter said with a drawl. 'I am thinking of the Wagner from whom you brought Szönyi an illegal message with a password!'

'Tibor Szönyi!' I exclaimed, surprised because, as far as I knew, Szönyi was still head of the Communist Party's cadres department, a post carrying at least ministerial rank in the state administration, as it was the cadres department that suggested, or even decided on its own authority, to what posts Communist Party-members should be appointed in the state administration, the Party, the army, or the so-called mass-organizations. When I was transferred from the Foreign Ministry to the Ministry of Agriculture, it had been Tibor Szönyi and his assistant, András Szalai, who informed me of the decision and discussed it with me. Szönyi had explained to me, in a dull party-jargon hardly in keeping with his erudition and intellect, why, though I knew next to nothing about agrarian problems, it was important that I should assume the direction of the press depart- ment of the Ministry of Agriculture instead of remaining at the Foreign Ministry. Had someone really brought this cold, rigid party functionary an 'illegal' message? Even supposing this someone was I, why should we have used a password as we did in the underground Communist movement, when contact had to be established between two party members or fellow-travellers who did not know each other? I repeated my train of thought aloud, but Péter interrupted impatiently:

'You'd better tell us the password.'

'I know of no password.'

'Then let me tell you what it was. It was 'Wagner notifies Péter. And what was the message?'

'I don't know anything about a password or a message.'

'Fetch Szönyi,' Gábor Péter ordered.

Any development of this farce would have surprised me less than Szönyi's appearance. Yet he appeared. Seconds later, there stood on my right, also at the foot of the T, the head of the Communist Party's cadres department, in a somewhat crumpled grey suit and a blue jersey sports shirt without a tie.

'Did this man bring you a message?'

'Yes, he did' Szönyi nodded, taking care not to look at me.

'One with a password?'

'Yes. One with a password.'

'What was the password? Tell him to his face!'

Szönyi, though he turned his face towards me, avoided my eyes.

'Wagner notifies Péter,' he said.

'And when did I give you that message?'

Szönyi looked up in perplexity, his gaze crept up from my shoes to my face, then slid away above my head. He stared into the air as if he were thinking, then said slowly, in a low voice:

'Last year, on the 4th of May.'

'And where did I give it to you?'

'In my office,' Szönyi replied, this time without hesitation.

'Well,' I said, relieved, 'this makes matters infinitely more simple. I went to see Szönyi quite a few times, so I know that his office keeps a record of every incoming telephone call, whether Szönyi takes it or not, and of every visitor, whether he is received by Szönyi or passed on to one of his subordinates. This record will show whether or not I saw Szönyi on the 4th of May last year. And there is something else too! As I had no permanent pass, I would have had to ask for an entrance slip at the gate. If I entered Party Headquarters at that period there must be a record of it. Unless I had business there, I didn't go to Party Headquarters for months at a time, so it should take you only a few minutes to find out that Szönyi is not telling the truth.'

'Do you maintain your statement?' Péter turned to Szönyi.

'I do.'

'And you too?' he asked me.

'Naturally.'

'In that case,' Gábor Péter shrugged impatiently, 'give them both a soling.'

Soling, an expression borrowed from the shoemaking industry, was already used in the vocabulary of the pre-war Hungarian police to describe an ancient but piously preserved mode of interrogation. The bare soles of the suspected person were beaten, first with a cane, later with a rubber truncheon, until he declared himself ready to confess. Szönyi presumably knew from experience what *soling* meant, for at Gábor Péter's words his features twisted into a plaintive begging expression, he raised his shoulders and held out his hands, palms upward, towards Péter in a gesture of helplessness, but a guard grasped his arm and led him out. This was my last meeting with the former head of the cadres department. Later, in one of the cells of the Markó Street prison, I discovered traces of his presence. He had scratched his name into the ancient layer of whitewash, connecting it skilfully, in a wreath of vines, with the words, 'Little Flower'; next to it he had kept a diary which showed that his arrest had taken place one week before mine. By the time I came across Szönyi's handwriting, my own bouquet of recollections and the words 'Little Flower' had reconciled me to him; but for the present I was still resentful, I was still angry with him, rather than the secret police, because I felt he was deliberately fooling Gábor Péter and his men and was accusing me falsely, perhaps to protect someone else.

I was still convinced of this when I entered the small room where a powerfully built man was waiting for me. Later I had occasion to see him repeatedly and from information gathered and remarks dropped, I discovered that his name was Detective Inspector Gyula Prinz, that once upon a time he had been a detective in Horthy's criminal police, but having supported the rather weak Hungarian resistance movement he was, after 1945, rewarded by being promoted detective-inspector in the ÁVH. Prinz, with the rubber truncheon swinging from his wrist, pointed almost apologetically, almost mildly, to the floor:

'Take off your shoes, please, and lie down on your stomach.'

We were alone in the room. Prinz muttered something and shrugged his shoulders with embarrassment. Perhaps it was his irresoluteness that disarmed me. After all, I thought, he's only obeying an order and I complied readily. Prinz hit the soles of my feet ten blows each with his truncheon. I took hold of myself so as not to groan but I think that if I bore this first *soling* more easily than the subsequent ones it was not merely because the truncheon came down on healthy, still unbroken skin, still uninjured tissues, but also because Prinz swung the truncheon from at most shoulder height, not in a three-quarter arc, like the experts I encountered later.

I was led back into the big room and again made to stand at the foot of the T.

'Well, do you admit it now?' Péter asked sneeringly.

'Szönyi is lying,' I replied, 'and you can prove it in half an hour if you examine the entrance slips at Party Headquarters and the diary of Szönyi's secretary . . .'

'I didn't ask you for advice. You had better realize that you can count on nobody's support, nobody's protection here. You understand? The Party has delivered you into our hands. Will you admit that you brought Szönyi an illegal message?'

'How can I admit it . . .'

'Give him some more of the same,' Péter shouted, pointing at the door.

This time I was taken to another room where I found myself surrounded by five or six men. I believe I never told anyone during my long imprisonment something that, at the time, seemed absolutely natural to me, namely, that when one of the detectives hit me in the face, I returned the blow with equal force. A couple of years later my action appeared improbable to me: more than that, as if invented by myself.

I was obeying some ancient impulse, maybe the bidding of my

upbringing, or perhaps I was living up to the code of honour prevalent in the provincial environment of my youth, though intellectually I regarded these interpretations of honour as comically obsolete and unrealistic. According to the standards of that code my first experience of the bastinado almost amounted to a voluntarily undergone test, but the first blow in the face was so obvious a humiliation that retaliation was instinctive, regardless of the consequences.

It did not take the five or six men long to overpower me with their fists, kicks and blows with truncheon and gun-butt. Then they stamped on me, sat astride my back, bent back my legs and held them while one of their colleagues beat my soles, swinging his truncheon through three-quarters of a circle. When I was led back to the big room I was unable to open my right eye and my face as well as my clothes bore witness to what had happened in the next room.

'What did you do to him?' Péter asked his men.

'He fell,' a rough voice behind me replied, drawing out and deepening the vowels so as to lend the answer, with its surburban overtones, a shade of vacuity.

The upper group at the T-shaped table rewarded this wit with hooting laughter, then Péter looked at me mockingly:

'Will you admit it now?'

'Not even if you put me through this treatment a hundred times. Szönyi is lying and you can easily prove it.'

'Take him away,' the head of the secret police commanded and my guards led me back, pushing and pulling me down the darkened staircase to the cellar, where they flung me into the cell.

While I was pacing to and fro in the little cell, or trying to squat on the bunk with my head between my shoulders, then lie on it with knees bent, two ÁVH squad-cars stopped in front of No. 11, Üllöi Street, the large block of flats where I lived. At a barked command, troops armed with rifles and tommy-guns jumped out. One group, so the inhabitants of the flats told me later, spread out in open formation, then cautiously, hugging the wall, worked their way up to my flat on the fifth floor. Armed troops occupied the landings, the back-stairs and, with an encircling manoeuvre, blocked the exits. Plain-clothes security men, accompanied by uniformed police with tommy-guns, opened my flat, and the search began.

What was the purpose of all this? When the squad-cars arrived I had been in the hands of the ÁVH for two solid hours. I think the principal aim was not to intimidate the civilian population, but to create tension in the ÁVH organisation and fill both officers and men with the sense of an immediate threat to their safety, if not their lives.

No ÁVH man could ever have supposed that his superiors would engage in such a large-scale operation as this raid on my flat in Üllöi Street, were it not to trap some utterly determined and unscrupulous conspirator.

After their military exercise they locked my rooms, then, for almost three months, two or three plain-clothes men visited the flat every day. The neighbours closely observed the ideological and practical results of these visits in the ÁVH's interpretation of the notion of private property; they always arrived with conspicuously flat briefcases and departed with equally conspicuously bulging ones. Key-hole inspection, systematically maintained by the neighbours in the absence of the ÁHV, noted the gradual disappearance of important pieces of criminal evidence, such as my table-lighter, candlesticks, embroidered cloths and such-like items.

About a hundred days later, the ÁVH must have grown tired of this piece-meal looting. Lorries arrived and took away those articles that wouldn't fit into briefcases: my furniture, pictures, carpets, books. They dismantled even the shutters in my little son's room and left nothing in mine except a small heap of rubbish, among it, a few photographs of my child.

All this I learned, of course, only half a decade later. At the time I was busy turning over in my mind every possible explanation of Szönyi's reasons for throwing such grave suspicion on me. It did not even occur to me that it might not have been Szönyi's accusations that compelled the ÁVH to act but, on the contrary, that ÁVH treatment might have compelled Szönyi to bear false witness.

Marking time in the cellar I still hoped that Gábor Péter would examine the diary of the cadres department's secretariat and the entrance slips issued by Party Headquarters, and if this part of Szönyi's statement proved untrue–for I had not visited the cadres department or even Party Headquarters on the 4th of May–Péter would give little credence to the second part of the statement, namely, that on that fictitious visit I had brought Szönyi an illegal message. However, the demeanour of the detectives when, long hours later, they at last opened the door of the oppressively airless cell, gave no hint of any such official doubts.

Again my four attendants led me towards the staircase. We passed the double door on the first floor, left the second floor behind, then climbed on up the narrowing staircase between black-curtained windows. To the right, in a recess, I noticed an iron door which, I suspected with a shudder of unreasoning fear, opened straight into the void. But we passed it, and half a storey higher, they pushed me

14

into a six-sided room. Each wall of the room, except the one into which the door had been built, consisted of a huge, flat, oblong window, blind and dead-black like its fellows on the staircase. Yet the circle of windows indicated that we were in a tower-room from where a heart-warming view must open on the mountains of Buda and perhaps even the town below.

The detectives silently surrounded me. Then, one struck me across the back with his rubber truncheon. As if this were a sign, all fell upon me, threw me on the floor, stamped on me, kicked me all over my body. They did not aim at the sensitive, delicate spots with the cold, calculated expertise of professional batterers and torturers, with the sadism of those enjoying their craft, like many of my future interrogators, but acted rather like a party of drunks, intoxicated with rage. They hurled abuse at me and belaboured me ceaselessly with their truncheons. Not for a moment did their fury appear simulated. They considered it natural that I should try to defend myself and catch hold of one or other of the raised truncheons. So it was that at times we were all rolling around on the floor, arms, legs intertwined, then they would pull me to my feet and go on with their job until, at last, the grey-haired man threw himself into the only armchair in the tower-room and asked me, panting and wheezing:

'What was the message Wagner sent Péter?'

'Szönyi is lying. There was no message.'

Swinging the truncheon between his knees like the pendulum of a clock and pretending not to have heard my reply, the detective repeated his question with added emphasis:

'What was the message Wagner sent Péter?'

Then the voice of the young, fat one, cut in like a whip:

'When did you join the American secret service?'

The next question came in a screaming chorus:

'Who hired you?'

My denials brought them on me in full force; questioning alternated with attack, till finally they hurled me to the floor and concentrated their attention on my soles. Somehow I succeeded in shaking them off, upon which they rolled me into the carpet, with the help of a fifth man who had, until then, stood by the wall as a mere spectator. One knelt on the back of my neck, one sat astride my neck, and two raised the soles of my feet under the swinging truncheon. After twice twenty-five blows they unrolled the carpet and kicking, pushing, hitting the nape of my neck, compelled me to run in circles round the room. While I ran they kept firing the same questions at me, endlessly. In the meantime the fifth man had slunk from the room, but by the time the others had again rolled me into the carpet he returned with a large spoon full of salt. They prised apart my clenched teeth with a pocket knife and pushed the salt into my mouth, then concentrated on my feet again. Only now they no longer hit out with the energy-squandering passion of drunks, but used their muscles and truncheons with systematic economy. They beat my soles, my kidneys and the more sensitive parts of my body with expert skill.

The fifth man disappeared once more but I was to meet him again several times at this secret ÁVH villa. His function, it seemed, was that of caretaker and general help. He opened doors, catered for his superiors and stood guard when a prisoner was taken to the lavatory. This middle-aged, pot-bellied man reappeared later in our prison-life. His name was István Lehota. But just now his withdrawal did not mark the end of my first day, we had merely reached half-time in our evening gymnastics.

The ÁVH did not add to the three original questions—what was Wagner's message, when did I join the American secret service, and who recruited me—but they embellished them with far from complimentary adjectives, describing Wagner, myself, and particularly my female ancestry, with conspicuously poor imagination. Still, when one or another enriched the vocabulary with a new obscenity, the others howled it after him with enthusiasm. Nor did the methods of criminal investigation vary. They rolled me twice more into the carpet, to tickle my soles, as they said, in order to improve my memory, but finally, assuring me that I could look forward to much more convincing methods of memory-improvement, they led me down from the tower-room. Dawn was breaking. Through the open door of the lavatory the reflected light of a grey morning fell on the cellar steps.

A short man with a long nose and a trimmed moustache, wearing a sort of ski-cap and a fur-lined coat, stood idly before the cellar door. It was he who locked the cell door after me and from then on his sad, dark eyes appeared every four or five minutes at the Judas-hole. He watched me inspecting my swollen, black-and-blue soles and trying to find some way of settling down on the bunk so that the hard, narrow board should not intensify the pain. Half an hour later he opened the door.

'Do you want some water?'

I did. I raised myself with difficulty to a sitting position. My tongue and palate were still burning from the salt forced between my teeth. I swallowed two mouthfuls. The water tasted salty. I spat it out.

'What's the matter?' the man asked.

'It's salt.'

'You don't imagine I'd give you salt water to drink, do you?' he asked, offended.

He must have felt that I was repaying his almost illegal lenience with ingratitude. Mangled as I was and locked in a damp underground cell, I was still keenly aware of how comic was the parallel between his resentment and mine; I must have smiled, for the long-nosed one asked me in a harsh but low voice:

'Is there anything else you want?'

I asked him if he could leave the lid of the peep-hole open. It was only through this pocket-watch-sized round hole that a little of the musty cellar-air penetrated into the vapour-filled cell. The man shook his head disapprovingly as if I had made an utterly unreasonable request. All the same, he left the lid of the spy-hole open for a considerable time.

Thus, the first day of my long imprisonment ended, one might say, with honours even and, therefore, reassuringly; for not only had I been accused, but I too had accused, even unwittingly shocked someone, and thus identical emotions had created a kind of kinship between myself and another human being. For a long time to come no more such conversations giving rise to arbitrary – and perhaps self-deluding – imaginings were to fall to my lot.

2

To Sleep or Not to Sleep

THE investigators proved to be conservative. They remained true to their truncheons all through the second day. If this time they concentrated on my kidneys, they did not neglect the soles of my feet, for which purpose they repeatedly resorted to the carpet-rolling process. There were six or seven of them taking turns in such a way that there were always four in the room with me.

They must have realized that my purple-blue, swollen soles, as well as the other parts of my body that had been belaboured with the truncheons were, in their maimed condition, incomparably more sensitive than on the first day. One even hinted at this by declaring that increased exertion was superfluous as the truncheon was becoming more and more effective and the pain I suffered more and more unbearable, so that it could be only a question of time, a short time at that, before I would give in and confess to anything including multiple homicide.

I took these allusions to be simply rhetoric; it seemed to me that Szönyi's accusations must really have convinced the investigators that they had caught a spy. However, it seemed somewhat suspicious, even bewildering, that they made no attempt to check even the most easily ascertainable evidence in Szönyi's accusation, that they took no steps to find out whether I had indeed been to see Szönyi or entered Party Headquarters at all at the time in question.

I believed, like hundreds of others, that I was the victim of a 'fatal' error and it never entered my head to admit even part of the false accusation in order to gain temporary, or perhaps even permanent respite from physical torment.

It must have been on the night following the second day that, rolled in the carpet, I at last lost consciousness. By the time I came to, the room was crowded with people, some of whom I knew, some I had never met. Among those I knew, apart from my usual interlocutors, were Dr. Bálint, Chief Physician of the ÁVH, and Colonel Ernö Szücs, Péter's deputy. Dr. Bálint must have given me an injection; soon after I regained consciousness, he disappeared, but Szücs remained sitting on the arm of the easy-chair watching me make vain attempts to rise, only to fall back, dizzy, on the floor. Then he remarked that he, too, had had his soles beaten bloody by the Fascists more than once.

I replied in a low voice that, even according to the Colonel then, there were no essential differences between the present methods and those applied by the Fascists. One of my interrogators raised his truncheon to hit me but Szücs held him back. He stood up, gazed at me for a long time, then asked:

'Do you know Ferenc Vági?'

'I've met Ferenc Vági, the Head of the press department of the Prime Minister's office. Is he the one you mean?'

Szücs nodded, then added:

'I mean him. Only he is no longer press department head, either of the Prime Minister's office or anywhere else because we've arrested him. Do you know Földi, Dobó, Dálmán, Demeter?' The Colonel listed a few more names, looked at me expectantly and said, 'Because we've arrested them too.'

As I learned later, in prison, all the persons mentioned by Szücs had been Hungarian exiles in Switzerland during the Second World War, where, under Szönyi's leadership, they had formed an anti-Hitler group. Most of them I had never met but those I had come across, men like Vági and Kálmán, had appeared to me to be dyed-in-the-wool communists!

Once, when I was still at the Foreign Ministry, I discussed with Vági how many copies of Western newspapers should be allowed to enter the country. At the time, the régime was still boasting that in the streets of Budapest you could buy *The Times* as well as *L'Humanité*, *Le Figaro* as well as the *Daily Worker*, and that not only *L' Unitá* was available but also the *New York Times* and the *Zürcher Zeitung*. Vági had showed every inclination to whittle down the number of copies available to the public to practically nil.

Nor were my recollections of a discussion I had with Kálmán more agreeable. He and I had clashed at a meeting of the ideological seminar-instructors. Rather ironically, perhaps, I had criticized one of the speakers who, with noble simplicity and relentless consistency, kept calling the United States 'Fascist'. I spoke against the constantly multiplying over-simplifications and conceptual mystifications of Party jargon. Well, András Kálmán hastened to the defence of the speaker against my 'unjustified irony', and what is more, went on to express his approval of the terminology that branded the United States as fascist. A few weeks after this event I was informed by the Party group of the Foreign Ministry that I could not be allowed to take part in instructor seminars because, according to the official party organ my views betrayed Trotskyite deviations. Two or three months later, without my having done anything about it, the prohibition was withdrawn.

All this flashed through my mind at the mention of Kálmán's name, and the charge of Trotskyite deviation, which less than a year ago had made me smile, now filled me with unpleasant foreboding. Yet, while sitting on the floor I sought Ernö Szücs's tiny, hardly discoverable eyes in his beefy, red, face, the arrest of these two blinkered Communists seemed to me even more mysterious than my own. Szücs must have misunderstood my glance, or pretended to misunderstand it, for he said:

'So you see, we've rounded up the whole gang. It surprises you, doesn't it? Do you still think it is worth while standing out? Why don't you tell me what kind of letter you brought Szönyi from Wagner?'

My face must have assumed a pretty dumb expression for even the surly Szücs laughed out loud:

'All right,' he said in an almost fatherly tone, 'let's leave it at that for the moment. But you'd better give this matter of the letter some thought.'

Then he drew one of the ÁVH men aside and gave him instructions in a low voice.

Soon two investigators took me under the arms, lifted me from the floor and half-carried me down to the cellar. Later, when Lehota opened the door to hand me a plate of cold, slimy, poppy-seed noodles, I realized that I hadn't eaten since my arrest. Last night they had given me no supper, and today no breakfast, no lunch and no dinner. Yet I returned, almost untouched, the plate on which the noodles, sparingly bestrewn with poppy-seed, lay stiff like worms in *rigor mortis*. Instead of eating, I reflected that in the meantime Szönyi must have supplemented and filled out his story, for Szücs was already demanding from me an account of a fictitious letter.

The discouraging idea that the ÁVH men were giving full credit to Szönyi's fabrication matured into conviction during the promptly resumed hours of manhandling which they carried on till dawn. Again my interrogators behaved like belligerent drunks rather than inquisitors conscientiously plying their trade. They surrounded me in a tight circle in the tower room and assault followed assault like waves breaking on the shore. In the rather infrequent pauses between showers of blows and screamed curses they enquired only about Wagner's letter and seemed to take it as proven that I had been the connecting link between Tibor Szönyi and the mysterious Wagner. From first to last it was obvious that these primitive men, beside themselves with rage, were not shamming–their ingenuity would hardly have run to such good acting–they were firmly convinced that they were dealing with a dangerous, stubborn spy, a determined enemy of the State, who refused to confess out of unwillingness to betray his contact line.

As, to my mind, Szönyi's false accusation largely explained the behaviour of the ÁVH men–officers and investigators alike–I still sought no secret purpose behind the application of means intended to break me physically but believed it was for the sole purpose of uncovering a truly existing espionage ring. In the short pauses between the concentrated attacks I confined myself to reiterating again and again that Szönyi was not telling the truth. I went on repeating this until dawn broke. Then my investigators, seeing that I was unable to leave the tower-room under my own propulsion, dragged me down to the cellar.

A few hours later they handed in some luke-warm slop resembling tea and a thin slice of bread, then, towards noon, they fetched me from my cell. Again I was surrounded by five or six hard-faced men. Lehota hit me in the back, then bandaged my eyes with a damp towel. The iron door of the cellar was flung open and reaching under my arms, two men dragged me up the concrete steps. In the garage they pushed me into a car, its engine already running. We drove to the Andrássy Street headquarters of the ÁVH where I was once again locked in an underground cell.

Compared with the mouse-hole in the cellar of the Buda villa, this cell seemed like a ball-room although it could not have been longer than eight or wider than four feet. The furnishings consisted of a wooden bunk with metal legs embedded in the concrete floor. Above the door of the windowless room, just as in the villa, an electric bulb glowed day and night behind a wire net, throwing its light straight into the eyes of the prisoner lying on the bunk.

Two ÁVH-guards stood at every turn in the labyrinth of cellar corridors, one in civilian clothes with a revolver stuck in his belt and one in uniform with a rifle slung over his shoulder. When a prisoner was being led to an interrogating room, or even to the lavatory, the guards posted at the corners of the corridor signalled to each other with a hiss whether or not the coast was clear, so as to prevent any two prisoners coming face to face. During the eighteen months of my preliminary detention, most of which I spent in this cellar, the rules and regulations of the underground prison, as well as its staff, were frequently changed. The uniformed guards were the first to disappear, then the plain-clothes men either carried no guns or concealed them in their pockets; they also began to wear felt slippers over their shoes to deaden the sound of their approach. In these eighteen months the premises of the ÁVH, below and above ground, were repeatedly rebuilt then changed back to their original condition, but each time they increased the number of interrogation rooms and underground cells, and moved the secret staircase leading from the cellar to the ground-floor and the floors above. But the hissing which served as a signalling system was preserved to the end.

Apart from this hissing, no human sound was audible in the corridors, though they were frenziedly noisy. Instead of the pocket-watch-sized Judas-holes, usual in prisons, there were here six-inch lids on the wooden doors, and hinged iron plates on the metal ones. The guards, making the rounds, would open these lids every eight or ten minutes, particularly at night, then slam them shut with such force that the clanging sounded almost like gun-fire echoing in the catacombs. If any prisoner was not awakened by the sound, the guard would kick his cell-door until the prisoner raised his eyes. Thus, however exhausted the prisoner, he could only doze for a few brief minutes.

The humid cold in the cellar was such that the ÁVH guards wore overcoats or even short fur-lined coats but it was a long time before I was given even a blanket. The food consisted of approximately half a pint of flour-soup in the mornings and around four o'clock in the afternoon, a little over half a pint of beans. With each meal the prisoners were given roughly an ounce and a half of bread. Not once during my first six weeks was the monotony of the diet broken. If, as frequently happened, the prisoner was not crouching shivering in his cell at four o'clock in the afternoon, but was being put through his paces in one of the interrogation rooms, he was deprived of even this cruelly insufficient food.

After the morning soup and the afternoon beans the guards would put the empty dixie-cans outside the cell doors and conduct each prisoner to the lavatory. If a long-standing prisoner, passing the row of cells at such times, noticed left-overs in a dixie, he knew with absolute certainty that a newly arrested person was brooding behind the brown-painted door, unable–as he himself had been at first–to consume even the small quantity of food granted him.

Compared with the atmosphere of the interrogating rooms, the starvation, the cold, the oppressive silence and even the exasperating hissing in the cellar passages seemed restful. At least, that is how I felt every time I was led back, in that first week, from the floors above to my cell. I was now in the hands of the three men who had arrested me. This time, instead of my feet, they hit the palms and the backs of my hands, swinging their truncheons through three-quarters of a circle, or forced me to do squatting exercises until I collapsed with exhaustion. All the while the grey-haired one would read out questions from a slip of paper from which it appeared that they took it as proven, not merely that I was a spy who had established contact between Szönyi and the mysterious Wagner, but also that I had organized an espionage ring when I was at the Foreign Ministry. After one of these periods of physical training lasting two and a half hours – I remember their duration exactly because, in self-defence, I tried ignoring the questions and concentrated my attention on the black-faced wrist-watch of the grey-haired interrogator – when they grew tired of the fruitless baiting and handed me over to an armed guard to take me back to the cellar, I stumbled and jack-knifed over the bannister. The guard dragged me down to my cell where, a few minutes later, the grey-haired man made his appearance and rated me for my alleged attempt at suicide, as though for personal reasons of revenge I had tried to involve him in a painful situation. By the time he had relieved his indignation by striking me across the face, I felt it was superfluous to explain in detail why, exactly, I had collapsed over the bannister. However, from then on, the lid of the Judas-hole was opened more frequently and I was escorted on the stairs by not one, but by two or even three guards.

Early next morning, I was taken to another wing of the building. At the desk facing the door sat a remarkably handsome, characteristically Transdanubian young man, with a black moustache. He eyed me darkly, then, for the first time since my arrest I was offered a seat. He opened a file, leafed through the documents it contained and then declared that I would have to give an exact, detailed account of my life – for the moment, only up to the day when I became an agent of the British or American – it didn't matter which – secret service. I could only repeat that I had never been a member of any secret service, British, American or Russian; all such insinuations were totally unfounded, mere inventions. The young man took a rubber truncheon from the drawer of his desk and rose. He was well over six foot tall, a giant with a splendidly proportioned athletic body. He walked up and down in front of me, then, as if restraining himself, sat down again behind his desk. But the truncheon remained on top of the desk, near his right hand.

For a while he stared at me silently, then he began to speak ponderously, with the accent of the uneducated. And yet, his sentences had a ring agreeable to my ear because the lad spoke the dialect of my county, County Vas in western Hungary.

'Look,' he said, 'we are on to something really big. Some people may get more than they deserve. That's tough. But, you bet your life, the guilty ones will not slip between our fingers. Our people's democracy is still too young; it cannot afford such luxuries. Look, I am a worker . . .'

While he paused for breath, I added in a low voice:

'From County Vas, at that . . .'

'How do you know? Or rather, what gave you the idea?' he corrected himself guiltily, retracting his confirmation of my guess.

'I can hear it. You probably come from the eastern part of the County.'

The giant looked at me dumbfounded, because ÁVH officers were always careful to conceal their identity and, when necessary, used cover names before their prisoners.

'You know a lot,' he remarked, 'too much. Still, it seems that there are things even you don't understand. So let me enlighten you by telling you a little story. It happened in the Soviet Union . . .'

As if reciting a well-prepared text, the giant related how at some undefined time, in some undefined place, an act of sabotage had been committed in the Soviet Union. Three people were suspected, none of whom would confess to the crime. What was to be done? All three suspects had to be executed. Regrettably. But a socialist state surrounded by hostile capitalist powers, cannot afford to let a saboteur go unpunished. So, the young man from County Vas concluded, hitting the desk with his truncheon for added emphasis, I should not imagine for a moment that my obstinate denials would save me from the scaffold. The only way in which I could help myself was to repent and admit my guilt.

I had no wish to quote another Russian example, Dostoevsky, and repeat the story of Christ and the Grand Inquisitor. I couldn't have done so even had I wished, because at that moment the overfed, brutal-faced ÁVH man who had participated in my arrest, entered the room. He sat down without a word and opened a large envelope addressed in a rather awkward female hand to 'Comrade Vajda'. Whether this was his real name or not, from then on this vulgar featured young man was Vajda to me. He tore open the envelope, perused the contents with great attention, then locked them away in his desk. In the meantime the lad from County Vas began to unwind the thread of my life.

First came my family. When I readily acknowledged that my father had been General Manager of the Electricity Works of County Vas, the two men exchanged meaningful glances, then they delved with gusto into my mother's background, with special emphasis on the army officers in her family. From their attitude one might have thought the mere fact that four of my cousins had chosen the army as a career – two as long ago as the days of the Austro-Hungarian monarchy – was in itself unequivocal proof in support of Szönyi's allegations. They commented in the same way on the Catholic private school I had attended, the once famous University College where I studied in Budapest and my two terms at the Sorbonne. Vajda remarked darkly that even in the absence of other information, it was obvious to him that someone brought up in such an environment could never have joined the then illegal communist party in good faith. Fortunately, there was sufficient evidence to show that in my university days, in 1932, I had wormed my way into the communist movement on behalf of Horthy's political police as an *agent provocateur*. It would be better for me if I told them of my own free will how I began and how I carried on my activities as a police spy before they were forced to confront me with the information at their disposal.

When I expressed doubts as to the ÁVH or anyone else being able to prove something that never took place, they reached for their rubber truncheons. After some preliminary skirmishing they pressed my forehead against the uneven gritty wall. They ordered me to keep my hands along the seams of my trousers and hold my body stiff as a poker so that it formed one side of a right-angled triangle between the wall and the floor. They took off my shoes to prevent me from slipping. The handsome lad from my county squatted down near me and beat my toes with his truncheon. It was not long before the right-angled triangle, of which my body was the hypotenuse, collapsed. But my interrogators soon restored me to the classic geometrical form. Still, this ingenious innovation that would have amazed Euclid, did not prevent the couple from indulging in the usual pranks: the kidney-blows, the palm-rapping, with 180° swings of the truncheon, and the bastinados. This time they did not use a carpet for the performance. Not only because there were no such luxuries in the bare interrogation room, but also because my weakened physical condition rendered such props unnecessary.

A few days later, at dawn, after a less violent night than usual, Vajda sat down to the typewriter to draft my first statement. They required only a few ordinary facts: date of birth, the schools I attended, my visit to Paris in 1937 and from there, in 1939, to the Argentine; my return to Budapest in 1946. After the first sentences we reached a deadlock, for Vajda wrote, 'In 1937 I went to Paris to seek adventure.'

I insisted that I had gone to Paris not to seek adventure but to study, so he had better delete that part of the sentence or I would not be in a position to sign the statement. It may have been utterly unreasonable to dig in my heels because of this mildly pejorative sentence but somehow I felt that if I gave in at this point, if I once started to slide down the slope of submissiveness, I might go all the way and would soon admit not only that I had established contact between Wagner and Szönyi, not only that I had created an espionage ring in the Foreign Ministry, but also that in early youth I had set out on my political and moral career as a police spy.

Vajda jumped up from his chair in fury and, joined by the youth from County Vas, was reaching for his instrument of persuasion, the truncheon, when the door flew open to admit two plain-clothes security men and a uniformed guard with a rifle on his shoulder. The two civilians conducted a whispered conversation with my interrogators, then led me away. Glancing back, I saw Vajda tear the paper from the typewriter, crush it in his hand and fling it into the waste-paper basket.

We walked through an intricate system of corridors until, at last, we entered a pleasantly furnished study. A man with thinning reddish-blond hair and the mild face of a priest sat behind the desk. He wore gold-rimmed glasses and his blinking, myopic eyes gave his features an expression of cunning. His smile was almost friendly as he pointed to the armchair facing the desk and motioned me to sit down. When we were alone he yawned deeply, removed his spectacles, rubbed his eyes, then leaned back in his armchair, visibly exhausted; a few minutes later he placed his elbows on top of the desk and addressed me:

'Well,' he began, placing the glasses back on his nose, 'how do you feel?'

I shrugged my shoulders.

'That black ring round your eye looks quite amusing. What was it, a boxing match?'

Ignoring this question, I declared that in my opinion we could get at the truth much quicker if the ÁVH relied on facts, not on slander, and if, before accusing someone, they took the trouble to check verifiable information, as, for example, Tibor Szönyi's deposition. The man with the glasses laughed ambiguously:

'Forget Szönyi,' he said, waving his hand. 'We are concerned with something entirely different. Szönyi is a side-issue, so are you. Do you smoke? Do you want a cup of tea? With lemon?'

I accepted the cigarette. The priestly-faced individual rang the bell. An attractive secretary came in. She listened to his instructions in silence and after a short while returned with a cup of lemon tea and a piece of cake which she put down before me. During her absence we sat in utter silence. The bespectacled man rose from behind his desk and threw himself, with an air of great weariness, into a deep armchair. He was of medium height, thicker around the waist than his age warranted. Later, I was to see that pink face, those blunt-fingered, soft hands, often enough. His name was Mátyás Károlyi, and although at the time he was only a major, he belonged to Gábor Péter's inner circle. This inner, or to use the ÁVH name for it, conspiratorial circle, directed the most secret activities of the political police. Its members were selected by Gábor Péter personally; they were not chosen according to rank but from his most loyal followers that he considered best fitted for the job. Thus it frequently happened that a lieutenant, drawn into the conspiratorial circle, wielded far greater power than many a major or lieutenant-colonel. A member of the inner circle could at times even give orders to his superiors.

When the secretary had quietly closed the door behind her, Károlyi scrambled to his feet and went back to his desk.

'Drink your tea first,' he said, staring at me short-sightedly. Then, unexpectedly, he asked:

'When did you first meet László Rajk?'

I did not attach great importance to the question, believing it to be of an introductory nature. I replied off-handedly:

'At the University. We were there together. I think we met for the first time around 1930.'

'Did you know that Rajk was a police spy?'

I glanced at Károlyi quickly–the suspicion flashed into my mind that he was laying a trap for me for some obscure purpose of his own.

After all, László Rajk was looked upon as the top man among the communist leaders, neither trained in Russia nor sent home by Moscow. Already in 1945 his past in the underground communist movement, his role in the Hungarian Brigade fighting in the Spanish civil war, and his activities in the Hungarian Resistance movement during the German occupation had won him such prestige that he was entrusted with the most important portfolio, that of Minister of the Interior, and in 1948 was appointed Minister of Foreign Affairs. When László Rajk took over Foreign Affairs, and the moderately gifted János Kádár was made Minister of the Interior, the communists in the know did not regard Rajk as demoted. On the contrary, they thought that consolidation in the country had reached a point where it was no longer important to have anyone as outstanding as Rajk to deal with domestic affairs; instead of presuming that Rajk had lost prestige by becoming Foreign Minister, they believed that the Party leadership had delegated Rajk to this post because foreign policy had increased in importance.

This was the line that Mátyás Rákosi took in the narrower circle of the leadership, but it may well be that even he was as yet unaware of the fate awaiting Rajk. This supposition seems confirmed by a telephone conversation between Rákosi and one of the leading officials of the Foreign Ministry. Shortly before Rajk's appointment, Rákosi telephoned Dr. György Heltai, head of the Foreign Ministry's political department.

'Well, have you heard the great news?' he asked Heltai.

There had been rumours that Erik Molnár was to be replaced by László Rajk, and Heltai replied truthfully that he had heard whispers of certain impending changes. Rákosi then informed him squarely that Rajk would be the new Foreign Minister and added, by way of explanation:

'The Foreign Ministry has been a Kindergarten long enough. Now you will have an adult to lead you.'

The word *kindergarten* was an ironic reference to the activities and attitude of the departing Foreign Minister, Erik Molnár. Molnár, although he had been a member of the Communist Party for several decades, had never been to Moscow. He had participated in the underground communist movement not so much as a militant as by contributing historical and agrarian-political essays to crypto-communist periodicals. His brother, René Molnár, however, who had acted for a considerable time as defence counsel for the imprisoned communists in Budapest and was later compelled to flee to Moscow, had there fallen victim to the 1937 Trotsky trials.

Whether this was the reason, or whether the administration of the Foreign Ministry held but limited interest for Molnár, he was careful to avoid taking any independent action or of forming decisions. Even on the most insignificant questions, he would turn for instruction or advice to Party headquarters or the Soviet authorities. It often happened that Molnár would interrupt the usual reports of the departmental heads and in their presence – and often in mine – would ring up Rákosi, Révai, or the Soviet Ambassador, Pushkin, on the secret, so-called 'chaika' line, before informing us of his decision. In the middle drawer of his desk he kept books to read during office hours. If anyone entered his room, he hastily shut the drawer, his face wearing the expression of a schoolboy caught using a crib.

Thus, not only Rákosi regarded Rajk, Molnár's junior by a good many years, as more 'adult', but so did everyone who placed more value on a practical politician than on a scholar of theoretical bent. Although it was no secret among the well-informed that Rajk had suffered some loss of prestige when the Politbureau of the Communist Party had sharply criticized his views concerning the role of the party group within the Ministry of the Interior – criticism followed by his transfer to the Foreign Ministry – no particular significance was attached to the affair in 1948, for in the course of that year which Rákosi called 'the year of change', the entire state administration was undergoing large-scale reorganization.

The trend of the changes taking place became increasingly clear. When, at the end of 1948, I was transferred from the Foreign Ministry, where I was deputy head of the press and information department, to the Ministry of Agriculture to head the press department there, many of the old officials, even those appointed after 1945, were recalled from their diplomatic posts abroad or discharged from their jobs, and replaced in the Ministries as at the Embassies by party functionaries of working-class origin or, even more frequently, by men from the ÁVH. The salaries of those who had been in the secret police were usually supplemented from ÁVH funds. Among these, for example, was ÁVH-Major Tamás Mátrai, appointed, in the summer of 1948, ministerial counsellor at the Ministry of Foreign Affairs. Mátrai's salary at the Ministry amounted to approximately 900 forints but at the same time he drew an additional 1500 forints from ÁVH funds. He once rang them up in my presence, to demand a remittance.

In the course of the reorganization of the Foreign Ministry, Mátrai built up a so-called administrative department with himself as its head. This department did no more than perform the duties of

two consular officials but Mátrai inflated it into a powerful bureaucratic control organization. He took over the issuing of diplomatic
passports that had, until then, been outside the jurisdiction of the
secret police, assumed direction of the courier service in order to be
able to use the diplomatic bag, and so take advantage both of the
passports and the bag for the purposes of the ÁVH. At the same
time, his department, on the pretext of administrative reorganization,
sought to bring every department of the Foreign Ministry under
police surveillance.

Years later, from hints dropped in prison, I gathered that even
then the Minister of Foreign Affairs himself had long been under
surveillance. The principal *commissar*, however, did not report to
Gábor Péter, like Mátrai, but in all probability directly to the
Russians and took his instructions from them. This *commissar* was
the Muscovite, Andor Berei, who became Undersecretary of Foreign
Affairs in 1948, when Rajk took over the Foreign Ministry.

Between the two world wars, Berei had functioned as a so-called
'instructor' in the Communist International and as the Comintern's
trusted emissary had assisted in the foundation and running of the
Belgian Communist Party. These Comintern instructors were
almost without exception representatives not only of the Comintern
but also of the Soviet secret police, the NKVD. Berei's erudition,
broad intellectual horizon and quick mind raised him above his
fellow-instructors. Perhaps it was because of these qualities – considered highly suspect in Moscow – that, though he had always been a
conformist, he never rose to the front rank. The most he achieved
was to act as prompter to less discerning people, persons without
stature, who could never be suspected of conceiving, by any un-
fortunate mischance, ideas of their own.

It was obvious from the first that the Foreign Ministry held
as little interest for Berei as it did for Molnár. Berei's loyalties were
still with the National Planning Bureau of which, before his appointment as Undersecretary of Foreign Affairs, he had been head. But
former instructor Berei of the Comintern could hardly have been
acting on his own initiative when he issued orders behind Rajk's
back, countermanded the Minister's instructions and took charge of
affairs in which only the Minister himself should have had powers of
decision. This – as I later learned – had caused several clashes between
Rajk and Berei in March and April, 1949. At the time of my interrogation, I was still unaware of these behind-the-scene conflicts as I

had spent the last few months before my arrest at the Ministry of Agriculture. But I recalled all the more clearly the May-Day celebrations when, standing on a rostrum in front of the gala-tribune next to the Party's first secretary, Mátyás Rákosi, Foreign Minister László Rajk greeted the demonstrators.

This scene had imprinted itself on my mind because, side by side with the tall, handsome, slender Rajk, the squat and neckless Rákosi had cut a ludicrous figure as, with his hat pulled down over his ears, he stood red and sweating in the sunshine. Rákosi was always very careful lest the contrast between himself and others should increase the aversion inspired by his unprepossessing appearance. If, in spite of this, he had invited Rajk to stand at his side, this meant in the flower-language of Party protocol that next to Rákosi, Rajk counted as one of the foremost leaders of the Party. What then, I wondered, was the purpose of the interrogator's leading question? – 'Do you know that Rajk was a police spy under Horthy?' After a while Károlyi grew tired of my silence.

'Answer me! Did you know that Rajk was a police spy?'

'In my opinion that is utterly impossible,' I replied.

Károlyi broke into loud and long false police-laughter.

'Of course!' he cried, 'the two buddies protect one another. I hope you realize that this makes you look even more suspicious?'

I was about to speak but he silenced me.

'I know, I know. Szönyi is lying. But in the face of his and other similar confessions, your denials won't be worth much. That's obvious, isn't it? However, if you agree to help me, I may be able to help you too.'

'What do you mean by helping?' I asked suspiciously. 'I cannot testify that Rajk was a police spy.'

'We don't require that from you. All you have to do is tell the truth. Isn't it true that in 1931 you were one of the initiators of the communist student-movement?'

I nodded.

'When did you come to Budapest?'

'In 1928, after I left school.'

'And you enrolled in the Faculty of Letters?'

'No. First in the Faculty of Foreign Affairs of the School of Economics.'

'In short, you were one of the privileged. You were raised in a hot-house where they nurtured the diplomatic shoots of the Horthy régime.' Károlyi, who was about the same age as myself, and was, therefore, familiar with conditions in those days, smiled ironically.

'How did you come to be a communist? At that time, the party was still underground!'

Yes, it was at that time the party had gone underground and the universities were ruled by right-wing student organizations called *fraternal societies*. Their members wore flat, visored caps – each faculty and organization a different colour – and participated in para-military manoeuvres and demonstrations. They received semi-official support from the government and were given preference among those applying for state scholarships. The patrons of the *fraternal societies*, so-called *domini* (usually outstanding right-wing public figures) lent them a helping hand after graduation. With an energy worthy of free-mason solidarity these patrons threw their weight into the scale when it came to finding jobs for these young men 'reliable from the point of view of national loyalty'. They were promised rapid advancement in the state administration or with the more important private enterprises. Neither the semi-official mentors nor the *domini* objected on moral grounds – though they did not relish the reaction abroad – when at the beginning of the academic year, the *fraternal societies* launched noisy and brutal 'Jew-beatings' in the otherwise sleepy and uninspired halls of science, to scare off the Jewish students already admitted in limited numbers to the universities.

To politically-minded young people who viewed the rule of the *fraternal societies* in the universities with deep revulsion, and who were driven into sharp opposition to the *fraternal societies* and their patron, the Horthy régime, the perhaps realistic but cautious opposition of the other parties including the Social Democrats seemed luke-warm and opportunistic. They wanted something more radical. Particularly those who, like myself, went on lonely walks of exploration at night in the streets of the capital and looked around with a feeling of guilt at the slums of Budapest, because they blamed their families, and even themselves, for what they saw. So after a year, I left the Faculty of Diplomacy, left the College with its white-gloved footmen, took a room in town and enrolled at the University. I became an habitué of the literary cafés, made friends with left-wing writers, wrote poems, essays and short stories, and edited, in company with other young writers, a number of short-lived literary periodicals. I joined the Jaurès-circle, contributed to left-wing publications appearing abroad, dug deep into Marxist literature, and then enrolled for a term at the Sorbonne.

Of all this I told Károlyi only that I had spent two terms at the Sorbonne in 1930, made friends with French communist students and on returning home, had sought contact with the underground Hungarian Communist Party. To further questions I answered that at first I took part in the activities of the so-called party 'apparatus'. I carried typewriters, stencils and printing ink to illegal printing shops, acted as courier and contact man and, at the same time, had instructions to keep my eyes open at the university and form a communist cell with the students sympathetic to our cause. The first man I won over for the movement was István Stolte, who had been a class-mate of mine for ten years, right through primary and secondary school, and whose thinking ran along the same lines as mine.

'We have now come to Stolte,' Károlyi nodded, then he offered me another cigarette.

'And Rajk?'

Rajk was a tall, slender, very masculine-looking youth. With his inordinately high forehead, protruding cheekbones, sharply-drawn features, he bore an astounding resemblance – as American newspapermen remarked later, when he was Foreign Minister, to Abraham Lincoln, and from the Foreign Minister's *curriculum vitae*, the journalists learnt that he was born exactly 100 years after the American President. This chance parallel was, of course, never referred to in the corridors of the Budapest University, but Rajk's bright eyes, his radiant, charming smile and calm, unhurried way of speaking inspired confidence among fellow students of the most varied backgrounds and intellectual levels.

'Well, and Rajk?' Károlyi repeated impatiently.

'Stolte drew my attention to the fact that László Rajk's attitude was similar to ours.'

'So you recruited him for the movement?'

'No. Until then my relations with Rajk had been only superficial, though friendly. So I approached him with caution. All the more so as I had strict instructions to be careful that no-one at the University should suspect me of being a communist; should I arouse suspicion, I would endanger my immediate contacts as well as the underground network attached to me.'

'What was the subject of your first conversation with Rajk?'

'We talked mainly about our studies. It was only gradually that we shifted to sociological and political subjects.'

'Didn't Rajk introduce his friends to you?'

'He did. Rajk was a member of a small circle formed around a fellow student called Mészáros. This circle read and discussed sociological, mainly Marxist works. Mészáros held that it was sense-less to join any kind of movement or party, to say nothing of exposing oneself to the dangers of illegality, before one had a thorough insight into the theoretical side of it.'

'Did Rajk approve of this attitude?'

'My impression was that though Rajk regarded this attitude as sensible, his practical turn of mind as well as his temperament were driving him, like most young men, towards action. I felt that I had to let him make his own choice and so I made no attempt to persuade Rajk to join us in our first action.'

'What was your first action?'

'We distributed leaflets at the College of Technical Sciences, the Faculty of Letters and a few student hostels. On the same day the yellow press announced this small incident in huge headlines, proclaiming that the communists had infiltrated into the universities. The régime, convinced as it was that it had the students under its thumb, partly through the *fraternal societies*, partly because of the thorough screening before admission, was in a flaming rage.'

'And then? Was anyone arrested?'

'No-one. But next day the corridors were crawling with secret police. A couple of us took their presence as a challenge and, behind the backs of the preposterous, stupid, bowler-hatted detectives, we stuffed leaflets into the desks in the empty classrooms and in the window-recesses before lectures began.'

'We don't wear bowler hats,' Károlyi remarked, feeling perhaps that my scorn was addressed not only to the secret police of the past; then he added significantly, 'And we're not stupid, either. Now give me a detailed account of what happened next, and also when you met Rajk again and how and by whom he was recruited into the movement.'

I tried to sum up my recollections of the next few days. 'Yes, the members of the *fraternal societies* made everyone entering the building identify themselves; only students were admitted. After the second distribution of leaflets it thus became evident that the theory advanced by some of the newspapers–that the leaflets had been smuggled in by an outsider–could not be true. The *fraternal societies* organized search parties for several days in succession. They combed the classes and in order to prove that the student body they led along the path of loyalty to the nation could not be responsible for the leaflets, they handed over to the police a few innocent elderly scholars who came to attend Professor Gerevich's lectures on the history of art. False rumours spread and, at times, the corridors were more crowded than the class-rooms. It was in this atmosphere that I met Rajk again.

'Even today I don't know whether or not he had guessed that I had had something to do with the events of those days, but it is certain that he asked no questions and we mentioned neither the leaflets nor the articles appearing in the press, nor the alarms and excursions of the flat-caps. As far as I can remember we were talking about a recently published essay on the French revolution. We were walking up and down the corridor when the warning bell before lectures interrupted our conversation. Rajk stopped short, spoke my name, then added without any preamble:

' "... there is only one solution: Lenin."

'We entered the class-room but did not sit together. The next day I told Stolte to contact Rajk openly, in the name of the communist student group.'

'So it is absolutely clear that it was Stolte who recruited Rajk for the party?'

'There can be no doubt of it. I myself instructed him to do so.'

'Are you ready to repeat this to Rajk's face?'

'Why? Does he deny it?'

'It is not for you to ask questions,' the major declared coldly. 'Are you, or are you not ready to say this to his face?'

'It is true. Therefore I am ready.'

'All right,' Károlyi nodded, 'let's get on then. How did the student movement develop?'

I described how the movement took shape. Stolte formed another group at the Eötvös College which was considered a significant success because this college, modelled on the French École Normale Supérieure, drew unchallenged upon the intellectual élite, students whose voices were listened to by others. Later, I was instructed to establish contact between Stolte and the league of young communist workers, and then to withdraw from the university movement because the work I would have to do in the rural department of the party–to which I was being transferred–ruled out a doubling of jobs that might prove dangerous from the conspiratorial point of view. Thus, Stolte became secretary of the University group, but my friends kept me informed concerning the development of the student movement.

'And what happened to you?'

'I was arrested in 1932, together with the leaders of the rural section.'

35

'Did you continue to obtain information concerning the activities of the student group?'

'Yes. My friends outwitted the censors by sending me books in which certain letters had pin-point marks under them. From these letters I could decipher their message.'

'You don't say!' Károlyi exclaimed laughing. 'Changed days!' Then he became serious again.

'And when did Stolte become a Trotskyite and police spy?'

'As far as I know Stolte's party membership was suspended in 1933, after the arrest of the University group. I think I am right in saying that was when Rajk was appointed secretary of the student movement. Later, Stolte was expelled from the party as a Trotskyite and police agent.'

'And Rajk continued to maintain contact with this Trotskyite police spy. Didn't he?'

'My information is that when Stolte was merely a suspended party member and was working on an historical essay, the party instructed Rajk to read and review Stolte's work, partly in his capacity of secretary of the University group, partly as a historian.'

'Did you meet Stolte in those days?'

'I did.'

'You must have been wonderful communists, both of you, to maintain friendly terms with such a suspicious character. Naturally, Rajk went on seeing him even after he had been expelled from the party?'

'I have no idea.'

Károlyi grinned. 'You will. You'll tell us a great deal more about this. Well, for the time being, write down in detail about your meeting with Rajk, your conversation. Mention who recruited Rajk for the underground movement, when and how. That's all for the moment. Do you want a cigarette?'

Károlyi struggled heavily to his feet, made me sit at the typewriter and put paper, pencil and a few cigarettes in front of me. Then he summoned the guard.

'I'm not giving you any matches', he called back from the door, 'if you want to smoke, ask the comrade for a light. And report to him when you have finished.'

He left the room and I smoked a cigarette. Only then did I begin to wonder about the possible implications of our conversation. In the meantime, however, coolly and objectively, I set down my recollections.

Late the following night, two ÁVH guards came to my cell to fetch me and took me to an office much more elegantly furnished than Károlyi's. Here Ernö Szücs received me. He was nervous, tired, impatient. After a few questions about the student movement, he wanted me to tell him who established contact between Rajk and the league of young communist workers. He sat down at his typewriter and drafted a brief statement merely saying that it was Stolte who recruited Rajk to the movement. He asked me whether I would maintain my allegation if I were confronted with Rajk. I said 'Yes, of course I would.'

I was led back to my cell, but soon they fetched me again, shackled me and made me get into a curtained car, standing in the courtyard. I was flanked on both sides by ÁVH men. Even though the curtains completely shut out the world, they placed on my nose a pair of sunglasses, carefully lined with black paper. We must have travelled the same road we had travelled before, we were driven into the same garage and I was dragged down the same steps to the cellar, for, when they took off my glasses, I found myself in the identical cell where I had spent my first day of captivity. After a few minutes in this damp hole, the door opened and I was led up to the first floor. A moment later I was again in the large room I had been in on my first afternoon. Now as before, the head of the T-shaped table was occupied by Gábor Péter and his general staff. But, standing at the foot of the T, slightly to my right, was László Rajk. They pushed me somewhat to the left, so that I was facing him.

On the table in front of Rajk lay several sheets of paper and he was holding a sharpened pencil in his hand. He wore neither jacket, nor tie, his shirt hung crumpled, half-unbuttoned, his medium-grey trousers—he wore no belt—had slipped down below his waist. His usually rugged but now ashen face was turned towards me but his eyes, gazing at me, were sightless. The lines on his forehead had deepened into hard hollows and three straight parallel furrows marred his exhausted face, as if drawn with a ruler. No-one except the interrogators and their superiors will ever know what Rajk went through during this first period of his imprisonment; it is still a mystery to me what could have caused the three parallel furrows searing his face.

Years later, comparing dates, I came to the conclusion that the day of our confrontation must have been Rajk's third day in the hands of the ÁVH. Three days before, late in the evening, he had been sitting talking to his wife, watching her feed their little son László, then a few weeks old, when Julia Rajk's mother came into the room to tell them that Gábor Péter's men had come to see László. The ÁVH officers were waiting in the hall. Rajk invited the unexpected guests, who had arrived at such an unusual hour, into his study, but one of the officers said brusquely that the nature of what Gábor Péter wanted to discuss with the Minister made it necessary for him to accompany them to headquarters. Rajk protested (he had already heard of my disappearance). Finally, Gábor Péter's men seized him and dragged him away by force. From the window, Julia Rajk watched her husband, still resisting, being pushed feet first, into the waiting black car.

Standing there at the foot of the T-shaped table, staring at my former university colleague, I gave not a thought to our grotesque situation, nor to what lay in store for us. My attention was concentrated on the three horizontal furrows that disfigured him. I was obsessed with the idea that Rajk's face would disintegrate. When Gábor Péter shouted my name, I turned my eyes away from Rajk's face and looked at Péter. Stressing every word, the head of the secret police now asked me:

'Who recruited László Rajk for the party, and who established contact between him and the young workers' movement?'

'István Stolte,' I replied.

'Say it to his face.'

Rajk's eyes strayed across the room as I repeated my statement.

'László Rajk! Do you admit it?'

Rajk flung the pencil he held in his right hand on to the blank sheets of paper lying on the table and said in a low voice:

'I maintain that it was Mészáros.'

'Do you maintain that it was Stolte?' Gábor Péter asked me.

'I do.'

I was led away and at daybreak was taken back to the cellar at 60 Andrássy Street.

Although no-one spoke to me during the day that followed, although I was not taken up for questioning, I found no peace. Could I possibly be mistaken? Was it conceivable that Mészáros had only been pretending to keep himself and his group aloof from the communist movement, and was it dissimulation when he preached the priority of theory and seemingly avoided practical action? Had I falsely accused Rajk at the foot of the T-shaped table where Szönyi had falsely accused me ten days before? For a long time I was unable to rid myself of these doubts although there were many arguments against them. It was not impossible that Mészáros should have had some vague connection with the party that my section knew nothing about, but as far as I knew, Mészáros had stuck to his convictions to the end and refused to participate in any kind of underground organization; what is more, when most members of his group had already joined the student movement his closest friends were still trying in vain to win his co-operation. Thus, both psychologically and organizationally it seemed entirely impossible that Mészáros could have established contact between Rajk and the party, even had he wanted to. Still, the faint chance that I had been mistaken tormented me for years, and therefore, both while in prison and afterwards, I did my utmost to check my recollections, which were later confirmed as true by other prisoners.

But even if Rajk did have some contact with the communist movement through Mészáros, why should he deny his connection with Stolte–something I myself had arranged? This denial awakened my suspicion of the former Foreign Minister, all the more so as its motives appeared obvious.

To be branded a Trotskyite in the Communist Party was equivalent to excommunication and, to the mind of a loyal party-member, Trotskyism seemed as dangerous an infection as did the plague to our mediaeval ancestors. Very often, those repudiated as Trotskyites had not even read Trotsky's works, and had they been familiar with his ideas they would certainly not have sympathized with them. Often their only crime was that they did not unconditionally approve of Moscow's tortuous political line or–like myself in the party organization of the state administration–criticized or made ironical comments on the widespread Stalinist jargon. But Stolte was an authentic Trotskyite. One of the most authentic in Hungary. After his expulsion from the party, he organized a small Trotskyite group, and as its leader, established contact with the regional Trotskyite centre set up by Sedov, Trotsky's son, in Bratislava.

It was therefore clear that László Rajk considered it dangerous to admit his connection with Stolte. No doubt he was more familiar than I with the methods and protocol of the ÁVH. He must have realized that his words would fall on deaf ears if he tried to explain that when he was secretary of the student movement, Stolte was not a Trotskyite and that it was only years later that he established his opposition group. By then Rajk must have known that this negligible difference in time would be completely ignored by the dialectics of the secret police and, regardless of the preposterous nature of such an interpretation, the final statement would contain words to the effect that Rajk had been recruited into the Communist Party by a man expelled as a Trotskyite and Horthy police agent; and this was proof, according to ÁVH logic, that Rajk also must have been a Trotskyite and police agent.

But to my eyes, it was not the connection between the twenty-year-old Stolte, and the twenty-one-year-old Rajk that compromised the former Minister but the fact that he denied that connection. As it was impossible that he should have forgotten this decisive moment of his life–for it was then that he set out with admirable consistency on his career as a professional revolutionary–I believed that Rajk had some ulterior motive for denying the facts. Szönyi must also have been driven by some malicious intention–I argued–when he insisted that his lie was the truth, and, as the behaviour of both gave ample grounds for suspicion, the ÁVH must have had something concrete to go on when they started their investigation.

The accusation made by the head of the cadres department had, objectively, put a rope around my neck, and the suspicion aroused in me by Rajk's denial of facts known to me put me subjectively into an ambivalent frame of mind. I had now found an explanation for the methods of my interrogators in their attempts to unmask spies. I thought that I had no right to draw general and final conclusions from my own experiences as long as I had no way of determining to what extent these brutalities were inspired by genuine indignation or momentary police hysteria.

My relatively abstract reflections were not interrupted until evening when I was again taken up for questioning. During the days that followed the groups of interrogators were frequently changed, though the questions and methods remained unchanged. Only one exception occurred. One night I was led into a very large room. The young man behind the desk made me stand straight, facing him, turned a reflector lamp full into my eyes and began to speak in calm, almost conversational tones. Behind him, to the right, a woman sat at her typewriter in semi-darkness as if she were waiting for dictation. Her face was turned towards me but in the blinding light I could not make out her features, only the shape of her head, hair and shoulders.

The young man began by saying that to him I was obviously not a spy in the generally accepted sense of the word. I belonged to a species he would call communists of Western orientation. His cultured selection of words, his intelligent, well-rounded sentences and civilized voice formed a surprising contrast to the manner of my previous interrogators. He did not ask questions, he lectured.

He argued that those who had returned to Hungary from the so-called bourgeois democracies had brought with them an alien and dangerously destructive mentality, an ingrained prejudice. In the Western countries where, like myself, they had often spent many years, they had attended universities, formed friendships, and so became deeply attached to the West.

He did not doubt that we sincerely regarded ourselves as communists; however, in truly socialist countries we constituted a harmful element, a foreign body. Perhaps unconsciously so. All I had to do was look back over the two and a half years since my return, at the period spent at the Foreign Ministry, and more especially at my term at the Ministry of Agriculture . . .

I replied that I should be grateful if he would be good enough to inform me what incorrectness or act of disloyalty I had committed. The young man laughed.

'Incorrectness and act of disloyalty? You see, this very question justifies me. Just think how destructive you are with these bourgeois notions of yours, your bourgeois scruples and prejudices. Think, man! Think and remember . . .'

While my interrogator elaborated his theme in several variations I tried to steal a glance round the reflector and make out the face of the woman behind the typewriter, for her contours seemed familiar. But all the while I thought and remembered. I recalled particularly something that took place in the middle of March that had really annoyed me at the time. Some party functionary by the name of Baráti, whom I knew only slightly, summoned me one day to Party Headquarters. After a few preliminary sentences he came to the point, saying with friendly directness:

'We want you to issue a communiqué stating that the *kulaks* (the rich farmers) are sabotaging the sowing-plan in the northern counties.'

I explained to him at some length that there was no question of sabotage. The press section of the Ministry of Agriculture had about one thousand agricultural correspondents throughout the country who sent in expert reports on weather conditions, the possibilities and progress of work in the fields and harvest expectations. These reports, which I had carefully studied, unanimously stated that in the northern counties the soil was frozen and in many places covered in snow. In such conditions the Hungarian peasant does not plough, he waits for a thaw–and this was expected within a few days. But even if there were signs of sabotage, of which there were not, I should hesitate to issue such a communiqué which, as it would be published in every newspaper in the country, would cause unnecessary alarm.

Baráti raised his hand. 'You don't think politically, comrade. According to the sowing-plan, ploughing should have been finished by the middle of March and in the northern counties the *kulaks* have failed to accomplish the plan.'

'Any communique,' I had replied, 'could, in all honesty, blame only the weather for the delay.'

Baráti had shrugged his shoulders, and declared that in his opinion I was misjudging, even underestimating, the significance of the struggle against the *kulaks*. For my part I produced new facts in support of my contention that the sabotage charge was purely fictitious. I emphasized, hoping that this practical reasoning would carry more weight, that the communiqué they wanted me to issue would discredit not the accused but the accusers, and in addition might be used as a pretext for acts of personal revenge, violence and manhunts. I had no intention of supplying such a pretext and, I hoped, neither had he.

After we had both argued hotly and for a long time, Baráti pronounced the words that had now brought him to mind, the exact words used by the young ÁVH officer:

'You are a man full of scruples and prejudices, comrade,' he said, looking me up and down reflectively.

I rose and with all the calm I could muster, replied in a low voice:

'That is quite possible. However, as long as I am head of the press section of the Ministry of Agriculture no such communiqués will be issued.'

I was convinced that it was I, not Baráti, who represented the political interests of the Communist Party and protected its moral values. I believed that I had been appointed to the position I held, not to function as an automaton directed by the pushing of various buttons, but to perform my work responsibly, conscientiously, and in the way I thought right.

Still, I was beginning to be discouraged by criticism and misunderstandings and so I had already taken steps to exchange my political post for a desk in a scientific or semi-scientific institute, removed from everyday politics. I felt I had a right to this decision, to this withdrawal. One or two of my old friends might grumble and shake their heads disapprovingly, but the hide-bound, narrow-minded party functionaries would eventually, without my help, fall through the sieve of time.

The phraseology of the party functionary and that of the ÁVH officer bore evidence of such close kinship that I should not have been surprised had the young man orating behind his desk called me to account for the communiqué I had refused to issue. But he mentioned no concrete facts, he was content to enlighten me with generalities.

'The communists of Western orientation,' he continued, 'destructive as they are, however unwittingly, must realize that the Party has to defend itself against them. Though they may not be saboteurs and spies in the military sense, their bourgeois mentality supplies more grist to the enemy's mill than the saboteur who works in a factory or blows up bridges. Thus, these men infected by the West are, in essence,' and he stressed the words *in essence*, 'saboteurs, diversionists and spies, and the Party has no choice but to remove them, especially if they are in high positions, to prevent them spreading the contagion.

'As far as I am concerned,' he declared, 'I am sorry for you when I think what is waiting for you.'

Then, raising his voice, he described in vivid detail how we prisoners would grow old, go off our heads and rot away in our lonely cells while the People's Democracy advanced towards unprecedented prosperity. Suddenly, one of his cleverly turned phrases was interrupted by a loud, sobbing sound. The girl behind the typewriter jumped up from her chair and ran out of the room. Unfortunately, I was unable to see her face.

We could alleviate our lot only, the young man continued unperturbed, by telling sincerely and openly everything we knew, or even suspected, of our acquaintances, by putting ourselves at the disposal of the Party and the ÁVH to help them fight the Imperialists more effectively.

'If you stop being so stubborn,' he concluded 'the Party will show you mercy. Already, tomorrow, you'll get better treatment. For instance, you will be given another cell, a blanket, decent food, meat. Think of it, man! meat! And you'll be spared a few things you probably don't enjoy too much. If not,' he shrugged his shoulders, 'you will have only yourself to blame. You will pay dearly. The choice is yours. I hope you understood me?'

My eyes were running in the blinding glare of the arc-light, my knees shook with exhaustion. I nodded to signify that I had indeed understood him. In franker, more unbiased language, reporting guesses or suspicions was equivalent to accusing each other on fictitious pretexts. And putting ourselves at the disposal of the ÁVH meant that we were to admit, without protest, any charge invented against us. Yet at that moment, all this appeared unimportant, uninteresting to me. Important, exclusively important, was to shut my eyes and stretch out on the wooden bunk of my cell, if only for a few moments.

These short rests always restored me a little, although when the interrogation took place at night, I could only rarely enjoy a brief nap during the day because the guards spared no effort to keep the inhabitants of the underground cells awake by banging the lids of the Judas-holes, and kicking the doors. In addition, I was suffering from constant, tearing pains in my chest and back, and particularly in the region of the kidneys, so that I had to muster all my strength to rise from the bunk. The skin on my swollen soles had cracked open in places; the rubber truncheons had burst the veins in my hands so that my palms had become inflated into dark purplish cushions and my fingers into sausages. For a week my kidneys discharged only blood, but my physical condition and the possible consequences of it caused me hardly any anxiety at all. My immediate concern was whether or not I would be allowed to sleep a little and whether they would take me up for questioning at the very time when they were distributing the morning soup or afternoon beans.

As I found out later, most of my fellow-prisoners in circumstances similar to mine were preoccupied, first and foremost, not with the problem of 'to be or not to be', but with the question to eat or not to eat, to be tortured or not to be tortured, and finally, to sleep or not to sleep. This was the state we were in when the young ÁVH officer indicated that basically it was up to the prisoner himself whether or not his lot improved. His concluding remarks offered a brittle golden bridge: the prisoner would yield not because he was afraid of torture, starvation and lack of sleep, but because he was eager to help his Party. The prisoner understood that though he himself was innocent, there were psychological reasons why, in a period of increased tension between East and West, the communists were suspicious of people who had studied and grown up in the West and who, during the war, had in any way co-operated with the Western allies.

In my eyes, Szönyi's statement, and even more Rajk's denial, justified the party's suspicions. However, this not only aggravated but also alleviated my situation in that it permitted a gleam of hope. If I remained firm, I might contribute to the separation of the innocent from those perhaps truly guilty among the communists of Western orientation who were, as a category, suspect; but if I admitted to trumped-up charges or, if simply by reporting guesses or suspicions, I furnished material for false accusations against others, I too would be responsible if suspicion and fact, truth and fiction, become inextricably mixed.

One night I was led up and down staircases, through corridors and a panelled passage-way into a part of the building that was wholly unfamiliar to me, though later I came to know it well. Turning sharp right on the landing we entered a spacious, oblong ante-room, passed a secretary bent over her typewriter, and the half-open door of the lavatory, and reached the chief's room. A fair-haired man in his mid-thirties, wearing the insignia of a Colonel, sat behind a desk. He told the guard to remove the chair facing the desk, then sent him from the room.

The Colonel's undistinguished but almost agreeable face was worn with fatigue, just like Károlyi's. His bloodshot eyes stared at me severely. For a few seconds I hoped that perhaps, at last, my case had reached the hands of a responsible person; that the ÁVH had compared the true facts with Szönyi's statement and that my interrogation would take a new turn.

'Who recruited you as an agent?' the Colonel asked suddenly.

After my now sterotyped reply, he barked at me:

'What was Wagner's message to Szönyi?'

When again I had nothing new to say, he did not wait for my answer to his third question: what letter had I brought Szönyi?–but produced a rubber truncheon from his desk drawer and issued an order:

'Hold out your hands! The other way round!'

The blows rained down on the backs of my hands, not on the palms. Then came the bastinado. While I was lying on the carpet, the Colonel bent over me:

'If you only knew how nice it looks when the truncheon sinks into your soles . . .' he whispered, then he gave my kidneys a few heavy blows with it.

He went back behind his desk, buttoned up his jacket and looked at me out of cold fish-like eyes.

'When did you meet Field? Noel Field?' he asked, enunciating every word precisely.

'I don't know him,' I replied.

'This Field is in our hands,' the Colonel declared loudly. 'That surprises you, doesn't it?'

I could only shrug my shoulders. I had never before heard the name of Field.

'But you will be even more surprised to learn,' my interrogator continued with a sarcastic smile, and his eyes lost their glassy stare, 'that we have also got hold of Field's archives. Amazing, isn't it? Even we were astonished at such carelessness on Field's part. Tell me, what was the text of the recruiting document?'

'I haven't the slightest idea.'

'Didn't you read it?'

'I never read such a document.'

'Not even before you signed it?'

'I never signed it . . .'

'And what would you say if I put this document, with your signature on it, on the table here? If I stuck it under your nose?'

I made no reply, but the Colonel insisted:

'Answer me! What would you say?'

'I should be surprised,' I answered in a low voice, although it would hardly have astounded me by now if I had been shown my own signature on a document leading straight to the scaffold. After all, if an unproved and unchecked statement was to be taken as evidence, why should not even the most obvious falsification be accepted as an authentic document?

The Colonel appeared to reflect; then, as if it had just occurred to him, he asked:

'How did you come back from America? Tell me in detail.'

I told him that it was because of visa and passport difficulties that I had remained in Argentina until 1946. In order to return home, I had to get permission, issued in Hungary, from the Allied Control Commission. To obtain this I corresponded with my friends in Budapest. I made no secret of it that I had written to László Rajk. However, this did not seem to interest the Colonel.

'By what route did you return home?'

'I went to France by ship, from there by train.'

'Through Switzerland, perhaps?'

'Yes, through Switzerland,' I replied. My interrogator was so pleased with my reply that his face brightened.

'Well,' he cried, 'then the whole thing is simple. Field was in Switzerland at that time. When you were passing through Switzerland, Field boarded the train and recruited you as his agent.'

I still don't know which nonplussed me more, the fact of the suggestion itself or its amazing naïveté. Both were frightening. More frightening, however, was the air of naturalness with which the Colonel suggested that I should confess to something he had just concocted with a complete disregard for even the shadow of truth.

It was hair-raising that he should be content with such a transparent fairy-tale. When I said that it appeared unimaginable to me that anyone should permit himself to be recruited into a foreign secret service by a complete stranger on a train, the Colonel shrugged his shoulders.

'If you don't like it, write something more convincing. I'll let you have paper and pencil. Write down who recruited you, when and how, and what was in the letter you brought Szönyi. Write down when and how frequently you met Szönyi since your return home; tell all you know about him and what you and he talked about. Write also about Field. We'll leave Rajk for another time. That should be enough for today.'

He made me sit down at a small table in his ante-room. He placed paper and pencil in front of me. A guard with a rifle kept watch. The secretary locked her drawer and left. I was often to sit hunched over that light-coloured, worn little table until daybreak. On the wall hung a large, idealized photograph of János Kádár. At the time, Kádár was still Minister of the Interior. A year and a half later he, too, became a political prisoner.

During the night there was little coming or going in the Colonel's ante-room. Once, however, I was interrupted by a young man clutching a large, brown envelope. He seemed in a great hurry. He looked around helplessly. The expressionless, exhausted, wooden features of the armed guard did not appear to inspire the newcomer's confidence, and in spite of my unshaven face, he must have thought I was one of his colleagues, for he turned to me, instead of the guard, and asked:

'Is Comrade László Farkas in his office?'

This is how I learned the name of the Colonel, though he continued to use the pseudonym Kovács when he telephoned in my presence.

No session passed without László Farkas making special mention of his proletarian background; this, together with his brief and insignificant participation in the anti-fascist resistance movement, he considered his greatest virtues and he liked to compare himself with my bourgeois family, education and interests. In fact, in his stiff, angular manner, he was always playing a part, except when he took out his truncheon. At such times a fierce, authentic flame blazed in his eyes and he was undoubtedly sincere when he hissed in my face:

'You just can't imagine how I hate you!'

On his desk, with typical petty-bourgeois taste, he kept a framed tinted photograph of his wife and small daughter. And on the wall of his office hung a portrait of the ascetic, bearded F. E. Dzerzinski, head of the Russian Cheka and afterwards of the GPU, whose murderous zeal even Lenin found exaggerated in 1923. At the peak of physical torture, Farkas's otherwise winsome smile, showing two rows of healthy teeth, distorted into a rigid, demonic grin. He would accompany every blow of the truncheon with remarks erupting from his infantile and vulgar sexual imagination; these, in the pauses between disconnected, obscene words, he would whisper in my ear or murmur to himself with enjoyment. After such scenes it took some time before he was able to shake himself back into his Dr. Jekyll state of mind, his everyday, eager, boyishly naïve, provincial garrison-officer personality, gazing out of dreamy, innocent eyes at the idyllic family group on his desk.

I must admit that I feared none of my interrogators as I feared Farkas. Once, after my release from prison, I ran into him at the entrance of the Kútvölgyi Sanatorium. I was sent there for a general check-up and met Farkas leading an elderly lady down the steps to a car bearing an official registration plate. The former ÁVH colonel had grown fat; his face was no longer pink but yellow. He reminded me now not of the boyish garrison-officer but rather of a prematurely aged, obese Russian general, fearful of being arrested. László Farkas was then organizing secretary of the Greater Budapest Party head-quarters and a member of the Central Committee—and even in 1956, just before the revolution, his name was often to be seen in the press and on posters announcing prominent speakers. When, for a moment, our glances met at the sanatorium entrance, his face did not break into the self-assured smile I had so often seen. It darkened.

On this first day of our acquaintance, too, the Colonel's face darkened as he read my draft.

'This is nothing,' he said, 'nothing at all!'

It was true the notes contained nothing new. I had summarized a few conversations I had had with Szönyi, and gone on to refute his statements first made at the foot of the T-shaped table, pointing out their utter absurdity. Of Noel Field I only said that I had never come across a person of that name. To be truthful, I did wonder for a moment whether it might not be more rational to fall in, partially at least, with the Colonel's suggestions. All the more so as the picture he had painted—Noel Field boarding the Arlberg Express and attempting to recruit a complete stranger for the American secret service, a Hungarian communist at that, returning home from the other side of the globe–might have furnished an amusing plot for a satirical film, but could never claim credence from normal human beings.

If I rejected the temptation it was by instinct rather than by careful consideration of the possible consequences. Since then, however, I have had the opportunity of comparing my experiences with those of others and today I feel certain that the idiotic suggestion concerning Field was a trap set not for the first time, the cleverness of which lay in its very guise of stupidity. As a matter of fact, some people, believing that even a People's Democratic court of law would feel ashamed at allowing such arrant nonsense to be taken seriously, laughed up their sleeve and accepted the role for which they were cast in the puppet-show. Then, in most cases, the silly story having served its subtle purpose, it was discarded without ever reaching the court; and, on the first admission, skilled artisans of the ÁVH constructed an inverted pyramid of fantastic charges, and though the bricks may have been baked from the soap-bubbles of imagination, their very weight sufficed to crush a slave of formal logic. Then, out of artistic pride rather than tactful consideration for the judge's sensitive conscience, the ÁVH investigators would drop the hotch-potch of nonsense and concoct a somewhat less incredible story to which the victim of logic–who had, by then, admitted to even graver crimes–would sign his name without protest.

As yet, my reflections had not strayed towards such possibilities when I ignored the Colonel's suggestion to write something more plausible. I don't know what he could have expected from me, nor do I know whether it was with feigned indignation or sincere fury that he flung my draft on the table, shouting:

'I'll show you how we deal with spies, traitors and police agents! From today you will stand, even in your cell! You will not lie down, either by day, or by night. No food. No water. No washing.'

He picked up the receiver then changed his mind and called the armed guard:

'Take the prisoner down.'

Then he followed us into the corridor.

'Don't let him get near the bannister,' he told the guard. 'Keep him close to the wall, he's already tried to finish himself off once.'

As the apprehensive guard took my arm and pushed me to the wall of the staircase, Farkas broke into hooting laughter. His guffaws echoed in my ears all the way down to the second floor.

3

The People's Educator

THAT night was followed by a period certain details of which it is vain to try to bring back from oblivion. This may be due in part to psychological factors, particularly the emotional economy of forgetfulness enabling a man to rid himself of tormenting memories and passions that could render him sleepless. Still, I may not be mistaken if I suppose that my physical condition was mainly to blame that my recollections become, here and there, hazy. But certain scenes and critical moments remain imprinted on my memory, both visually and acoustically, with the exactitude of a synchronized sound-film, and I can quote every word spoken at such moments. Therefore, I have no reason to fear that either forgetfulness or emotion will lead me astray.

As a result of the Colonel's order, I was once and for all freed from the anxiety whether or not I would get a few minutes sleep or whether I would miss the flour-soup in the morning and the beans in the afternoon. I was led to a remote cell, which nobody ever passed; the lid of the Judas-hole was left open and an armed guard stood almost uninterruptedly in front of the door. Later the door was left open, a bench was placed before it, and this is where the four members of a one guard-unit, uniformed men and civilians alike, set up quarters when on duty. Whether on instruction or simply for fun, they used me to relieve their boredom. They ordered me to stand motionless, then yelled at me or kicked the door, and on the pretext that I had moved, fell upon me and struck and kicked me all over. Other groups of guards left only the Judas-hole open, and one of the armed guards made me stand in front of the small opening so that he could spit in my face every time he went by.

After a few days, these spectacular doings must have gained fame in the cellar-township, for from time to time an expert audience assembled in front of my cell. Sometimes the guests grew tired of being merely spectators and took an active part in the proceedings. This is how, one day, I came to be visited by a broad-shouldered man in his mid-forties, whom the others called Tarján—in England, they would perhaps have called him Tarzan. His flattened nose and cauliflower ears betrayed that he had devoted his youth to the excitement of the ring rather than to the study of Virgil's Bucolics. Although he hardly came up to the level of my eyes, his physical strength was such that, to the delight of the grateful audience, he lifted me by the hair, swung me back and forth, and when my heels touched ground again, held me away from him at an angle of 45 degrees and bashed his fist several times into my face.

There were times when they made me stand facing the lamp, then again facing the whitewashed wall, sometimes with my back, sometimes with my side towards the door and the Judas-hole. On the third day I longed for water but had no longer any wish to eat.

On the fourth day, my eyes discerned a medley of colours on the white wall; then these pale and uncertain greens, yellows and pinks began gradually to form into pictures. One I particularly remember is the picture of a crowded terrace of a Champs Elysées café where, among mediaeval poets and contemporary painters, I saw Walt Whitman sitting at a small, round table, wearing a hat the size of a mill-stone and sipping lemonade through a long straw.

I realized even then that my eyes were conspiring with my imagination; that they were playing a game of benevolent cunning to distract my attention from the present. But when, through the open door of the cell, I stole a glance at the corridor wall and there, under a neo-classical bas-relief I read the signature of a sculptor friend of mine, it suddenly occurred to me that I might be having hallucinations. I wondered why they had arrested the sculptor and felt glad that he had a privileged position here, in the cellar, since he was permitted to work, if only with plaster. I observed with pleasure the slender female figures walking with a basket or a jug on their heads, though I wondered with some disapproval why my friend had reverted to his earlier, neo-classical style. It did not seem in the least strange that I should now notice his work, though the day before, the wall had still appeared smooth and empty.

It did not appear to me any less real than the bas-relief when I noticed that not only did the concrete floor of the cell show patches of dampness but that great puddles were forming on it; then my feet and the entire cubicle were flooded with a filthy liquid, the level of which rose gradually, until it reached my chest. There it stopped, began to recede, rose and receded again, and when, after much ebb and flow, once more there remained only tiny puddles on the floor, I observed that out of the concrete floor the water had washed century-old newspapers with old-fashioned typography and pictures of the nobility dressed in the fashion of our great-grandparents.

It is at this point that my recollections become hazy; I don't know when and how often I was taken up for questioning, I don't know how often the water in my cell rose to my chest then receded again, all I recall is that when the grey-haired interrogator opened the door and I made some remark that the old newspapers on the floor should be in a museum, and complained about the spitting guard, he pointed to the bunk and told me to lie down.

With this single exception, made memorable also by a full dixie of beans, I stood for nine days and nine nights without food and without water. These nine days must have been an event worth recording; perhaps they were set down in my file side by side with the date of my birth, since they were repeatedly referred to later by various investigators and, approximately a year and a half later, one of them promised that he would make me stand for another nine days, 'but this time on one foot'.

Since my arrest I had not been shaved, had not cut my nails, nor had I changed my underwear. Even before those nine days, the guards had frequently deprived the prisoners in the cellar of the few pleasant minutes of ablution; perhaps out of laziness rather than malice. But now Farkas's orders had put out of my reach even this modest possibility of cleaning myself. I touched with distaste the three week's growth on my face and looked with nausea at my swollen, deformed hands, my blackened nails. The extreme torment of filthiness was augmented by the fact that, as a result of the complete lack of food and water, my mouth was filled with a glue-like, sticky fur that impeded even my speech. Soon I was as unbearably disgusted with my own physical state as with the Colonel's frequent personality changes and obscene play of imagination when excited by cruelty.

Days and nights flowed into each other. Every time I heard the noises of the morning soup distribution I drew another line on the calendar scratched into the humid wall. At dawn, when I was being led back from an interrogation, I kept an exact record of the number of bastinados and palm-beatings, like a conscientious journalist, a chronicler, who may, sometime, somewhere, have to account for his experiences with professional honesty and reliable exactitude. Yet I wished nothing more ardently than never to see that cell-wall again, nor the guards nor the Colonel, and it would have seemed to me a saving joy if my heart had at last stopped beating. Of this I now saw some hope, for my ankles had swollen to the size of elephants' and my knees were like large melons, almost completely filling my trouser-legs. I concentrated all my energy upon interrupting and terminating my biological functions. Yet during those nine days, only once did I collapse and lose consciousness. But however hopeless I knew my situation to be, or perhaps just because of that hopelessness, I sometimes found the transports of rage, the primitiveness and cynicism of the Colonel, and even my own pedantic and utterly purposeless statistics amusing, and there were moments when I entertained myself, almost self-forgetful, with my time-killing games.

The permanent dialogue between the instinct of survival and the wish for liberating death was frequently interrupted by the knowledge that what the investigators and the Colonel were constantly repeating, namely that they were acting with the full approval of the Communist Party, was indeed true. They committed deeds of extreme cruelty in the name of a party that I had joined in my early youth because of a groping, radical humanitarianism. And yet, I felt that I had no more spiritual affinity with the guards in the cellar, the investigators, Vajda, Tarján, the Colonel, Károlyi, Ernö Szücs or Gábor Péter, than with an amoeba. I had never accepted the philosophy that considers the end justifies the means, and I therefore regarded it as all the more self-evident that the means applied by the ÁVH compromised any end whatsoever, for all time to come. As I myself would have prevented such procedure as theirs everywhere, at all times and against everyone, with passionate indignation, had I had the power to do so, I considered myself caught in a trap, betrayed, because, in however small a degree, and however indirectly, my communist past had been grist to Gábor Péter's mill. This realization only increased my wish that my breathing should at last stop.

For this reason, the death-wish remained dominant, but at the same time, the instinct of survival, and even more the immediate torment of thirst, compelled me to commit a shameful act. At certain times the guards conducted even me to the lavatory although on the third day of starvation and thirst my metabolism had almost completely ceased. I went only for the pleasure of moving about. But on one occasion I could no longer hold my animal desire in check; I pulled the chain and stuck my face into the bowl to get at least a few drops of water. In vain did my gaoler press the barrel of his revolver in the back of my neck, as long as the water was running, in vain did he kick me, pull me, and hit my head with the butt of his gun.

The physical agony and tormenting need of sleep, water and food, were supplemented by threats and promises. Farkas took particular pleasure in depicting in great detail various methods of torture inspired partly by his reading (for example, a translation of Octave Mirbeau's *Le Jardin des Supplices*), partly by his own imagination. He frequently described an instrument the invention of which he claimed for himself, the execution to the brilliant technicians of the ÁVH. This instrument, complete with straight-jacket, could, according to the Colonel, lift the eye-ball from its socket and introduce electrodes into the eye-hole thus causing inhuman suffering and insanity. While threatening me with the most varied tortures Farkas also declared several times—as his predecessors, particularly the grey-haired investigator had done before him—that not only myself but also my family would suffer the results of my stubbornness. My mother was already under arrest and my three-year-old son would be sent to a camp for children: neither I, nor his mother, nor our friends, would ever see him again.

'Do you think,' he asked me again and again, 'that we have to account to anyone for your family, your child or even your own life? Nobody and nothing obliges us to send a spy and a Horthy police agent for trial. If we don't get a statement, you will either rot away in this cellar or we shall take you out one night to some deserted place, make you dig your own grave, then shoot you in the back of the head. I can assure you that no-one will look for you. You will have disappeared, and that will be that.'

After this several times in the middle of the night my cell door was unlocked. Five or six grim-faced men would put me in irons, bundle me into a car and drive me out of town. Blinded by dark glasses I sat in the speeding car cramped between two security men and the car cornered sharply, first in the deserted streets and later on the winding road leading up the mountain; only the humming of the motor and the squeaking of brakes were audible, there was no sound of human voices or other traffic. At such times I thought not only of Farkas's threats, but remembered my religious childhood when I had prayed for an easy death. A bullet in the back of the head now seemed indeed easy. Usually however, I landed in the cellar of some secret villa because, especially in the mountains of Buda, the ÁVH had commandeered a large number of summer villas, like the one with the T-shaped table where I had spent my first days and had been confronted with Rajk. Gradually, I became inured to these nightly excursions and if, at first, I felt a shiver run down my spine, later I no longer even wondered whether I would return or not.

It could not have escaped the Colonel's attention that neither the prospect of having to dig my own grave before being shot, nor even the carrying out of this threat, was likely to appear more uncomfortable to me than my present situation. So, early one morning, after an exhausting all-night session, he put his little flat revolver on the desk in front of him and delivered the following speech:

'I am perfectly aware of your state of mind. You feel that everything has come to an end. That there is no way out. We know that you are a spy and were a Horthy police agent, and you know what is coming to you. We have sufficient proof. That reminds me, tomorrow I shall show you your recruiting document. But even so, if you decide to help me, if you make a statement, I promise that I will show you mercy. I shall leave you alone for five minutes with this gun. There will be one bullet in the magazine. Naturally, I shall remove the others.'

For a while he fumbled with the clip of his gun, then he looked at me.

'Don't you believe it? You don't believe me?' and he broke into loud laughter.

This scene was repeated several times in several variations, at dawn or at night. But once, as if no-one had ever said anything about a bullet in the back of the head, or out of mercy, leaving me alone with the revolver, the Colonel went to the wireless which stood next to the divan. He switched it on, and sank down on to the divan. It was late, most stations were broadcasting dance-music. The Colonel waited for the announcer to speak.

'Well, Mr. Scholar,' he asked, 'is that Spanish?'

'Italian.'

Farkas narrowed his eyes, examined the dial of the wireless closely, then turned the knob. The strains of a *jota* filled the room. We heard the Madrid announcer.

'It wouldn't be bad, would it,' the Colonel laughed, 'to sit on the terrace of a Madrid café, and perhaps stretch out on the sands on the Spanish coast. In the sun. And then bathe. Imagine! Bathe. For, no doubt, you know that you stink like a skunk?'

Then he grew serious, jumped up from the divan and began walking to and fro.

'If you make a statement involving yourself and others, we shall sentence you to a few years. You won't have it bad in prison, I'll take care of that personally. Because I need an able man to work for me, one I could send to Spain. You speak Spanish, you'd be most suitable. In a year, a year and a half, or even much earlier, I shall get you out of prison. Your family stays here, of course, and if you try to play any trick on me abroad, your boy . . .'

The Colonel stretched his arms forward and made a movement as if he were wringing a heavy, wet sheet. Then he looked
at me.

'Well, would you like to work for me? Work in Spain?'

'I wouldn't know how,' I replied.

'Of course you would. You'd be excellent! I couldn't find anyone
better. But you don't believe me. You don't want to work for me.
Isn't it true that you don't believe me? Isn't it true that you don't
believe I would release you from prison?'

I made no reply.

'All right,' said Farkas reaching for the rubber truncheon. 'You
don't believe me and you don't want to work for me. In that case we
shall get back to our good, old, reliable people's educator.'

Before swinging it, the Colonel tenderly caressed his favourite
instrument which he had christened 'the people's educator', and for
which he had a wide variety of loving nicknames. In those days, the
people's educators of the Communist Party were the agitators who
went to factories and other places of work, and even from house to
house, trying to convince the doubters of the correctness of communist policies and of the uniquely redeeming quality of the ideals
of Soviet socialism.

Colonel Farkas obviously regarded the ÁVH's blunter methods
of persuasion as more expedient; though the fact that he made fun of
a party institution like the people's educators with such impudent,
cynical irony, might have led one to suppose that he believed in
neither the communist dogma nor the world-transforming power of
socialism, but had put himself at the service of the system merely as a
mercenary. Though I think that such a supposition would not
reflect the whole truth.

From the devout and emotional respect with which he recalled the
events and personalities of the past when attempting to build a
credible background for my alleged activities as a former police
agent, I gained the impression that Farkas's cynicism was interwoven
with some sort of bigoted and sentimental blind faith. It is question-
able whether this flicker of religious enthusiasm was kept alive
artificially, or whether, at times, he unconditionally and sincerely
believed that he was a believer. I seemed to discover signs of the
latter in numerous sudden softenings and indignations which
reasons of duty could hardly have led him to put on, and in the
tensely expectant, even anxious way in which he waited for my reply
and watched for the effect, when by way of a detour he referred to
some aspect of socialist ideology to show off his extensive reading.

But another duplicity was to have a more direct effect upon my fate than the ambivalence of Farkas's emotional make-up.

The Colonel urged me more and more openly to invent some story that would help to prove that I was a spy and a former Horthy police agent. He dreamed up, then discarded, different stories, suggested others, then discarded those as well. The variants excluded each other mutually, not merely psychologically, but also as far as place and time were concerned. This made it evident that his intention was to construct a false charge against me with complete disregard for the facts. At the same time, he had no doubts whatsoever as to my being a suspicious individual, not merely harmful but dangerous from the point of view of the Communist Party, a person to be eliminated; and that I had indeed committed acts that the political police were justified in punishing. At times, Farkas reminded one of a child given a puzzle to solve; he sought more and more savagely for the solution, knowing all the time that it must be a simple one, but, unable to find the right answer, he resorted to cheating rather than admit the shameful fact of his impotence.

He wanted results at any price; he must find compromising episodes in my life, give me a bad conscience over some insignificant detail, so that I would acknowledge the justification of their suspicion and thence draw the conclusion that I must, to appease my feeling of guilt, admit to a capital crime. Finally Farkas did indeed discover the damning evidence he wanted.

When he enquired into the circumstances of my various travels I readily recounted every detail, nor did I conceal the fact that when, in the spring of 1939, it was no longer easy for a Hungarian citizen to obtain an overseas visa, the military attaché of the Hungarian Legation in Paris, Colonel Karátson, one-time class-mate of a close relation of mine at the Military Academy, had helped me, at the request of my army-officer relatives, to obtain an entry permit for the Argentine.

Farkas made me relate with hair-splitting accuracy my conversations with Colonel Karátson. Although my talks with the military attaché turned almost exclusively on our common interest, film-making, Farkas made me repeat again and again what Karátson had said, what I had said, how I came to introduce the attaché to the chairman of the French amateur film club; when and how we attended exclusive meetings when, at the film-club, they screened the prize-winning avant-garde films of the year. I also recounted

E 57

repeatedly and in minute detail my exclusively formal visit to the Argentinian military attaché for, naturally, Karátson introduced me to his Argentinian colleague, and innumerable times I described my brief talk with the Argentinian consul to whom, in turn, I was introduced by the Argentinian military attaché.

The very fact – Farkas concluded – that I had come into contact, socially, with people of that sort, put me in a doubtful light. He, for instance, could never have entered such suspicious and compromising circles. It put me in an equally bad light, and this even I had to admit, that since 1933 I had had no direct organizational contact with the Communist Party either in Hungary or in France; all I did was to contribute a few articles to leftist publications and deliver a few lectures in fellow-traveller clubs. It was characteristic, Farkas added, that even for these articles and lectures, I selected art subjects and not political or sociological ones. Even so, according to his information, my lectures had aroused general uproar and indignation. I ought to see the condemning depositions made against me by communists who had returned from France and Argentina; my hair would stand on end if I knew what a vile and despicable Trotsky-ite they took me for.

It must be clear even to me, Farkas continued, that no man in his right mind would believe that a military attaché would do someone a favour merely out of friendship. Military attachés are professional spies, therefore, there could be no shadow of doubt that Karátson would help me only if I did espionage work for him in exchange. At the same time, a military attaché must protect his reputation. He would not openly ask a complete stranger for information, in case by doing so, he should be led into a trap. It was quite obvious that the attaché knew I was an old and experienced agent. All he did was take me over from Peter Hain, the head of the detective branch of the Hungarian political police. For as far back as 1932, when as a young communist, I was arrested, Peter Hain had recruited me into the service of the Horthy régime as an *agent provocateur*. Karátson helped me to obtain an Argentinian visa, partly in reward for my services, partly to spy for him in South America, but by no means selflessly, or without an ulterior motive.

How could I have been Peter Hain's agent, I asked, if, as the Colonel himself had disapprovingly remarked, 'I maintained no close contact with the communists?' What could I have told Hain about them? What information could I obtain for Karátson in the class-rooms of the Sorbonne?

'Just at present,' the Colonel interrupted me, 'we are not discussing your espionage activities but the circumstances under which you were recruited as an agent.'

He had shaped, then re-shaped, changed and pieced together the story of my recruitment for several days now. He referred no longer to Szönyi's statement, he asked no questions concerning Wagner, Field, or Wagner's fictitious message to Szönyi. He was content to prove that I was a man of doubtful antecedents, that they were justified in suspecting me, and that it should be entirely a matter of indifference to me how the deposition expressing the party's suspicion of me was formulated, for even if that suspicion remained no more than suspicion, I should never again be released. I was in the power of the ÁVH, they could do with me as they pleased, they could starve me to death in the damp cellar, and if they finished me off more quickly I should owe them a debt of gratitude.

After I had been standing for seven times twenty-four hours, they no longer led, but half dragged, half carried me to Farkas's room. If, after the now ritual bastinado I was unable to rise, the Colonel pushed a chair towards me with his foot. To make me understand how much he loathed me he did not touch it with his hands. I would then get hold of the leg of the chair, pull myself up to the seat then grasp the back of the chair and straighten up relying solely on the strength of my arms. Two of the lower ribs in my chest had completely caved in and now rendered my stomach muscles almost useless.

'Are you shamming? What's the matter with you?' Farkas asked, pretending surprise.

'I must have some broken ribs,' I replied.

'If you had, you wouldn't be able to stand,' he declared with the superior assurance of the expert.

He was wrong. A good five years later, side by side with other injuries the X-ray pictures showed the ungainly scars of two broken ribs in my chest, and three in my back. However, during my interrogations it never even occurred to me to bother about such petty details. What did I care who was right, when, on the eighth and ninth day of constant standing Farkas was promising me pleasures undreamed of. As soon as he had finished his statement dealing with Colonel Karátson, he said, I would get a jug of hot cocoa and a piece of plain cake.

And on the night of the ninth day he summoned his secretary, sending his car to fetch her. The frighteningly ugly, bespectacled girl took her place beside the Colonel's desk. She stared grimly at the keys of her typewriter as if she feared the fate of Lot's wife, should her eye accidentally fall on me. In marked contrast, the Colonel giggled happily, allowed himself childish jokes, and sucked lumps of sugar while dictating his notes which–if I remember rightly–dealt with my family background, university years and the events of the student movement, particularly László Rajk and my conversations with him.

I was lying on the floor, dozing, and came to with a start only when Farkas yelled at me, called my name, or reminded me of the cocoa and cake. Though I looked up at such times, I had no hope whatever of touching that cocoa or that cake. Not only because I had little faith in the Colonel's promises, but also because in my half-stupor it seemed to me utterly inconceivable that such pleasures should ever again exist for me in reality, instead of in the realm of fantasy.

I was no longer able to follow Farkas's dictation or to concentrate my attention for more than a few seconds. Only the memory of my earlier reflections still turned round and round in my mind. Slowly, with great effort, I attempted to piece them together. The methods applied in the past three weeks had the purpose of reducing me, the suspect, both physically and mentally, to such an animal condition that my momentary needs would deprive me of human dignity and render me blind; they were aimed at distorting my judgment of values, at falsifying my standards when differentiating between rational and irrational, so that an hour's sleep seemed a greater treasure than life itself, and where, in exchange for a little peace or a jug of cocoa, or to escape from the terror of physical pain, I would confess even to a charge involving the noose. But by now, all things had become a matter of indifference to me. As long as I could close my eyes, lying there on the floor, I gladly forgot even the cocoa. I was awakened by Farkas. He called my name several times in succession:

'You are not paying attention,' he said without anger, then screwed up his eyes ironically, 'though we shan't be long now. We have reached Péter Hain. Come, tell me how he recruited you? Did he give you a cover-name?'

Though I made no reply Farkas continued to dictate; then like a railway guard bawling the name of the station, he called to me again:

'What did that Karátson look like? Describe him again. Get up!'

I crawled to the chair, got hold of its leg and pulled myself to my feet in the usual way.

'We are having a beautiful dawn, or rather morning,' Farkas smiled almost benevolently and rubbed his eyes, bloodshot from lack of sleep. 'You may look out.'

Indeed, the Colonel's balcony was bathed in brilliant sunshine and the sun shone on the floor of the room, too. Farkas came to my side.

'You may look out,' he encouraged me, 'certainly you are not able to jump out,' he added; nonetheless, he followed me as I stumbled towards the light.

The whole length of Andrássy Street was sparkling in the sunshine and red geraniums were sunning themselves on the window-sills and on the balcony.

'Another hour, and you'll have your cocoa and cake. I am a man of my word,' Farkas assured me, then went back to his desk to continue dictating to the grim girl.

I don't know how many more pages he dictated. But though I never saw the promised cocoa I cannot say that the Colonel was not a man of his word, that he deliberately deceived me, because, for my part, I never signed the final text of the legend concerning Péter Hain and Colonel Karátson. But on this brilliant morning, the struggle was not yet over; it was merely interrupted by the sudden ringing of the telephone.

Farkas lifted the receiver, and answered with military brusqueness; he was almost standing to attention. Then he quickly arranged his papers and locked them up. He whispered something to his secretary, buttoned and smoothed down his tunic and gave me a signal:

'Let's go!'

As I was stumbling down the stairs he came to my side, grasped my arm and spoke in a low voice:

'Don't try to play it smart with the Lieutenant-General! If you do, you'll pay for it.'

When we turned from the corridor into the ornate mirrored lobby leading to Gábor Péter's ante-room, the Colonel stopped for a second. I stopped, too. And then, from the long mirror on my right, I saw a stranger looking back at me from hollow eyes in an unkempt, bearded face. He wore my grey suit and it was many sizes too large for him; when I touched the button of my jacket, he copied the action. It was some time before I could convince myself that I was facing my own image in the mirror.

Behind the padded door, Gábor Péter sat at a desk facing the entrance; next to him and behind him, a few leading ÁVH officers. I recall Ernö Szücs's face, Vladimir Farkas's and Dr. Bálint's, but others may have been present also. László Farkas placed himself some distance away from me, near the left-hand window opening on Andrássy Street. To the right of me stood a round table. On it were some twenty-five telephones of various shapes and sizes, which, for a second, suggested that the grim men assembled here were engaged in arranging some modest technical exhibition.

I can scarcely remember what Gábor Péter asked me, for, as soon as he offered me a chair and I could sit down, I suddenly felt as if curtains of spider-web thinness were being let down before my eyes, one behind the other in quick succession, and from second to second it became more difficult to penetrate them. Soon, I caught myself falling and had to hold fast to the seat of the chair. Still, I went on answering the questions put to me, until Gábor Péter lost patience:

'Nonsense,' he cried angrily at one of my answers, then added after closer observation:

'What's the matter with you?'

When I remained silent, he insisted on knowing what had happened. I told him that I was tired, exhausted, because I had been standing for nine full days and nights, and, with the exception of one break, without food or water.

'On whose orders?' Ernö Szücs's and Gábor Péter's voices rose in wrath simultaneously.

All eyes turned towards László Farkas, then the Lieutenant-General looked at me and pointed to the door:

'Leave the room,' he said.

I stumbled out into the ante-room, then, without asking for permission, threw myself into the same deep purple armchair in which, on that first day, I had waited while the security man telephoned from Gábor Péter's room. Within seconds I fell into a deep sleep.

I was awakened by a diminutive little man. At the time he fulfilled the functions of an orderly and valet to the Lieutenant-General. Later, in reward for his services, he was appointed director of the Gyüjtö or Concentration Prison housing political prisoners. It was there I learned that he was called Antal Bánkuti, and my cellmate, a social-democrat steel-worker from Diósgyör, told me that during the war years Bánkuti had been an employee at the Diósgyör steel-works, a sort of record-keeper. At that time he boasted of his clerical job just as he did later of his past as a manual worker. Bánkuti led me back to his chief's room. I sat down. Dr. Bálint addressed me:

'What kind of drug are you addicted to?'

I did not understand the question and when Bálint insisted on knowing whether I had not been taking some drug, or some medicine containing a drug, I thought this interrogation was also part of the cat and mouse game. Gábor Péter did not seem particularly interested in this interlude, for as soon as Bálint paused, he motioned to him to be silent and turned to me:

'Look here. You are going to sleep now and you will also get some food.'

'I should like to shave,' I said.

'You can't, but someone will shave you.'

'And take a bath . . .'

'You can take a bath and you'll get clean underwear.'

Bánkuti took me under my armpits again and led me to a bathroom where I could take a hot shower and cut my nails. He brought me a clean shirt and pants. Then they took me to a small room where I was shaved and afterwards they put me to bed on an iron cot with a sheet and blankets, in an office or inspection room, with an armed guard to watch me.

At regular intervals, they woke me. I was given tea and biscuits, coffee with lots of milk and rolls, and later mashed foods. It was evident that the diet had been prescribed by a physician. Did Gábor Péter remember, and in a sudden burst of enthusiasm take seriously what Mátyás Rákosi, the First Secretary of the Hungarian Communist Party so often proclaimed, namely that 'in the people's democracy man is the greatest asset'? Hardly. And though Colonel László Farkas may indeed have been taken to task by his chief, it was presumably not for his application of the classical ÁVH methods, but because the Colonel's ideas on people's education had endangered a life still of value to the ÁVH. Not, of course, in the general meaning of Rákosi's slogan but because it seemed suitable material to fit into a plan that was beginning to take shape.

On the sunny morning when the Colonel accompanied me to the Lieutenant-General's room, even the newspaper-reading public may have guessed that something was afoot, for the official organ of the Hungarian Communist Party, the *Szabad Nép*, published the following brief but conspicuous communiqué under the heading: 'Resolution of the Hungarian Workers' Party's Central Committee and Central Control Commission', and sub-heading: 'Unmasking of a Trotskyite espionage ring':

The Central Committee has expelled László Rajk and Tibor

Szönyi, as spies of foreign imperialist powers and Trotskyite agents from the ranks of the Hungarian Workers' Party.

The prisoners of the ÁVH were not informed of this sensation; no newspaper ever reached their hands. And if, by any chance, I had not been sleeping in a bed, on a sheet on that day, but had still been standing in the cellar, I should have done nothing other than engrave on my calendar the date: June 16, 1949; and in my statistics, under the heading *soling*, I should have marked the thirty-sixth (neglecting to add that one *soling* consisted of 15–25 blows of the truncheon, though if performed by the Colonel only 15–18) and under the heading *palm-beatings*, I should have reminded myself with five thick lines that I had, with luck, weathered half a thousand.

For over two days and two nights, I slept in a stupefied torpor, yet in an agony of restlessness. I opened my eyes only when they woke me to give me food. On the third day, one of the guards spoke a few words to me; I replied, and then immediately, as if there were no more important task imaginable than keeping a diary and I had to make good a criminal omission, I asked what date it was. The armed guard proved kind and allowed me to share the secret that it was the 18th of June. In all probability the second communiqué which both party-members and non-party members were to read on the 19th of June on the third page of *Szabad Nép* was already written:

> The press-department of the Ministry of the Interior announces: For espionage carried out on behalf of foreign powers, the State Security Organization has arrested László Rajk, Dr. Tibor Szönyi, Pál Justus and 17 accomplices. There is no industrial worker or peasant among those arrested.

The concluding sentence, which, by the way, did not coincide with the truth, 'there is no industrial worker or peasant among those arrested,' created panic, overt and covert, among white collar workers and intellectuals.

In the following weeks, *Szabad Nép* and other newspapers carried reports of hundreds of spontaneous demonstrations and mass-rallies, of an avalanche of letters and telegrams received, in which citizens, factories and organizations of the country expressed their 'savage hatred for the Trotskyite traitors' and begged the Party and the authorities to 'strike down with ruthless energy this vile gang of spies and imperialist agents'. The Party's central organ opened a permanent column for protests and attracted attention to the more important ones by giving them banner headlines: 'There is no room for mercy for the traitor Rajk and his gang. We request the Political Committee and Comrade Rákosi to leave not even the seed of treason in our Party', (*Szabad Nép*, 24th June, 1949). At their meeting, Greater Budapest Party 'condemned the traitors with ardent hatred, and expressed their unlimited confidence in and devoted loyalty to the Central Committee and Comrade Rákosi', then, in a draft resolution, congratulated Rákosi who had set an example in militant communist vigilance', (*Szabad Nép*, 26th June, 1949). At the same time, however: 'The filth of the country, the reactionaries of all walks of life still living among us, have suddenly begun to speak of Rajk and his gang with pity', (*Szabad Nép*, 24th June, 1949). Not so the members of the Women's Federation: 'The working women loathe the gang of spies now unmasked because it is an enemy of the powerful socialist Soviet Union and the Party, the pledges of our peaceful, free future.' Therefore, the Women's Federation besought the party and the authorities 'to deal the imperialist agents a heavy blow', (*Szabad Nép*, 26th June, 1949).

While the interrogations were in full swing at the ÁVH, in the secret villas, and in the cellars of 60, Andrássy Street–where I, too, was taken back on the morning of 18th June–while tormented, lonely, starving men and women sat gazing at the electric bulbs and the dripping walls, the Monday journal of the Communist Party declared: 'The Judas Tito and the executioner Rankovich have introduced a fascist reign of terror in Yugoslavia', (*Független Magyarország*, 20th June, 1949), and *Szabad Nép* came out with the sensational headline: 'Witch-hunt in America–eleven communists in the dock', (*Szabad Nép*, 26th June, 1949). While the ÁVH were arresting approximately two hundred persons, reports appeared in the Hungarian Party press: 'The UDB–Tito's Gestapo–carried off its victims like a beast of prey. In Montenegro, in the environment of Andrijevica, sixty persons disappeared in a single day.' Then came heart-rending descriptions of the Yugoslav prisons where only rarely was permission given for 'families to bring in food and clean under-wear', (*Szabad Nép*, 29th June, 1949). In the meantime, party-members and non-members alike were given ideological instruction. 'At an inspiring ceremony marking the commissioning of new officers of proletarian background', the Muscovite Milhály Farkas, Minister of Defence, following in the ideological footsteps of the pioneer theoretician József Révai thus clarified the concept of patriotism on behalf of these worker and peasant lads:

Only he who deeply loves the Soviet Union, the great protector of the world's peoples, the powerful and invincible vanguard of progress and peace, is a good Hungarian patriot. Only he is a good Hungarian patriot who reveres and loves our great teacher, Generalissimus Stalin, who successfully leads the struggle of the peoples for a lasting peace and the triumph of freedom in the entire world. (*Független Magyarország*, 18th July, 1949)

The reader was informed also that, in unhappy contrast to the Soviet Union fighting for the triumph of freedom, there were also police states. 'The USA is the greatest police state,' proclaimed a fat headline in the party organ, and this is how it summed up its proofs: '. . . the FBI drives thousands of innocent persons to suicide, terrorizes the entire country and in fact legalizes every successful gangster-trick, from threats to anonymous denunciation', (*Szabad Nép*, 24th July, 1949).

While the inhabitants of Budapest and the people of the Hungarian countryside were supplied with such exact information concerning an overseas country, they could not even guess what was happening to those of their relatives arrested by the ÁVH. Not only was it impossible to take them, even once in a while, such food or clothing as was accepted by the jailers of 'Tito's Gestapo'; they did not know whether those who had disappeared were held prisoner in Hungary or in the Soviet Union, or even if they were still alive. At 60 Andrássy Street, all information was refused.

4

'Imperialist Agent. Establish This!'

IT seems to me that communist state-management could best be depicted not as a static pyramid but rather as an area of concentric magnetic rings in which centrifugal and centripetal forces fluctuate simultaneously. This scheme of things is ideal when a single person – a dictator – stands at the centre. Where the hub of the concentric fields is no longer a fixed point but a small inner circle, each constituent element of this inner circle will generate separate concentric fields around itself which will frequently cut across each other. This illustrates the conflicts, alliances and struggles between the various factions which, in the outer circles, usually manifest themselves merely in the form of competition for authority.

In 1949, at least as far as appearances were concerned, the paradigm could be regarded as ideal because at its centre stood Stalin who, according to Mihály Farkas, was 'successfully' leading not only the Soviet Union and her satellites, but 'the struggle of all peoples for a lasting peace, the triumph of freedom throughout the world'. Which, being interpreted, means that Stalin was trying to extend the power-line network of the magnetic fields generated around himself, to the entire world. Because the world's population is the outer circle. According to communist theory, Stalin was the only begotten leader of the hundreds of millions; forming the closer circle is the working-class, or, to be more exact, the industrial workers. And the élite of the working class, to use Lenin's now liturgical formulation, is the Communist Party.

The printed pamphlets, the devout proclamations, invariably coupled the concept of the Communist Party with Stalin; and in Hungary they tagged Rákosi's name on to Stalin's. It was never mentioned that the ÁVH considered itself to be the élite of the Communist Party just as, according to the dogma, the party was the *avant-garde* of the working class. Yet, in 1948 it had already become clear in Hungary that, as far at least as the seizure of power was concerned, it was not the one million strong Communist Party, of heterogeneous composition, that was heir of the former underground élite. It transpired that the real successor of the secret, conspiratorial party, demanding blind discipline, was none other than the equally secret, conspiratorial political police who demanded the same kind of blind discipline. The ÁVO, and its successor, the ÁVH.

From 1945 to 1948, following Rákosi's infamous 'salami-tactics', the Communist Party strove to dismember all other political parties and fill key positions in the state organization with its own men. After 1948, the same fate overtook the group of communist leaders not trained in Moscow. For by then, numerous bridge-heads of the state organization, seized by the communists from the bourgeois and other parties, had gradually been taken over by the political police. This was done in two ways: by transferring many members of the ÁVH to posts in the state administration; and by coercing into its service as informers many communists, though preferably members of other parties – formally still in existence in 1948 – and non-party members working in the various ministries.

The expansion of the political police was not even concealed. For example, several of us were transferred from the Ministry of Foreign Affairs immediately after Tamás Mátrai and other secret police had inundated the various sections of the Foreign Ministry and the Hungarian Embassies abroad. By the time I was appointed to the Ministry of Agriculture, the ÁVH reorganization there was more or less complete. The head of the personnel-department was a former ÁVH captain, who had been a shop-salesman, the transport section was directed by a former ÁVH captain, the control section by a former ÁVH first-lieutenant and the administration department by a former ÁVH major who had, in the past, been doing a shady business in cameras in Budapest's flea-market, the infamous Teleki-Square. These ÁVH officers, together with many of their colleagues of lower rank, had been transferred to the Ministry of Agriculture more or less simultaneously. Not one of them knew anything about agrarian problems; on the contrary, all were city dwellers who had never so much as smelled a village. They qualified for the high positions they held in the Ministry of Agriculture by having had a hand in staging the show-trial of the old and expert Ministry officials.

These former ÁVH officers continued to be as ignorant in matters of agriculture as they had been before their promotion, but they built up a network of spies in various sections of the Ministry, co-operated with other ÁVH agents who had been smuggled in earlier and less conspicuously, and recruited new agents – as for instance one of my secretaries – and, like Mátrai in the Foreign Ministry, maintained direct contact with the ÁVH headquarters. They always turned to the ÁVH for advice and always carried out the instructions of their headquarters, to the infinite despair of the party and non-party experts in the Ministry.

It was by these and similar methods that the ÁVH won ground in the state organizations and public offices. Naturally, this could not have been done without the knowledge of Moscow and the Muscovite party leaders. It was, in fact, carried out under direct orders from Moscow, on the basis of plans long elaborated. For the Hungarian secret police was set up in 1944 by MVD officers who arrived from Moscow with the Soviet armies and remained under their control. While the war against Hitler was still being waged on two fronts, direct Russian control could be established relatively discreetly, owing to the conspiratorial character of the secret police, and it was allowed to develop even while the democratic parties still held some power in Hungary. Thus, by 1949, the Russian MVD and the Hungarian communists who had returned from Moscow, most of whom were closely linked with the MVD, had made the ÁVH into a party within the party. It was not the one-million-strong Hungarian Communist Party, nor its successor, the Hungarian Workers' Party that made possible the Russian seizure of power in Hungary, but the party within the party: the political police and its trusted agents. For in Hungary the secret police was not merely an accessory of the Russian seizure of power, but an indispensable prerequisite, a *sine qua non*.

The last phase of the ÁVH seizure of power took place in 1948-9, when it occupied the key positions of the state administration in order to provide Moscow with a direct *chain of command* from the inner circle to the outer, and now no deceptive façade was necessary any longer. We must agree with Rákosi: this was, indeed, the 'year of change' in Hungary.

In the interests of the smooth functioning of the controlling structure, it became necessary for all persons suspected of, or capable of, resistance to be removed as a preventive measure. By 1949, Rákosi had succeeded in excluding the representatives of the democratic parties from the state administration. Those who remained no longer represented their parties but only themselves, and most of them had given in to the Muscovite leaders. Thus, thanks to their position in the state administration, it was, in the first place, the old Hungarian communists like Rajk and his friends, never recruited by the MVD, who were liable to resist, men who had lived in the West, who had learned the democratic rules of the game, and believed that their posts not only allowed them, but obliged them to think for themselves and even to show initiative and form decisions according to their notions of justice and fairness.

In utter contrast to these men, the young ÁVH officers were trained by their superiors for devotion, blind discipline, and were at the same time filled with a consciousness of mission and professional pride. In 1949, these young and usually newly-fledged communist ÁVH officers not merely regarded themselves as a select body, but their arrogance vied with the haughtiness of the mediaeval Hungarian bannerets. Their self-confidence was further inflated by the fact that they could fill their pockets with various allowances, bonuses and benefits, adding up to many times the earnings of a Hungarian office-worker or skilled industrial worker. Colonel Gyula Décsi, a member of Gábor Péter's inner circle, once told an official of the Ministry of Foreign Affairs that, on a realistic basis of comparison, the rank of a young ÁVH lieutenant equalled that of a legation secretary, that of a first lieutenant the rank of a legation counsellor, that of a captain the rank of an Ambassador; that a post in the Foreign Ministerial Service could equal the rank of an ÁVH major was not conceivable.

This financially pampered organization indoctrinated with a consciousness of mission, regarded the steering of the communist state as its natural privilege and was not only theoretically an élite, like the Hungarian Workers' Party, but in reality an élite within an élite, because, by 1949, its hand undoubtedly controlled the most vital switchboards of the state machinery. Therefore, for the members of the ÁVH, 'Party' was not merely an abstract idea, a theoretical and practical framework of ideas, as it was for the faithful Party-members; it was also a collective term, embracing the concrete notions 'our power', 'our prosperity,' 'our career,' which was raised by some of the ÁVH officers to the rank of some kind of mystical religious ideal.

After my release, in the summer of 1956, when Stalin had been dead for over three years, and Gábor Péter, Károlyi and Décsi were in prison, when Beria had already been executed and Rákosi sacked, and it seemed as though the unchangeable was, after all, changeable, several ÁVH officers indulged in self-justifying, even unsolicited, declarations. This is how I came to know, among others things, what took place inside the political police organization before the arrest of László Rajk and his fellow-accused.

In the records of the ÁVH, the Rajk affair differed from the previous show-trials staged in Hungary by involving members of the Hungarian Communist Party, and especially veteran communists.

Until then, the secret police had arrested and brought to trial almost exclusively persons like Cardinal Mindszenty who had often openly opposed the régime. In the Rajk affair only communists were arrested and leading communists at that, of whom, for people in their right minds, it was difficult to believe that they could be enemies of the system. Nor could the head of the ÁVH find anything in their files, apart from fictitious spy-reports and transparent hints and guesses, often from dubious sources.

Therefore, on the eve of the arrests–as I was told in 1956 by an ÁVH officer who was present–Gábor Péter called together his conspiratorial circle, stiffened with some of his most reliable men. He appealed to the party-loyalty of those assembled, to their un-limited trust in the party leaders, in Stalin and his Hungarian disciples. He stressed that the persons invited to this confidential conference, the élite of the élite within the élite, had been greatly honoured because the Party had selected them to accomplish an unusual task. The Soviet and Hungarian party leaders–Gábor Péter explained–had uncovered within the Hungarian Workers' Party an anti-party group, a monstrous conspiracy which, had its plans succeeded, would have endangered the very existence of the party. However, thanks to the communist vigilance of the leaders, the tables could still be turned and the communists could deal the imperialists, and their hireling, Tito, a terrible blow. The Russian and Hungarian comrades possessed confidential information as to the persons involved in the conspiracy; they knew who the agents of the foreign powers were. The unravelling of the details would be the task of the ÁVH. Gábor Péter expressed his hope that they would be worthy of the trust that had been placed in them.

Apart from the assurance that the party was infallible, Gábor Péter could put no fact, no proof, at the disposal of his men. Still, it was inconceivable for any ÁVH officer to reply in the negative to the question: 'Don't you believe the Party?' For, on the one hand, the existence of the ÁVH, the moral justification for any deed they committed, rested on their faith in the party; on the other hand, every communist secret police officer is fully aware that he is risking his life if he replies: 'No, I don't believe the Party', or even if he expresses the slightest doubt concerning the reliability of the informa-tion possessed by the Party. He may lay himself open to suspicion of protecting the so-called anti-Party group, or even of being a member of that group.

Péter stressed emphatically that the unmasking of the conspirators

71

was of vital interest to the Party. To the members of the élite, there was nothing equivocal about that speech. It was clear to them that if they refused the honourable task, or attempted, under however cunning a pretext, to evade putting their services at the disposal of present party-interests, they would, in fact, be refusing to protect their own power and financial privileges, and their colleagues would regard them as renegades and deal with them as one deals with a front-line soldier who tries to desert to the enemy.

But it did happen–although I know of only one or two isolated cases–that certain ÁVH officers attempted to withdraw from the task thrust upon them, and there was even one case of suicide; but these incidents could scarcely be regarded as typical. Yet, each ÁVH officer must have been rather surprised when he opened the file of the suspect entrusted to his care. Except for a few scraps of gossip concerning the love-life of the arrested person, all he found was a little slip of paper, bearing a brief instruction in the hand of Mihály Farkas, Muscovite Minister of Defence:

X. Y. Imperialist agent. Establish this! Farkas.

Which meant that the innermost circle, in close collaboration with Moscow, had already decided on its verdict. The business of the secret police was to construct an indictment that matched the verdict: *X. Y. is an Imperialist agent. Establish this.* They had to 'realize' the allegation on that slip of paper in the same way as centuries ago a King's messenger used to unroll a sealed document and read a coherent text to the illiterate peasants. To establish, or, as they liked to call it, to 'realize' is to execute the verdict as the builder executes the plans of the architect, in which not even the architect or the engineer prescribes how the mason should place one brick upon the other.

Not every ÁVH officer was privileged to see Mihály Farkas's written order. After the conference and the general pep-talk, once their tasks were allotted, Szücs or Gábor Péter would usually give the group-leaders individually a verbal account of the 'confidential information of the Soviet and Hungarian comrades', such as, for example, that the accused entrusted to the care of this or that group-leader had been a police spy under Horthy and had later become the agent of this or that foreign power. Péter and Szücs might sometimes inform the officer, but at other times they only hinted, with what other persons the accused should be connected, in what way or ways he could be compromised or made to compromise others. They might even add that the written documents concerning the recruitment of the accused as a spy were preserved in the Moscow archives and would, when the time came, be put at the disposal of the ÁVH.

The innermost ÁVH circle – Gábor Péter, Szücs, Károlyi, Décsi and their fellows – thought it important that the outer ÁVH circles – the investigators for instance who tortured me at the villa of the T-shaped table, and in the cellar of 60, Andrássy Street – should really believe that they were dealing with genuine spies. They were to believe this at least in *the first phase of the realization*. By various internal farces and utterly superfluous rules of a disciplinary nature, intended to create spectacular effects, they sought to carry out this aim. They even furthered it by dramatic manoeuvres such as the one carried out at my flat, after my arrest.

It seems that the inner ÁVH circle did indeed succeed in awakening in the investigators a sense of real danger and instil into them the belief that they were investigating a genuine, important espionage-affair. This explains why, at the villa of the T-shaped table, after the theatrical confrontation with Szönyi, intended partly to convince the security men, they attacked me with such apparently authentic fury, when trying to compel me, sworn enemy of 'our power', 'our prosperity', 'our career', to account for Wagner and Wagner's message to Szönyi.

But the Hungarian ÁVH leaders staging the drama, although a light-year away from the magnetic power-fields of the MVD inner circles, not to mention their centre, Stalin, did not imagine for a single moment that there was even a delicate link tying the verdict to reality and the charges of espionage and conspiracy were intended for the benefit of the outer ring of the ÁVH and the public. They were fully aware from the outset that the casual relation between the charges and the verdict was the exact opposite of bourgeois custom: the accusation was the consequence of the verdict, and not the verdict the outcome of proven charges.

The concentric ÁVH circles around the inner command either guessed or did not guess this. But, at least at first, the very outer circle of the ÁVH formed by the armed and uniformed men, appeared utterly unsuspecting. These men were often transferred from the regular army first to the frontier-guards of the ÁVH and eventually, to headquarters. Here they were tested and trained, and if they seemed suitable, were promoted to investigators, thus obtaining unlimited opportunities to make a career. This centripetal movement was made permanent by the constant increase of the ÁVH effective.

Though Colonel Farkas did not belong to the inner command, he came within one of the inner circles. He hovered on the periphery of the command and hoped that his ruthlessness and his results would one day promote his entry to the sacrosanct inner circle. When he took over my interrogation personally, Farkas, if I am not mistaken, did not as yet perform his duties with the disdainful cynicism of the top ÁVH men. He at first acted with conviction. During the months in which I frequently saw him he was advancing rapidly from a state of waning faith towards complete cynicism.

Later, the outer circles of the ÁVH also followed him along this road. I am relying not merely on my own experience; dozens of my fellow prisoners told to me how during their preliminary detention they witnessed the transformation of their ÁVH officers; how these exalted novices turned from enthusiastic believers into disillusioned, blasé and unfeeling craftsmen, manufacturing false charges. This process was unavoidable, because the more people were arrested, the more ÁVH investigators had to be employed, so the broader became the circle aware of what was happening behind the scenes until even the scene-shifters of the most limited mental capacity could no longer ignore it. But by the time the formerly convinced and enthu-siastic ÁVH investigator fully woke up to reality, he had become an accomplice–and therefore a prisoner–of the inner circle to such an extent that it would have been extremely dangerous to try and sever his ties unilaterally. This is why the ÁVH bosses did not mind the gradual enlightenment of the outer circles, or, to use another expression, their reaching 'police maturity'. They had, presumably, reckoned with this process and even promoted it, knowing that complicity forges stronger bonds than any faith or ideal.

After the first month the prisoners became increasingly aware of this gradual change. The communiqué announcing the arrest of Rajk and his accomplices had already been issued, the population of the country had already demanded in panic-stricken spontaneity the liquidation of the imperialist agents, there were already signed admissions, compromising depositions. So the ÁVH leaders relaxed in self-confident calm while the initial wave of police-hysteria spent itself.

True, the statements and notes of the individual suspects seemed rather confused and did not fit together. But once these prefabricated elements were in the hands of the ÁVH *the first phase of the realiza-tion* could be regarded as complete, for the sole purpose of this first stage was to break down those under suspicion and extract from them statements involving themselves and their fellow-prisoners. It was the task of the *second phase* to weld together these elements and fill in any cracks that remained; the *third phase* had merely to add the finishing touches, the decoration and furnishing of the edifice and its solemn presentation to the public: that is, the preparation of the show-trial for public hearing.

Of course, not all those arrested passed simultaneously through the same phases of the *realization*. Often the phases overlapped. At times, during the first phase devoted to breaking down the prisoners, the ÁVH was able to accomplish the task of the second phase, too, and even the first contours of the building may have appeared for a moment behind the separate elements.

The physical and psychological instruments of compulsion applied during the first phase were not always identical. The intensity of the means depended not merely upon the measure of resistance shown by the prisoner, but also upon the degree to which the ÁVH regarded the prisoner's past and personality as important raw material. In such cases the physical brutalities were kept within certain limits in order to preserve temporarily, in usable condition, material considered valuable in the final construction of the trial.

When, after forty-eight hours of sleep I was taken back to the cellar, shaved and bathed, I had no idea that Gábor Péter had preserved me for an uncertain future, driven purely by the instincts of a thrifty craftsman, but even he could have had no definite notion how this raw material was going to be used. He could not have known, partly because, as it soon emerged, not the ÁVH but the MVD leaders decided how to mould the raw material, how to piece together all the elements. Gábor Péter could not have known, partly because he was in no position to include me in his calculations, as in my case even the first phase of the *realization* was not yet completed. I had made no compromising statement. I had denied being a spy, and even László Farkas's notes, dictated in my physical presence but spiritual absence, as I dozed on his floor that sunny June morning, were as yet unfinished.

The ambitious Colonel did his best to make up for lost time. As soon as I was back in the cellar he had me brought before him. This time his questions centred almost exclusively around László Rajk.

I spent many successive nights at the worn little table in his ante-room. The guard, leaning on his rifle, kept a careful eye on me while I described over and over again details of our university years, but more particularly of my later meetings with Rajk, a few private conversations we had after my return to Hungary, my official reports to him at the Ministry of Foreign Affairs. Whenever Farkas read my notes he raged aloud as though he were certain that while I was describing a few unimportant details, I was concealing the essentials. He was insistent that I should supplement my statement and make changes showing Rajk in a suspicious light. When, in the ensuing version, he again failed to find any damning allusions or phrases, he would make me re-write the whole story again.

I added nothing to the truth but neither did I conceal a single detail. Not, of course, in the hope of clarifying matters, for by now my former notion that if I stuck to the truth I might, to some extent, prevent the tangle of fact and fiction from growing, seemed puerile even to me; but I concealed nothing merely out of practical considerations, namely, to save myself and Rajk from a painful situation should our statements conflict. I felt that by concealing insignificant details we should lay ourselves open to the suspicion of hiding something important.

Therefore, I described how, in 1947, when I was editor of a weekly paper, and Rajk was Minister of the Interior, he tried to persuade me to leave my job and join the political police. As the idea did not in the least appeal to me, Rajk immediately dropped his proposal. Later, he proposed in the executive committee of the Communist Party that I should be appointed to the Ministry of Foreign Affairs. Not merely because he did not consider editing a weekly much of a job, not merely because I had attended the Academy of Diplomacy, but because he thought—and expounded this in detail—that there were too few Hungarian communists in the Ministry of Foreign Affairs who spoke foreign languages, knew the Western way of life and were able to maintain contact with Western people.

'Naturally,' the Colonel commented, 'it is characteristic of you that you wanted to maintain contact with the West.'

Then he interrogated me in great detail on the special tasks entrusted to me by Rajk when I travelled abroad. I had to account for my time practically from minute to minute, say what I had talked about with embassy employees, ambassadors, foreign diplomats, at receptions, dinners, or, as the Colonel put it, how I conspired. Farkas continually tried to make me admit that in 1948, when I went to Italy twice, once via Vienna, by train, once via Prague, by air, I did not stick to the prescribed schedule but made it my business to visit Yugoslavia.

In the second and third phase of the *realization*, such a statement, broadened and coloured, could have been used as proof that Rajk had indeed conspired with Tito, and had even used the opportunities presented by the Foreign Office for his purpose. But as yet, I had no idea that the aim of the trial would be to convict Rajk of such a conspiracy. I was merely filled with suspicion and surprise at the emphasis the Colonel put on this alleged trip to Yugoslavia, and the promises of the reliefs, benefits and food I would receive, should I admit it.

Then, a day or two later, I suddenly saw through Farkas's intention. I was just describing in my painstaking notes my only difference of opinion with Rajk. It took place at the Ministry of Foreign Affairs after the Cominform had expelled Yugoslavia from among its members and the Hungarian press had already launched its campaign against Tito. The ammunition for the attacks was supplied by the Hungarian Telegraph Agency, partly from its own information, partly from information received either from the party or from the Ministry of Foreign Affairs, which was pieced together by Foreign Office officials from the reports of the Hungarian Embassy in Belgrade; I had to decide whether, and in what form, to issue the information to the Hungarian Telegraph Agency. As the reports from the Embassy appeared wild, unreliable and often even fictitious I sometimes suppressed what was obviously false, not because I wanted to act against the party-line but because of my scruples as a journalist. Because of this the Minister reproached me on two occasions and, when I tried to argue, he declared that my attitude and resistance affected him like a cold shower.

On reading this part of my notes Farkas roared with laughter. This must be the exact opposite of what really happened, he said, only the opposite could be true, for Rajk had already admitted he was Tito's agent. I had better re-write my notes so as to show that Rajk had forbidden me to issue the anti-Tito reports. When, on the following day, I again declined to do this, Farkas triumphantly produced a typewritten statement from his desk. At the bottom of each page he showed me László Rajk's signature. Then he read me a paragraph of the statement. In this Rajk confessed to having been an agent of the Yugoslav secret service, and having furnished confidential information to Major Cicmil, head of the Yugoslav Military Mission, and to Ambassador Mrazov. Farkas turned the pages, then read me another paragraph in which Rajk admitted that in his student years he had joined the communist movement as a police *agent provocateur*. When my expression betrayed my disbelief, Farkas covered up the rest of the page and held both paragraphs before my eyes. Then he said:

'You see, there isn't much point in protecting your buddy. You can do him no harm now, whatever you say against him. You will only harm yourself if you continue to be so stubborn. I can assure you, His Excellency the Minister does not spare his friends.' Farkas turned more pages, then, as if he had found what he was looking for, he pronounced my name and added something in a murmur. 'Yes,' he looked up after a little while, 'Rajk has some very interesting things to say about you. Of course, I won't read them to you. We are waiting for your own confession. For that will show us your attitude to the Party, to the People's Democracy, and whether you are ready to help us. Then we shall deal with you accordingly.'

This was plain speaking with a vengeance. Farkas no longer demanded that I confess to the accusations which for weeks had served as a pretext for torture. For some time now he had mentioned neither Szönyi nor Wagner nor Field, and what was more, he had recently even dropped Colonel Karátson and the insinuation that I had been an agent of the pre-war political police. Now, Farkas no longer asked me for genuine or even invented facts, he asked me only for a *willingness to confess*, a readiness to put myself at the disposal of the ÁVH; that is, to make statements involving myself and others. He repeatedly stressed that it made no difference as far as Rajk was concerned what charges I brought against him. If the former Minister admitted that he had been a Horthy police agent and a spy, he would also admit what I accused him of. This assurance was intended to make me understand that there was no risk whatsoever, no matter how incredible the story I invented.

While I was busy writing my nightly notes, the Colonel ordered vegetables, and sometimes even meat for me, perhaps on the instructions of Gábor Péter or the doctor, perhaps in order to be able to blackmail me later by depriving me of food. During interrogations, he still placed his rubber truncheon on the desk, threatened me with it and sometimes hit me a blow, but in general he restricted himself to making me execute squatting exercises. It cost Farkas an obvious effort to restrain himself. At times, his eyes still assumed their glassy stare and his lips tightened in the rigid grin that, at the climax of a beating, used to distort this provincial garrison-officer's face so frighteningly, and although his hand reached often, almost unconsciously, for the 'people's educator', the beatings accompanied by

78

bestial sexual utterances were not resumed. Farkas was now trying to come to terms with me, though not yet quite openly. He would not acknowledge that he was unable to produce any compromising fact against me and was, therefore, trying to establish a collaboration between our two imaginations.

'Look,' he would say, 'we know exactly what sort of fellow you are. We know exactly who your employers are, what espionage activity you were engaged in. It was the spy Rajk who tried to worm you into the people's democratic state security organization, it was the spy Rajk who insisted on your appointment at the Ministry of Foreign Affairs. Even the blind can see that you are Rajk's man, that you are birds of the same feather, that you can be nothing but a Horthy police agent and spy yourself.'

Here Farkas paused, then he added mockingly:

'Even if we didn't know all this, we could string you up whenever we wanted to on the basis of Szönyi's confession. We can wipe you off the face of the earth. As I said before, you shall dig your own grave and then a single bullet will fix you. But we never waste the public's money. We don't even need a bullet. In two years you will rot alive down there in the cellar. Shall I show you a fellow who has already been here for a year and a half?'

Without waiting for a reply, Farkas continued:

'All right. You shall see him. However, as we are not vindictive and are always rational in our thinking, we shall give you one more opportunity. You know what I mean, don't you?'

'I don't.'

'Of course you do. I've told you before. If you make a statement we shall sentence you to a short term in prison, then I'll send you to Spain to work for me there. But for that I need information with which to exert pressure. Information that will compromise you, so that I can keep you in check later. It is not enough that your family stays here. You must understand that.' He thought for a while, then, as if he had come to a sudden decision, he said: 'Now make a list of all your friends and acquaintances here and abroad who could have contact with British, Americans or Yugoslavs, and indicate which of them could be spies. We'll come back to Rajk later.'

'Some of my acquaintances did have contact with British, Americans and Yugoslavs but I have no knowledge of their having been spies.'

'Look,' Farkas replied with unusual mildness 'for the time being it is enough if you put down who, *in your opinion*, could have been a spy. Later . . . well, later we shall see.'

First I listed my friends living in Hungary. I scribbled for several nights but Farkas made a wry face every time he perused my notes.

'Isn't there a single spy among all these?' he asked gloomily.

'If there is, I'm not aware of the fact,' I replied cautiously.

'According to you, of course, everyone is honest?'

As I made no reply, the Colonel quoted a few names.

'These,' he said, 'have already confessed to having been spies. You must have known about them. And you did, too. But you deny it. You don't want to help us. I am warning you: you are heading for disaster.'

Then he made me list the names of my acquaintances abroad. The list was endless, as I had left Hungary as early as 1937, had spent two years in Paris attending the Sorbonne, writing articles, essays, short stories and, working as an assistant director in a film studio. In the course of these activities I had made many acquaintances and friends. And even more in South America. For, in 1939, a few months before the outbreak of the Second World War, I had signed an agreement with a French film company and had travelled to Argentina with a very advantageous contract in my pocket. But the war put paid to the French plans, so I wrote a screenplay for an Argentinian film company and then began taking photographs for advertising and catalogues. My active participation in politics began only when Count Michael Károlyi, whom I knew from my Paris days, launched a movement among Hungarians abroad to support the Allied war effort against Hitler, and for a new, democratic Hungary, to be created after the war. I joined Michael Károlyi's movement and soon became secretary general of the South-American branch.

After the collapse of the Habsburg monarchy, Michael Károlyi became President of the Hungarian Republic proclaimed in October, 1918, but when, in 1919, the communists seized power, Károlyi left Hungary. He lived in Vienna and Paris, and was at the outbreak of World War II, in London. In the eyes of the radical Hungarians living abroad, the integrity and political intransigence of the former President symbolized our democratic traditions, and also won him esteem and prestige in Western circles. The allies received our movement with approval and confidence, in South America, too. During the war years, in the course of various common enterprises, I came into contact, as secretary general of the Hungarian movement and editor of its journal, as well as in my private life, with British and Americans, Dutch, de Gaulle's French followers living in South America, Yugoslavs and anti-Hitler Austrians.

'Would you dare to allege,' Farkas asked, 'that there wasn't a single intelligence agent in these Inter-Allied Committees?'

'I wouldn't say that,' I replied, 'there may have been, but nobody dealt with me in that capacity.'

Farkas waved his hand dismissively.

'That's what you say, but I hope you don't imagine I believe it?' Then his face broke into a mocking smile, he breathed with relief and, like someone who had come almost to the end of a painstaking job but still had to apply the finishing touches, he asked me, 'And did you never talk with these Inter-Allied people about the affairs of the Hungarian movement?'

'Of course I did. We discussed and co-ordinated our common activities.'

'So, you informed them.'

'Yes, I informed them of everything that concerned them in the above mentioned connection. Delegated by the Hungarian movement's leadership . . .'

'That is, you informed them. You deliberately informed spies, therefore, *essentially*, you were a spy yourself.'

The same expression was used by the young ÁVH officer who devoted a whole night to a rhetorical explanation that the 'communists of Western orientation', though in the military sense not saboteurs or spies, were, with their Western mentality, bringing grist to the mill of the capitalist powers, and thus, *essentially*, were saboteurs and spies themselves. This *essentially* became one of the key-words of the ÁVH; it bridged the gap between the accusation and the supposedly capital crime. It served on innumerable occasions in the interrogation of innumerable fellow prisoners of mine to transmute harmless and insignificant deeds into crimes.

This formulation of a police conception had taken root in the jurisdiction of the Hungarian People's Democracy and the People's Court could sentence a prisoner at the bar on the basis of *presumption*. In various prisons, I came across many a prisoner sentenced to life imprisonment for trying to leave the country, but who instead of being charged with illegally crossing the border, was sentenced for espionage. Because, the indictment explained, had the accused succeeded in leaving the country it could be *presumed* that he would have contacted the espionage agencies of the Western powers and given them essential information concerning Hungary's internal situation and thus, *essentially*, would have engaged in espionage.

On the third floor of 60, Andrássy Street, I did not as yet anticipate this change in Hungarian legislation and therefore I entered into an argument with Farkas.

'It can under no circumstances be considered espionage,' I said, 'if someone discusses matters with his allies; besides, I never discussed with my foreign friends the disagreements within the Hungarian movement, or the regrettably frequent painful internal bickerings and intrigues among the emigrés . . .'

'Be kind enough to leave it to us to decide what is or isn't espionage,' Farkas interrupted, but with unusual politeness, feeling himself already in the saddle.

For the notes made during the last few nights and his endless interrogations had finally elicited certain details of my 'espionage activity'. As the Hungarian movement in Buenos Aires and our weekly paper possessed no addressograph, the office of the Inter-Allied Committee undertook, as a favour, to duplicate the list of subscribers to our weekly and at the same time also despatched to our subscribers the Committee's Spanish language publication. As most of the clerical and administrative work of the Committee was done by British citizens, I, according to Farkas, had, *essentially* handed over confidential papers of the Hungarian movement to the British espionage agency and as I had from time to time met the British head of the bureau and the British members of the Committee, Farkas established that I had maintained *contact* with the British *Intelligence Service*.

The term *contact* was the other magic word of the ÁVH. If an accused was even superficially acquainted with someone, he maintained *contact* with him. This is how I maintained *contact* not only with the spy and police agent Rajk but, by means of the addressograph, also with the British secret service; and one of my fellow-accused–a friend of mine since our teens–was compromised by the admission that he had *maintained contact* with me. With the help of this chain of *contacts* the ÁVH could link together dozens of accused –even if none of them confessed to a punishable offence–and could, *essentially*, make a mountain out of a mole-hill and turn a chat in a café into espionage activity. The sham-reality conjured up from a grain of truth by the magic power of the word *essential* was more ominous for the accused than the totally false charges. And because his fellow-accused, caught in a similar trap, gave up the struggle one after the other admitting, defeated, that *essentially* they were spies, the accused was compromised by having maintained *contact* with more and more spies until it appeared, in the end, as if he had exclusively frequented spies.

I know of numerous cases in which the accused, thus entrapped, was first subjected to the most violent methods of physical pressure, which then suddenly stopped and the lenient ÁVH officer appeared on the scene. From the very first moment of his first interrogation, this officer almost blushingly condemned the methods previously applied, adding, however, that the accused had to make allowances for the less sophisticated ÁVH men, since it was hard for anyone to believe that a man in the centre of an espionage ring formed by his friends and acquaintances, could preserve his integrity. This, at any rate, would be an alleviating circumstance. But the prisoner must think, he must try to remember. He would no doubt find evidence that others had taken advantage of his good faith.

While exploring such possibilities the mild ÁVH officer would offer the prisoner cigarettes, order him food, ask him if he was too cold in the cellar, whether he wanted a blanket. He would play the role of the warmhearted, humane man fulfilling a painful task, and sympathizing deeply with the prisoner. If it depended on him, he would release him. But the prisoner must see that there was certain circumstantial evidence against him. And if he did not comply, if he refused to help the ÁVH to uncover the details of the supposed conspiracy, those entrusted with the investigation might consider him obdurate, he might lay himself open to more suspicion and then even he, the lenient ÁVH officer, would not be able to prevent the application of violent measures.

The investigator and the prisoner would then consider, together, in what way the accused might have been used, naturally without his knowledge, how someone might have taken advantage of his good faith, and all the time the ÁVH officer would attempt to create a sort of benevolent complicity between himself and his victim. No sooner had they agreed on some kind of formula as a basis for an arbitrary interpretation, than the lenient ÁVH officer disappeared into thin air. The suspect was taken to another room, to another investigator, who looked him over grimly, appeared to know nothing of his ostensible good faith nor of the concessions made by his lenient predecessor. He turned the loose formula into a firm accusation, with the help of certain magic terms. He used the magic word *essentially*. If the prisoner had *maintained contact* with spies, he himself *essentially* became a spy. He then ordered the prisoner to account for his contacts.

Even if the accused was aware of the trap, he usually concluded from this changing of the guard that his situation was hopeless and he was now completely in the power of the ÁVH. It is quite possible that the chiefs of the political police applied this trick not because they hoped to deceive their prisoner but merely to make him realize how strong was the net in which he was caught, how hopeless any kind of attempt to free himself would be. All he could do was to resign himself to his fate, stop worrying about tomorrow and the day after tomorrow, because only the ÁVH could decide his fate, he himself could in no way influence the decision. He must accept the momentary advantages, the proffered benefits: the cigarettes, the food, the blanket, even the complicity with his interrogator. If he co-operated with the investigator in the drafting of a statement he might, perhaps, hope for clemency as a reward for his readiness to help. Why, for instance, should they deprive him of his life when they knew he was not really guilty and when, moreover, he had put himself at their disposal?

Many a prisoner arrived by way of considerations such as these, at the second phase of the *realization* and helped the ÁVH to piece together the prefabricated elements. As a result of his helpfulness he was, eventually, brought to trial charged with crimes so serious that his steps led from the court straight to the scaffold.

In my case László Farkas omitted to send the lenient ÁVH officer into the frontline. Not, I imagine, because he had no hope of achieving results by this method, but rather because the point of this exercise was merely to coax out the admission suitable for distortion of the truth. In my case, there was no need . . . Because, undeniably, in South America, I had been in contact with British people and this fact required only an insignificant addition, a slight turn, for *contact* to be reclassified as *espionage-contact*. However, to the Colonel's extreme annoyance, I was unable to bring myself to perform this short dance-step.

I regarded my position as hopeless and realized that Farkas might be right: that the court could pass sentence on me on the basis of Szönyi's statement, even though I denied it, and view the absence of a confession as an aggravating circumstance. Yet Farkas, who wanted to achieve quick results after having for so long made no headway, built too much on the magic word *contact* and made me recoil. For the Colonel insinuated not only that I had joined the British Intelligence Service in Buenos Aires and returned home upon their orders but also that in Budapest I was the *resident* of the British Intelligence Service.

This word I heard for the first time from Farkas's lips, having been rather unfamiliar with the terminology of the ÁVH and espionage affairs in general. But when I asked with interest, and not quite without malice, how I was to understand the word, Farkas told me to shut up and prescribed a good number of squatting exercises. From his following questions it became clear to me that the *resident* is a kind of chief spy who directs the activities of arriving, departing and local spies and collects and passes on information. If I admitted to having been a resident I should have to involve not only myself but obviously many others. Farkas must have been a poor psychologist if he believed that a man who had only survived thanks to the ill-mannered irony of fate, would be capable of shouldering the grave responsibility of exposing others to the sufferings he had experienced himself.

So I did not accept the complimentary appointment offered me, the position of resident, nor could I admit that I had carried on espionage activity in Hungary because that again would have started an avalanche of unpleasant questions. If I had carried on espionage activity, I relied, presumably, on informers and then the question would have arisen, who were they? Thus we got stuck with the *contact* I maintained with my British acquaintances and political friends and never reached the *essentially* formulation.

After many long nights of fruitless wrangling the Colonel resumed threatening me with the truncheon and pulled out once again the notes he had dictated on Péter Hain, Colonel Karátson and my activities as a police agent. It could not have escaped his notice that the accusation of having been a Horthy police agent filled me with greater loathing than the charge of espionage, and he may have hoped that should he insist on the former charge I would be more inclined to admit the espionage contacts. By now he was beginning his interrogations in the late afternoon, resting on his divan while I wrote answers to questions I had answered innumerable times before. My depositions began to assume the dimensions of a multi-volume novel.

As it happened, a very annoying and painful carbuncle had developed in my nose in those days, due to the lack of vitamins and cleanliness, for which, after waiting a full week, I had at last received some kind of ointment and a bandage. Wearing this almost mask-like bandage I was taken up, one afternoon, to Farkas's room. Followed by the guard I was trudging up the main staircase when at one of the turnings I came suddenly face to face with Gábor Péter. He was carrying a black attaché case; behind him were his body-guards. My guard grabbed me by the shoulder and turned my face to the wall.

'What has happened to you now?' I heard Gábor Péter's voice behind me.

I turned round and explained the bandage in a few brief words. Then it occurred to me that this was the least significant of the things that had happened to me, and, yielding to a sudden, obscure impulse, I added:

'I should like to ask you for a hearing.'

He looked at me, then motioned to my escort and his body-guards, upon which the ÁVH-men retreated a few steps, and kept a watchful eye on us beyond the range of our voices.

'Why?' Gábor Péter asked in a low voice.

I was at a loss for an answer; as a matter of fact, I didn't know why I had asked for a hearing, as it would be absolutely pointless to explain to Gábor Péter, of all people, that the charges brought against me had not a grain of truth in them. But now I was compelled to reply. I said, almost unthinkingly but with deliberation:

'Among other things because you know as well as I do that I have never been a Horthy police agent. Whatever happens to me I shall never, under any circumstances, confess to that charge.'

Gábor Péter looked at me again, more closely. Only much later did it occur to me that he may have taken my words as a promise to confess to the other charges. He nodded, deep in thought, then replied languidly:

'All right, you'll get your hearing.'

I entered Farkas's room after a longer than usual wait. The Colonel stood by the window opening on Andrássy Street, purple with fury.

'What did you want from the Lieutenant-General?' he bawled at me.

'I told him that I would on no condition confess to the charge of having been a police agent.'

'Do you think you're going to decide what you confess to and what not?' Farkas shouted and the veins stood out on his neck. 'Do you imagine you are at a country fair where you can choose among the boots on display?'

He stepped behind his desk and snatched his truncheon from the drawer, but he only gesticulated with it, then hit the top of the table several blows and commanded:

'Squat!'

He must have had a telephone call from Gábor Péter while I was waiting in his ante-room. Perhaps he had been instructed not to insist on the police agent charge but to try, rather, to concoct some

useful material from my Western friendships and contacts. Whatever had happened, the statement prepared with much devotion and
labour concerning Péter Hain and Colonel Karátson was never
mentioned again. Instead Farkas returned to my *contact* with the
British.

He regarded it as proven that I had been an agent of the British
secret service, and all he wanted to know now was who I had been
in touch with in Hungary, what information I had received from
them and by what means I passed on my information to my employers. When I denied having had any kind of espionage contact,
Farkas, with admirable patience ignored my protest and put the next
question, again in a way that assumed I had long ago admitted to
having been a spy and was only withholding the details. He went on
playing this psychological comedy for days and nights, at times
orally, at times by dictating questions to which he demanded a
written answer.

Farkas omitted the bastinado, spared my hands and kidneys and
restricted himself to threats. He sucked lumps of sugar and only
described to me with gusto, without ever applying them, the tortures
conjured up for me in his imagination. Nevertheless, his interrogations were not less frightening to me than those that used to lead to
the truncheon. Indeed, the Colonel's primitive play-acting struck
me as more blood-curdling than physical pain. In the beginning, the
period of guilelessness, I could still assume under the swish of the
truncheons, that if I resisted they might recognize that they had been
mistaken; later I could still hope they would realize that I was not
the man to admit false charges or bring false charges against others.
But now it seemed weightless in the balance of logic whether I
admitted their accusations or not, for the ÁVH was deaf to any
protest, argument or proof; for them, truth was a purely voluntaristic notion and in the end it would depend on the sovereign decision
of the ÁVH whether or not an assumption, or a slander, no matter
how stupid, would assume the status of incontrovertible evidence.

Therefore, although I had in fact admitted nothing, my situation
was just as hopeless in this net of false facts as if the facts had been
true, as if I had repentantly confessed that I had first been recruited
by Péter Hain as a police agent and then had spied for Colonel
Karátson, and had later become an agent of the British secret service
in Argentina, had established contact between Tibor Szönyi and the
American secret service, and finally conspired with the spy and
agent provocateur, Lászlo Rajk, to overthrow the People's Democracy.

Never, in the interrogations, did Farkas omit to remind me of the trap in which I found myself and warn me of my helplessness. What was the point of resisting? After all, he insinuated, my chance of escaping, of remaining alive, depended on my showing some tractability, some pliancy. I must at least admit something, he would frequently repeat, sign something that could serve as a basis for the charges. Then they could transfer me to the prison controlled by the Public Prosecutor's department and sentence me. Otherwise, they would keep me here in the cellar for years. I should know better than anyone that I would not last long on the diet of the Andrássy Street cellar.

I did indeed know. I was spending my sixth week in the cellar on half a pint of soup and half a pint of beans a day. My strength was deserting me at a frightening speed, there was always blood in my urine, I could walk, or rather drag myself forward, only with the most painful effort and even at the most cautious movement my broken ribs hurt me. Therefore, compared with the ÁVH cellar, I imagined the prison of the Public Prosecutor's department as a kind of rest-home. A barred prison-window through which one could catch a glimpse of the blue sky or which permitted a sunbeam to penetrate, measured against my walled-up cellar-window, now seemed to me a Dolomites panorama, and the scanty daylight of a prison cell, compared with the lurid electric bulb in my cellar-hole, shone with the brilliance of the Italian Riviera.

I yearned for that prison the way an ordinary prisoner yearns for freedom. All this must probably have contributed to the shuddering loathing with which Farkas's face, voice and antics filled me. Not to have to see or hear the Colonel again was worth almost any price. Suddenly I caught myself wondering which of the suspicions voiced against me I should admit.

Farkas undoubtedly knew that, compared with my present quarters, prison must have seemed an idyllic place; he no longer promised to send me to Spain. Instead, he would say:

'Very soon we'll be sending a carload of prisoners over to the Markó street prison. If you make a statement, I shall include you in the group. If not ... Well, you'll only have yourself to blame. I warned you, didn't I, that you were heading for disaster. Haven't I warned you a thousand times?'

He had indeed. What is more, his scareword, 'You are heading for disaster,' which he had always used unsparingly, had developed of late into a mania. He used it again to inform me that he had had enough of this dilatory sparring, would now send me down to the cellar and not have me brought up again for interrogation until I myself asked to be brought up to make a statement. It was absolutely indifferent to him whether it was months or years before I made up my mind. To me, however, it would not be a matter of indifference. And the Colonel really let himself go, describing in gruesome detail the symptoms of 'rotting alive'.

Like an artist gloating over his chef-d'oeuvre, Farkas tilted his head to one side, looked me over from top to toe, then remarked with mock pity that I must already have observed some of the symptoms of 'rotting alive' in myself; as he was more experienced in this field than I was he noticed it even more. Finally, he pointed his middle finger at the ceiling, stared at me grimly and shouted at the top of his voice:

'I am telling you for the last time: you are heading for disaster!'

After this, they really did not take me up for interrogation again. Farkas's theatricals had not helped my perplexity—which of the suspicions to admit—to ripen into decision. On the contrary, it gave me food for further thought.

At times it did seem rational that I should yield at least in part. But whenever I was able to divorce my thoughts from my miserable physical state, I knew that there was no escape from my irrational situation by the path of a logic that appeared—for the moment—rational.

I was not in a position to know the ultimate aims of the ÁVH, therefore I had to concentrate on a single rational effort: to preserve my physical and mental balance as far as I was able. If I obeyed Farkas's wishes I might, perhaps, gain physical advantages for a while. On the other hand, whichever of the accusations I admitted, I would have to name informers, collaborators, accomplices. If I were to follow in Szönyi's footsteps, I would, even if it meant more food and more sleep, lose my psychological balance because the realization that I had put a rope around the neck of others would quite surpass the limits of my moral endurance.

I think that my meditations were influenced in no small measure by the factor of my anger, and do not think I am mistaken when I ascribe this decisive word to it. I was nauseated by Farkas's repulsive play-acting and I felt it almost physically impossible to yield to such a man and thus, by yielding, justify his methods; but I rebelled not only against Farkas, but much more against the institutions represented by him: the ÁVH and the Communist Party.

If the secret police allegedly discovered that many of my friends and acquaintances, concerning whose integrity I would always, even now, have put my hand in the fire, had been police agents and spies, it could only mean that they had undergone the same treatment as I had before they signed or failed to sign the false confessions. Thus, I could no longer regard my case as unique, the result of some sort of police-hysteria, but only as a part of a deliberate, even systematic, action initiated by the Party. When after soup-distribution, they led me to the lavatory I saw at least one dixie in front of each cell, an indication that the spy-factory was working at full capacity.

That long line of dixies was comical but at the same time revolting. The sight made me laugh, but it also made me clench my fists. Although there were still moments when I cherished hopes of a miracle thumbing its nose at reality, and proving that the last month and a half had only been a savage joke, a ruthless test, my temperament dismissed any temptation to ask for a meeting with Farkas.

Just when I was resigned to a long wait, suddenly, one morning, I was taken to the Colonel. Again his room was flooded with sunshine. But Farkas's face outshone even the sun.

'Well, how do you feel?' he asked me with a gay smile as if he had invited me in for a drink.

Not by a single word or a single hint did he revert to his earlier threats, nor did he repeat his statement that I could rot in the cellar for years, or that he would never have me brought up for interrogation until I myself asked to be fetched to make a statement. On the contrary, he was almost friendly. He asked me in a conversational tone about my acquaintances in South America, then made me write down again the names of those I had met and where, and what we had talked about.

He was particularly taken with the unusual name of a Danish teacher of backward children.

'This woman sounds suspicious to me' the Colonel declared and made me write a special report on her.

He requested more and more information and then I happened to mention the name of an Englishman who, if my recollections were correct, I had met at the teacher's flat. This Englishman took an interest in my private affairs with somewhat Castilian verve, at any rate with an enthusiasm unusual in the British, and tried to convince me with great eloquence and many arguments that I was committing suicide by returning to Hungary. Perhaps it wasn't even at Vera's flat that I met him; in any case, it was no more than a fleeting acquaintance. I had forgotten his name but often remembered his predictions during the last few weeks. It was not for the sake of a meticulous completeness of my report, that I mentioned him to Farkas, but because I was curious to see how my interrogator would react to the already more or less fulfilled prophecy. I figured that he would ignore it, or shout at me for provoking him with the stupidities of soothsayers and fortune-tellers. I was wrong. The opposite happened.

Farkas demanded an exact description of the Englishman, remarking that to him it was as clear as daylight that my acquaintance had been an agent of the secret service, perhaps Vera's superior, because there was no doubt that the Danish woman was also working for the British secret service. These two had recruited me at Vera's flat. The Colonel demanded more and more details from which he could create an opportunity for the application of the magic word *essentially*.

He let me go in the middle of the night and this time he neither swore at me nor shouted impatiently that the interrogation had been fruitless.

'We shall continue tomorrow,' he said smiling at me gaily, amicably. 'Goodbye for the present.'

Next day I was not taken up for interrogation, nor did I see Farkas again. It was one of the basic principles of ÁVH methods that the prisoner must never know what is happening to him. He must constantly be given surprises, even sometimes relatively agreeable ones, as, for instance, the Colonel's façade of patient serenity when I expected the truncheon and more refined tortures or, at best, months of starvation in the cellar-hole.

It did not surprise me that I spent the twenty-four hours following the interrogation in my cell, but I was all the more amazed when on the morning of the second day they led me, through hitherto unknown passages, into a room I had never seen, photographed me from the front and the side, took my fingerprints, and then, with my face to the wall, made me stand in line in the corridor. I was just as astonished to discover in the line not only Otto Tökés, Rajk's former secretary, but also Péter Mód, counsellor in the Paris legation, Gyula Oszkó, former police Colonel, and even István Stolte who was living in West Germany and who could hardly have had any reason to return voluntarily to Budapest.

But I should have been even more staggered had I known then, that I had in vain refused to admit the accusations of having been a Horthy police agent and a spy, because from the higher point of view of the ÁVH I had completed the first phase of the *realization*:

though only rough-hewn, I was already a prefabricated element, a semi-finished product, a sort of building material, which would be used to glue together the polished, prefabricated elements in the *second phase of the realization.*

5

The Governor Appears on the Scene

OUR group was transferred to the Markó Street prison and–as far as I had the opportunity to observe–was put in cells on the same floor.

Compared to the cellar my new living-quarters were almost comfortable. There were two iron beds in it with straw mattresses, but neither a table, nor a bench, a chair or a shelf. Only in one corner did a lavatory pan proclaim the triumph of modern hygiene. However, I was disappointed in the barred window. Not merely because it was small and placed very high–I had expected that–but because its opaque frosted pane gazed down on me like a petrified, blind eye.

The dixie was handed in through an opening the size of a book cover and was approximately a foot and a half below the Judas-hole, which they kept locked. But when we were given fresh water the whole iron door swung open. It was unlocked twice, first when we put out the bucket, then when we took it in again. Only at such times did we see our guards face to face.

When the door of my cell flew open, unexpectedly, for the first time, four plain-clothes men stood in the corridor, shoulder to shoulder, glaring at me silently. Two were in their shirt-sleeves, a revolver-butt showing in their belts. For a while we looked at each other without a word. It flashed through my mind that one or another of Farkas's threats was going to come true when one of the gunmen spoke:

'Put out your bucket.'

As I moved to obey the instruction the three other men took a step backwards as if to cover their commander and one raised his hand to his belt. I don't know whether they were play-acting or whether this scene, too, proved that the heads of the ÁVH were trying to awaken a sense of danger in the outer circles of the secret police and make their uninitiated collaborators believe that they were facing implacable enemies.

Even if, under the influence of the adventure stories I had read in my childhood, it had occurred to me to attack the four guards, capture one of the guns and then break out through the multiple ring of armed men, my physical condition would have compelled me to postpone this romantic undertaking at least for the present. For I was still learning to walk. I rose from my bed moaning in agony, and at first considered it a remarkable achievement when I could stagger back and forth eighty or a hundred steps between the walls of my cell without stopping to rest. The food held out little promise that I would regain my strength. They gave us for the whole day half a loaf of sticky, black bread; in the morning a kind of dishwater made from roasted barley, at noon some thin soup and watery vegetable, and in the evening, a soup *called* vegetable. And of these only a tiny quantity.

Yet I could still have regarded the change as fortunate were there any sign to indicate that I was now a prisoner of the Public Prosecutor's department and that instead of Farkas and his colleagues, I would soon be brought before an examining magistrate sharing, perhaps, the convictions of the others but possessing more modest means of persuasion. Days went by and it was still armed plain-clothes security men and not uniformed prison guards who opened my door and handed in the food because, as I discovered later, the ÁVH had requisitioned two floors of the Markó Street prison for its own use and carefully isolated them from the rest of the prison. The prisoners of the Public Prosecutor's department looked with horror towards the ÁVH 'secret section', where no sound was ever heard except the clinking of the buckets and the slamming of feeding-holes.

The monotony of my days was soon interrupted by an agreeable surprise. The door was unexpectedly thrown open and the guards ushered in a burly man of medium size. The newcomer wore a conspicuously well-cut camel-hair overcoat and looked around shortsightedly before sitting down, opposite me, on the other bed. For a while he just sat there, gazing at his feet, then he rose, approached me and introduced himself:

'My name is Sándor Érdi,' he said, and began making sober enquiries concerning the prison and the prison rules.

He listened dejectedly to my report because, as he later admitted, he had hoped to find himself again in the custody of the Public Prosecutor's department as he had been on several occasions since 1945; he had presumed that I was some kind of gentleman burglar and not a political prisoner. Érdi went back to his bed deeply depressed, then he told me that until now, every time he was arrested by the Public Prosecutor's department, he had been able to obtain privileges by bribing the guards, had smuggled out letters to his lawyer and to his wife who had supplied him with food, cigarettes, clothes. But as a political prisoner, for now there was no doubt he

94

belonged to that category, he could no longer hope to do much in the interests of his comfort, physical well-being and release. And yet . . . here Érdi began to tell me about the excellent relations he had had with some party heads, especially Károly Kiss, the secretary of the Communist Party's Central Control Committee. Suddenly he fell silent, paced the cell nervously, and finally stopped before me.

'Tell me, do you know who this Doolesh is?'

He pronounced the name with the long, Hungarian 'oo' and an 'sh' at the end, so that at first I didn't know who he was talking about. I shook my head and asked:

'Why?'

'Because they suspect me of having maintained contact with him.'

'What kind of contact?'

'What kind? Espionage contact, of course. When I was in Switzerland.'

'And who is this Doolesh?'

'Some American chief spy. How should I know who he is? I've never even heard the name before.'

Érdi raised both hands to his head with a theatrical movement, then collapsed on his bed and began to moan softly. I put various questions to him, to which he gave evasive answers. Later, he sat down beside me and told me in a whisper that they accused him of having been the contact man between the Deputy Minister of Defence, György Pálffy, and this Doolesh. Érdi had no doubt but that they had arrested Pálffy, as well, and that some unprecedented spy-trial was being prepared. In the course of our conversation it turned out that the man Doolesh, whose name Érdi had for the first time heard from his interrogators and – as they did – pronounced in a way distorted beyond recognition, could be none other than Allen Dulles, head of the American Intelligence Service in Switzerland.

My companion looked at me anxiously and asked in a shaky voice: 'What do you think? They wouldn't give me a death sentence, would they? After all, I am a nobody and even the accusation says I was only a contact . . .'

I tried to reassure him but Érdi interrupted our conversation time and again to request, now with tear-filled eyes, now with deep sighs, some words of comfort and an endless repetition of my assurance that they would not hang him. At times he wouldn't even wait for me to finish my little speech of consolation but would, without any preliminaries, launch into anecdotes, describe his home, his family, or certain scenes from his life, all with great emotion. I liked listening to him. Not only because, talking about the past, he forgot the miseries of the present and, temporarily at least, his continual lamentations, but also because Sándor Érdi's career, particularly in the period following 1945, threw light on facts and interdependences which I had never even suspected.

My cell-mate, like the other prisoners, had been deprived of his spectacles to prevent him from severing his veins with the broken lens or attempting suicide in some way. Imagining the gold-framed spectacles back on his face, and ignoring his crumpled suit, his tired, fear-worn features, I could see that had I come across him in a hotel lobby in the West and tried to guess his profession from his face and bearing, I should probably have hit the mark when I decided that this flabby, dumpy and yet dynamic, cheerful man could only be a not over-scrupulous businessman. And so it proved. Érdi was a racketeer in the classical sense of the word.

Not that he had started out that way. He was the child of poor parents and, as he himself related with melancholy irony, when young he thought he had struck it lucky when he got a job beating the keys of an adding-machine from morning till night. In those days he didn't wear a light camel-hair coat, but a black one and a black homburg and he regarded it as inconceivable that on a cloudy day anyone should leave the house without an umbrella. But fate had linked the little cashier with an equally insignificant actress who, to him, was the most beautiful, most wonderful fairy-queen in the world. For her sake he left his wife, his child and even his job. The little actress transformed him, or perhaps awakened his true nature. Sándor Érdi set out on the road of the businessman walking the sharp edge between the law and illegality. The Second World War had brought him financial success and by bribery and cunning he was even able to evade the consequences of the Jewish laws which spelled death for hundreds of thousands. But it was only after the war that his real career began.

In 1945 the devastated and despoiled country possessed neither food, industrial products nor transport vehicles. Thus it was that the government and the political parties not only tolerated semi-legal or even legally prohibited deals, but themselves formed enterprises whose business activities in any normal country and in normal times would have been stopped by the police and the Public Prosecutor. At last Sándor Érdi was in his element. He established an export-import firm. At a time when everyone who could smuggled in everything from locomotives to synthetic fertilizers, from cocoa to stockings, and trafficked in them, my cell-mate was well ahead in the race. Indeed, he became so eminent in the field that soon he was contacted by official personalities.

On one occasion, György Pálffy, who must have been keeping an eye on Érdi's activities, approached him with a strange proposition. At the time, Pálffy, a veteran and well-trained army officer who had played an active part in the anti-fascist resistance movement, headed the so-called military-political department of the army, that is, the defensive and offensive espionage services. He told Érdi that the state budget could not cover the expenses of the military-political department and therefore, naturally with the full approval of the Communist Party and his superiors, he was compelled to find the financial means himself. He proposed to Érdi that they should engage in some business deals in common. Érdi was to smell out possibilities and make suggestions as to how they could be carried out. Pálffy would help with the smuggling and back Érdi against the authorities should anything go wrong. After each deal they would share the profits. This proposal referred, of course, only to illegal deals, for the export firm could take care of the legal business, such as the sale of electro-meters to Damascus or the delivery of lavatory pans to Beyrouth without Pálffy's help.

Érdi accepted the profferred deal and for some time the partnership between the racketeer and the head of the counter-espionage service prospered admirably, to the satisfaction of both.

When Érdi recalled his most memorable exploits, his eyes lit up with pleasure; the day, for instance, when with the help of Pálffy's men, he had brought in, without paying duty, a freight-train full of goods, or the time when he sold wagon-loads of articles in scarce supply on the black market. But thoughts of the good old times cheered him only temporarily. Like the stage, when the footlights start to fade and dim, Érdi's face assumed a gloomier and gloomier expression until with drooping mouth he'd murmur plaintively:

'And now they are going to hang me . . .'

After my now almost ritual reassurance, my cell-mate would wonder in dreamy melancholy what his wife, the pretty blonde ex-actress, was doing at this very minute, where she was, what she was thinking about? Then suddenly he'd thrust out his chest, put his hands in his pockets, and, strutting up and down the cell, he'd explain with arrogant self-assurance, like a banker reviewing his investments, what in his individual transactions and deals should be regarded as original, even brilliant, what would never have occurred to anyone else – except Sándor Érdi.

97

'Of course,' he shrugged, 'I am an idiot. I should have stuck to the sort of thing I understood. Why did I have to stick my nose into politics?'

Érdi's involvement in politics took place one day when Pálffy made him sign a pledge recruiting him as an agent of the military-political department. What is more, and of this my cell-mate was rather proud, he was given army rank. Érdi, well-known as a racketeer in Budapest, was not a member of the Communist Party, nor did his undertakings reflect the triumph of socialist economy over private initiative, and for this reason he seemed particularly suited to win the confidence of bourgeois politicians. Therefore, Pálffy used his new man mostly for provocation.

My cell-mate told me how he had tried to ensnare the Small-holder Undersecretary of State, Pater Balogh, a reputedly corrupt man. He could remember the exact price of the cases of champagne and French cognac he had sent Pater Balogh, as well as the cost of the lunches and dinners consumed at 'Uncle Stern's' famous, though outwardly not very elegant-looking, Jewish restaurant. He told me how, instructed by Pálffy, he had tried to provoke General János Vörös, the former Minister of Defence, into compromising himself. By then, János Vörös had resigned his portfolio, after having been deserted in the Council of Ministers even by his Smallholder fellow-ministers when he protested against the draft of the Hungarian-Russian commercial agreement, on the grounds that, as he saw it, the agreement delivered the country economically into the hands of the Russians.

Well, Érdi approached the general and suggested that in the course of his frequent trips abroad he could take letters and messages for the general. Instructed by Pálffy, he brought up the name of a former Hungarian military attaché living in the West, who, or so the military-political department assumed–was working for the Americans. I can no longer recall whether Érdi did in fact smuggle letters back and forth between the general and the former military attaché or whether the attempt at provocation failed; but Érdi's description of the general's cautious mistrust stuck in my memory. Whatever happened, his caution did not save János Vörös from prison. Three years later we worked, facing each other, at the same table in the button-factory of the *Gyüjtö* and had alternate puffs at the same cigarette rolled in toilet paper.

Érdi's public activities were accompanied by decidedly more spectacular successess than this and similar attempts at provocation. His political moves were always directed by Pálffy. He was acting on the orders of the counter-espionage chief when he bought a lot of shares in the weekly *Kossuth Népe* and also, when after the disintegration of the Smallholder Party, he joined Zoltán Pfeiffer's Independence Party and in the 1947 elections ran for membership in Parliament on the Pfeiffer ticket. As he told me, he had put 40,000 forints into the election funds of the Independent Party, on condition that they nominate him as their candidate. This is how, at the last free elections in Hungary, an agent of the military-political department controlled by the Communist Party entered the Parliament building as a representative of the most unequivocally anticommunist political party. Later, on Pálffy's instructions, Érdi, whose erudition and political acumen were much below those of an average accountant, may have collaborated in the destruction of the Pfeiffer-party, and thus contributed to the final liquidation of the parliamentary system in Hungary.

Érdi's sometimes disconnected stories did more than give me a brief glance behind the scenes of public life. They brought to light other facts of which I had been just as unaware as I was of the smuggling backed by the authorities or of the agents planted by the authorities in the ranks of the opposition. What preoccupied me most–I had a notion it might influence our fate–was the conflict and competition which I now learned existed between the leaders and organization of the military-political department as well as the leaders and organization of the ÁVH and which was gradually turning into a life and death struggle. Although what my cell-mate had to relate did no more than awaken a well-founded suspicion, my conclusions were later confirmed by information gathered in prison.

Almost from the very first, the GRO (economic police department), which is similar to the Fraud Squad in Britain, working hand in hand with the ÁVO (State security department–predecessor of the ÁVH), attempted to thwart Érdi's and Pálffy's illegal deals. Érdi and his men were repeatedly arrested, and at such times, Érdi's wife turned to Pálffy and Károly Kiss to obtain her husband's release. Kiss was then head of the Communist Party's Central Control committee; it was his task to watch over the political and moral integrity of the Communist Party members. He knew about the agreement between Érdi and Pálffy; my cell-mate had repeatedly shown him copies of their accounts. Thus the high-ranking Party functionary could personally supervise both partners and ascertain that the racketeer was not cheating the counter-espionage chief, nor the counter-espionage chief the Communist Party. It appears that Károly Kiss did not regard the heavy losses suffered by the state budget as an offence against communist morality for at the time the state was only partly in communist hands, and in order to seize it completely, it seemed expedient to strengthen the communist-controlled institutions. Therefore, Kiss interfered more than once to save Pálffy's agent from the legal consequences of the black-market deals, or even to stop an investigation into his affairs, and when he was imprisoned had him released—on orders from above.

After each arrest, the head of the GRO had Érdi brought before him and, before going into the merits of the case, offered to release him immediately, without further interrogation, if the racketeer pledged himself to work henceforth not for Pálffy but for him.

The military-political department and the economic police supported by the ÁVH would often arrest each other's men, try to annex each other's agents and extend their fields of authority. Originally the military-political department was entrusted with the work of offensive espionage and the ÁVH, as its most important task, with counter-espionage, that is, the removal of foreign spies. Undoubtedly, the two fields of activity met at numerous points, indeed, often overlapped and, under the conditions mentioned, clashes would have been unavoidable even under normal circumstances. All the more so as the ÁVH was linked to the Soviet MVD, and the military-political department to the counter-espionage and defensive service of the Soviet army, and there were, as it leaked out, conflicts and clashes of authority between the two Russian organizations, too. However, in 1948–9, motives beyond the obvious ones intervened in the struggle of the two Hungarian secret services and it was these motives that finally decided the battle.

The backbone of the military-political department was made up of anti-German officers of the old Hungarian army, men like Pálffy, well-trained officers versed in both the offensive and defensive services. Clearly, particularly in the early stages, the Russian military leaders had more confidence in these practised experts than in Gábor Péter, magically transformed from assistant tailor into police-general, for in the ÁVH, following the Russian example, every member was given military rank.

As in Hungary direct military considerations were gradually relegated to second place, and the maintenance of Moscow's chain of command became the most important consideration, the ÁVH was continually winning ground over the military-political department.

For it was the ÁVH, this organization formed in the meantime into a party within the party, that was called upon to execute the Russian seizure of power in Hungary. And as, from the point of view of the seizure of power, it was not professional knowledge that counted but reliability and loyalty to the Russian point of view, Gábor Péter easily triumphed over the old army officers, and the ÁVH over the military-political department. Whether or not the former officers would have been ready to subordinate themselves to the former tailor's assistant, they seemed, if not suspect, certainly capable of resistance, just like the old communists not disciplined by Moscow; they had therefore to disappear. This is why a few months after my meeting with Érdi, his employer, Lieutenant-General György Pálffy, joined Rajk in the dock.

Érdi was not in the least interested in these ramifications. The conclusions to be drawn from his stories and adventures left him cold, as cold as the fate of his likely victims. When I enquired how he would square things with himself if he learned that through him János Vörös had gone to the gallows, Érdi shrugged his shoulders:

'What else could I have done? Tell me what I could have done?' He spread out his arms and looked at me as an indignant adult might look at a child of hitherto irreproachable behaviour caught in an unforgivably stupid act.

Érdi considered himself a goodhearted, generous fellow and his eyes would fill with tears when he spoke of his family and the gifts he had showered upon them. He would have been not only astonished but indignant had anyone raised moral objections to his actions, for he was naïvely corrupt and harmed others by his fatuous harmlessness. It was with the same enthusiasm and unscrupulousness that he displayed in selling reject electro-meters to Damascus and damaged lavatory pans to Beyrouth, that he sold his fellow-men in Budapest. Thus, in his moments of panic, I could indeed have reassured him with even more sincere conviction; for after a bare two months course in the methods of the ÁVH, I could take it for granted that the People's Democracy would not hang Sándor Érdi, because it needed Sándor Érdi, the largest possible number of Sándor Érdis it could get.

Instinctively rather than deliberately I violated Hungarian prison etiquette where Érdi was concerned, because I did not call him by his first name, did not use this form of address to indicate recognition of our common fate. But even though we regarded each other as beings from different planets, even though it occurred to me that he had been put in my cell to spy on me, his stories not only enlightened me but also helped me to relax. I was fed up both with interrogation and with silence and he was the first person I had spoken to for a long time who had no authority over me and could not bully me. Thus, when one night our door was unlocked and I was ordered by our morose guards to put on my clothes and follow them, I felt not only apprehension at the thought of the unknown awaiting me, but also sadness at having to leave behind the familiar cell and even Érdi who had by now also become familiar to me.

While I was dressing my cell-mate watched me with pity and anguish, but as I walked out through the iron door he closed his eyes and kept them closed.

My guards took me down to the ground-floor and handed me over to two other plain-clothes security men. The latter handcuffed me, then made a sign to a uniformed gaoler, who came forward with servile haste to open the door. He raised his hand to his cap, but the ÁVH men paid hardly any attention to his salute. Even in the best of cases they treated the ordinary gaolers with arrogant condescension, as a feudal landlord might treat a flunkey.

A delightful breeze touched my face as we stepped out into the cool, starlit night. But I had no opportunity to look around as the ÁVH men pushed me hurriedly into the waiting car. My two escorts made me sit between them in the back and placed a pair of eye-shields lined with paper over my eyes. While the car sped across Margaret Bridge, and then took the steep mountain road, I could only think of Farkas's threats that, one night, they would make me dig my own grave and finish me off for having refused to aid the ÁVH.

Therefore I felt almost relieved when, just as on the first day of my arrest, I heard the wheels of the car rolling over gravel, when in the garage I smelled the odour of gasoline and finally when I set out with my two escorts down the stairs. In the cellar they removed the goggles, the handcuffs, searched me, then pushed me into the first cell. Hours went by but only the eyes of the guard appeared at regular intervals in the Judas-hole. It must have been late in the morning when they opened the door of my cell. Two guards led me to the familiar tower-room.

This time the windows of the hexagonal room were not covered in black curtains; they had only hung thick curtains over the lower three-quarters of them, but light and air penetrated into the room through the top of the windows. As I entered I heard a train whistle not very far away. From this I concluded that we were on the former Svábhegy, or Svabian Hill, re-christened by the régime Freedom Hill, not far from that pride of the people's democracy, the Children's Railway.

There was a desk by the left-hand wall, and behind it sat an already bald man about forty years old with middle-aged spread. Opposite the entrance a moustachioed, gipsy-faced ÁVH man sat sprawling in an armchair; it seemed to me that I had already met him in the cellar of 60 Andrássy Street. A gangling young man with tousled hair was just rising from the divan that stood on the right side of the room and, without looking at me, he busied himself tightening the belt of his dark-blue trousers, shiny with age.

A narrow table and a chair stood by the entrance. The bald man gestured toward the table and chair, indicating that I should sit down. He waited until I had taken my place, then he addressed me in a sonorous baritone. He asked me a question. Unfortunately, I could not answer as I had not understood a word of what he said. He was speaking in Russian. I must have looked at him rather stupidly, because he broke into laughter. Then he asked me with a strange, hard accent:

'*Sprechen Sie deutsch?*'

I nodded. Thereupon the tousled-haired young man, still busy with his belt, repeated the question more loudly in German and shouted at me not only to nod, but to reply loudly, clearly. Thus I replied in German:

'*Ja, ich verstehe und spreche deutsch.*'

With the help of the interpreter, the bald man took down my personal details, then laid his fountain pen down on the desk and delivered a lengthy speech. I did not even try to catch the meaning of his words but sat listening to his harmonious voice. I felt that even the man himself was carried away by the music of his words, that he paid little attention to their meaning but more to the striking rhythm of his speech, and that he was self-forgetfully enjoying the sonority of his voice, particularly the long drawn-out, throbbing, vibrating vowels. After a while he stopped orating and looked at the interpreter. Now the tousled-haired young man began in German:

'The Colonel says . . .'

At times he spoke of the baldheaded man as the Colonel, at other times as the Lieutenant-Colonel, but as they warmed to their collaboration the interpreter dropped the indirect form of speech, and just like Dickens's wooden-legged school-porter, not only repeated his master's words–naturally in German–but imitated also his intonation and even his gestures. At present, as an introduction, he contented himself with a cool summary of the speech.

From this I learned that the Lieutenant-Colonel was going to interrogate me in the name of the Soviet Communist Party and the Soviet authorities, on a matter of such importance that it concerned not only the Hungarian Party but the Soviet sister-Party, too. He asked me to reply openly, without prevarication, to every question. His Hungarian colleagues had told him that hitherto I had denied everything with the stubbornness of a mule. This was now over. He warned me that he possessed much more effective means of persuasion than the Hungarians. If I behaved, he would not apply them. On the contrary. His only wish was to deal with me in a friendly way. The way he saw it, I was drifting with the current in mid-stream. On one bank was the socialist world, on the other the world of the Imperialists. He wanted to save me from drowning, he was throwing me a life-belt to pull me out on to the socialist bank. If I struggled, the life-belt would slip from my fingers. I, too, must help, show my good faith. Therefore he asked me whether or not I was inclined to speak the truth, at last. But only the truth, because he was not interested in anything else.

The frequently repeated metaphor of the stream and the benevolence the Colonel assured me of did not encourage me to entertain ardent hopes. The mere fact that I was in the hands of the Russian MVD, interrogated by a relatively high-ranking officer, dealt a death-blow to the assumption I had still not quite discarded in spite of my two-months intensive crash course. Until now, I had thought it possible that the arrests had been carried out on the initiative of the ÁVH, to decide some local struggle for power, of which I knew nothing. The presence of the MVD rendered this idea most improbable and excluded also the assumption that the Russians were only here to arbitrate. It now appeared certain to me that the ÁVH had acted with the approval of the Soviet secret police, in accordance with the wishes, perhaps even on the instructions, of the Russians. Thus, my partly instinctive, partly intentional answer was so formulated as to sound the degree and nature of the Russian-Hungarian collaboration when, to the purely rhetorical question–whether or not I was ready to tell the truth–I replied: I had always been truthful and intended to remain truthful in the future. Until now, I added, my interrogators had given proof of an attitude sharply conflicting with mine. They were interested in everything–except the truth.

The Lieutenant-Colonel looked me over from head to foot and said something, upon which the interpreter thundered, doubling the volume of his master's voice:

'Don't provoke me! It will cost you dear if you do!'

Then the bald man shrugged his shoulders, the interpreter shrugged his too, but after a while they began questioning me concerning my interrogators. I think my characterization of Farkas was not exactly of the most uncharitable nature but neither was it complimentary. The Lieutenant-Colonel did not shut me up, he only smiled ironically and made some remark, perhaps about Farkas, perhaps about me, I don't know because the interpreter did not translate it. Then we came to the ÁVH officer from County Vas who, on the first day of my arrest, had told me the instructive story of the case of sabotage in the Soviet Union and how all three suspects had been hanged because none of them would confess to the deed. I then added that I was in the same situation as the two innocent victims.

The indignation of the Lieutenant-Colonel seemed almost sincere. He could not believe, he said, that anyone should have told me such a malicious invention, least of all an ÁVH officer. For no such thing had ever taken place in the Soviet Union and nothing of the sort could ever happen there. I must have invented the story myself. But if I had not invented it but merely believed it, then I was the same kind of vile, moronic, degenerate animal as the person who told it to me. The Lieutenant-Colonel wiped his perspiring forehead, then said something in Russian to the gipsy-faced detective sprawled in the armchair. The latter jumped up with alacrity, left the room and returned after a short while with tea and a plate heaped with sandwiches.

My Russian interrogator never used Gipsy-face as anything but a messenger or a waiter. As I had occasion to observe, the relationship between the MVD officers and the ÁVH interrogators was in general exactly the same as that between the ÁVH interrogators and the prison guards of the Public Prosecutor's department. The Hungarians smiled a flattering, servile smile when the Russians spoke to them; they reacted to the most witless jokes of the MVD officers with obsequious trumpetings of immoderate laughter. Thus, I had occasion not only to supplement my knowledge of protocol acquired in the Ministry of Foreign Affairs with significant new material, but to acknowledge that my notions concerning the equality of men demanded urgent revision, for socialist progress had long rendered them obsolete.

The bald man put two sandwiches and a packet of Hungarian

cigarettes in front of me. He himself not only used an American Parker fountain pen but also smoked American cigarettes, though as a concession to proletarian internationalism, he lit his cigarettes with Polish matches and selected from among the sandwiches those made with Hungarian salami. While he was swallowing them one after another with unconcealed greed, he declared that he was tired of this fruitless prattle and would now come down to essentials. He picked up his fountain pen and arranged some sheets of paper in front of him on the desk.

The interrogation by the Soviet Lieutenant-Colonel differed from that of the Hungarian Colonel in two essentials. The Russian never personally used a rubber truncheon or applied any other means of torture. He relegated this sphere of his office, as I had occasion to experience later, to his Hungarian underlings, and was not even present to see that the punishment was properly carried out. But even more surprising to me than the absence of the rubber truncheon was the fact that the Lieutenant-Colonel showed interest not merely in events that could be linked to the fictitious charges, but also in the truth.

I had to give a meticulous account of my childhood environment, my schooling, my university years, not only my activity in the student movement but also my studies, and of course, László Rajk. My interrogator was not familiar with the small scope and rudimentary methods of the Hungarian underground organization and, if only because of his age, he could not have participated in the Russian equivalent. His questions clearly showed that his information came merely from romantic accounts and high-flown propaganda and that as a result, he was measuring plain reality against idealized images. He shook his head repeatedly with an expression of unbelief.

At first he used to rouse the ÁVH-man slumbering in the arm-chair, to ask him whether it was possible that one or other detail was true, but Gipsy-face, although he was not too young to have participated in the Hungarian underground movement,* knew less about it than anyone could have learned from a conversation in a pub, although they had presumably tried to instil into him at least a few slogans and a few facts embellished for posterity, at the obligatory seminars. When the bald man asked him something in Russian, the investigator would discuss the question with me in Hungarian and only then would he give an uncertain, stammering, whimpering

* In Hungary the Communist Party became a legal party only in 1945.

reply. The Lieutenant-Colonel gave up consulting him and hence-forth restricted himself to sending him for tea. And now, with ever more obduracy and with increasing volume of sound, he tried to make me admit that I had been a Horthy police agent in the student movement and afterwards. The tousled-haired interpreter bawled the questions and insinuations at me even louder than the Lieutenant-Colonel, and I too bawled back my replies. Often all three of us bawled together. The tower-room rang with our voices like a country-fair where each stall-holder tries to out-shout the others.

When we had no breath left and had reached deadlock, the Lieutenant-Colonel suddenly fell silent, then he murmured the three obscene, four-letter Russian words inciting incest with one's mother, which side by side with the words *Khleb, Chas* and *Davai* (*bread, watch,* and '*come along*'), everyone in Hungary knows, re-gardless of age or sex. He signalled to the interpreter and rose. It must have been lunchtime. I was led back to the cellar. Although I was given no food, and returned to the small table about an hour and a half later with a rumbling stomach, I was agreeably surprised by the fact that the bald man continued the interrogation in a calm voice, put objective questions concerning László Rajk and made a note of my replies. I was on the verge of believing that henceforth the interrogation would be carried on in this reasonable manner in a genuine effort to get at the truth, when, without any warning, the Lieutenant-Colonel bellowed at me so loud that even the Hungarian detective sitting in the armchair took fright.

'You must have known Rajk was a police spy! Stop playing games with me!'

We resumed our earlier vocal competition which the Lieutenant-Colonel once again concluded with the same rustic Russian encouragement to incest. Then he delivered another long speech. Rajk, he said, had already admitted he was an *agent provocateur.* It was impossible that I should not have known this, or at least had my suspicions. But not only was I refusing to supply information, I would not even voice the suspicions I must naturally have enter-tained, and which would give the investigators something to go on. This was irrefutable proof of my bad faith. Here the Lieutenant-Colonel returned to his stream-metaphor: he would like to pull me out on to the socialist bank, but what was he to do if I refused to grasp the life-belt?

Why didn't I recall that Radek, although he had committed serious crimes, had not been executed in the Trotsky trials in Moscow, because he had given proof of sincere repentance during the investigation and at the trials, and, sparing neither himself nor his accomplices, had admitted everything. This was why, in prison, he had been allowed to read, to write a book and this was why, on his release, he had been given a not insignificant post, permitting him to work and live like an honest Soviet citizen. The Lieutenant-Colonel mentioned also other persons, politicians, scientists and one aircraft constructor caught in the enemy's net–as the Lieutenant-Colonel expressed it–but as he had not been stubborn, he did not have to finish his sentence but was soon released, sent back to work, and today is celebrated as a hero of the Soviet Union.

Outsiders, like myself, had no idea how well-informed the Soviet secret service was of even the most insignificant details. Therefore, the purpose of the investigation, apart from obtaining additional information, was also, and to a large extent, to find out whether I belonged to the incorrigibles or could later–like the aircraft constructor he had mentioned–be fitted into society. I made no reply whatsoever, although the Lieutenant-Colonel must have been expecting one for, after a short pause, he asked me suddenly in an irritated voice:

'Have you ever been in a cage?'

I said that my present cell could easily be called just that. The Lieutenant-Colonel shrugged his shoulders and so did the interpreter:

'I am speaking of a cage,' Tousled-head translated, 'in which you can only squat, where you cannot stretch out your leg or turn to one side, and your head, if you tried to raise it, would hit the ceiling. Four or five days in such a cage without food or water is not exactly pleasant. Have you tried it?'

'No,' I said, 'I have not yet been in such a cage.'

'Well then, you will.' The Lieutenant-Colonel laughed and the interpreter laughed even more loudly.

I was led away. I was not put into a cage but four detectives took me down to the ground-floor and, shouting and threatening, gave me a relatively brief thrashing with their truncheons. There was more smoke than fire. I had the impression they were instructed to frighten me but not to injure me too much. I was to be spared now. I was a prefabricated element. My second visit to that room on the ground floor, however, proved much more painful than this mild, and compared with what had gone before, almost symbolic beating.

I don't remember when it came about, in the morning or in the afternoon, but I recall all the more clearly the huge tin wash-basin the ÁVH-men brought in, filled with water. They ordered me to undress, then made me sit in the basin and used an instrument to conduct one pole of an electric current into the water; they then applied the other pole to my body, first to my back, then to more and more delicate parts, particularly those covered with membrane. An elderly, burly detective stood guard in front of me with a rubber truncheon in his hand; his stubbly red hair and thorny red moustache almost glowed in the semi-obscurity. At my side, also armed with a rubber truncheon, an athletic, bull-necked young man with dark skin stood, legs apart. The others called him Tiny. Every time the electric shock made me jump, Tiny and his elderly colleague would hit my shoulders with their truncheons and push me back into the basin.

I don't know what the Lieutenant-Colonel expected from this electrified intermezzo, because, just as before the bath-tub incident he had dropped the accusation that I had been a police spy, so after it he dropped the demand that I supply either proof or at least a basis for suspicion concerning Rajk's activity as an *agent provocateur*.

I doubt whether the priestly-faced Russian enjoyed cruelty by nature; I rather think he had a tendency to softness and sentimentality. When on the second day, he returned from his lunch, he placed three apricots in front of me on a piece of white paper. It was not so much in this and similar acts but rather in the way he did it that made me think I discerned in him some traces of generous humanism. This is why I believe that it was not out of bad temper, perhaps not even on his own decision, that he submitted me to the electric treatment, but was merely fulfilling an obligatory ritual. I think that had the Lieutenant-Colonel been his own master, he would have been content to deprive me of cigarettes, which he often did when my answers did not satisfy him or, worse, annoyed him. But the Lieutenant-Colonel was a prisoner himself, though not in the way I was. Perhaps he didn't even know he was, or refused to admit it.

The days went by, we stumbled along the road of my life from Budapest to Paris and Buenos Aires, then from Buenos Aires back again to Budapest. At times, other Russian officers would appear in the tower-room, particularly a tall, bald man with an intellectual face, and a short man of military bearing who looked like a sergeant but whom the interpreter addressed as Colonel. These men, too, would put questions to me with the help of Tousle-head, and at the same time, they were obviously egging on their priestly-faced colleague in Russian. At such times my interrogator would open his arms wide and point at me. But when we reached the last period of my residence in Argentina, he brightened visibly. The Russian must have been familiar with Farkas's notes and had carefully studied the one dealing with my Danish woman friend at whose house the Englishman and I had discussed my return home.

'Of course!' the Lieutenant-Colonel exclaimed, 'it was this Englishman who sent you home, he recruited you!'

'That Englishman,' I reminded the Lieutenant-Colonel of what I had told him a minute ago, 'tried, on the contrary, to convince me that it was madness to return to Hungary.' But the Russian officer indicated with cheerful laughter and ample gestures that this detail held no interest for him, for at last he felt victorious.

'All right, then,' he said patiently, 'he did not recruit you formally. But that doesn't count. Tell me, what did you talk about with this gentleman?'

I had only a faint recollection of my conversation with the Englishman and could not repeat it word for word. One thing is certain, I countered his arguments by pointing out that we Hungarians educated in the West had a particular task to fulfil, almost a mission at home which it was morally impossible to evade. For however small our country, however insignificant it was in world politics, it might be particularly suited for building a bridge–resting on the pillars of our dual tradition–between East and West; it might find a synthesis of two ways of thinking, two ways of life, and thus, by its very existence, relieve the tensions bound to bedevil international relations after the war.

'Build a bridge! Create a synthesis!' cried the Lieutenant-Colonel. 'Why don't you say straight out, and without beating about the bush: to be a bridgehead against the Soviet Union!'

'On the contrary . . .'

My interrogator waved his hand. 'Only an Imperialist agent could think up such a notion.'

'I am unable,' I said, 'to discover any causal relation between the two, and to tell the truth, even today I am not ashamed of this idea.'

'True to type,' the Lieutenant-Colonel nodded sadly but with satisfaction. 'And do you still consider it feasible?'

I must admit that I began to doubt it more and more. I did not mention that during the last week my doubts had become a certainty as a result of what was really an insignificant incident. This incident, I thought to myself, somewhat rashly generalizing, had thrown light, or rather shadow, not only over the past months, but also on the probable fate of those arrested, and even on the future of our country.

What had happened was that–perhaps a few days before my

present interrogation – a short man had entered the tower-room. He wore a plain-cut Stalin-tunic, but the silvery, bluish sheen of the material betrayed its Western origin, and also that its manufacturers had intended it for women's wear. The newcomer smoothed down his conspicuously curly, grey hair. An amusingly coppery nose protruding from his face proclaimed loudly that its owner was a chronic alcoholic. The Lieutenant-Colonel jumped to attention and whispered to me in a suppressed panting tone, in German:

'Get up! Get up at once!'

Copper-nose carried on a short, whispered conversation with my interrogator, glanced at the handwritten notes lying on the desk, shook his head, looked me up and down, then quickly left the tower-room. The Lieutenant-Colonel hurried forward to open the door for him. As soon as this squat person had entered, the Hungarian security man had stood motionless, almost petrified, and the interpreter had drawn back modestly to the wall. When the bald Lieutenant-Colonel was again behind his desk, he remained for a moment wrapped in silence, then remarked in German, with deep reverence:

'Believe me, this is a greater man than Horthy. He is the Governor.'

He wondered for a while whether he should continue, then added:

'For, as we know, Horthy was only Hungary's governor. But this man? He is Governor of Hungary and Austria, Germany, Czechoslovakia, Poland, Roumania, Bulgaria and Albania. I am telling you, in case you don't know, that the Comrade Lieutenant-General is the Commander-in-chief of the South-East-European MVD.'

In prison, where one of our principal pastimes was the mosaic-game with which, from scenes, incidents, details and remarks dropped, we reconstructed the various phases of the show-trial, I also learned that the Governor was called Fedor Belkin and that he resided at the Baden bei Wien Headquarters of the MVD.

A ———————————— megyei bírósági börtön vezetője.

Flh. :

———————— -19 ———— törzslapszám.

Értékletéjének száma : ————————— Ft ———— fill.

Elbocsátólevél

Szász Béla ———————— részére, akit a mai napon a börtönből szabadon

bocsátottam, mert a ———————————————— kihágás — vétség —

bűntett miatt a B ————————————— -19——— áú. ———————— számú ügyben

1954 évi *augusztus* hó *31* napjától elrendelt letartóztatását megszüntette.

Személyi adatai *Szombathely* született, *1910* év *julius* ———— hó

9 napján, *ujsagiró* foglalkozás, nős — nőtlen — különváltan élő — hajadon —

férjes — özvegy — törvényesen elvált, *1* gyermeke van, vagyon ———————— kapott.

Szabaduláskor : *Bp. II. Ullői-u. 11*

Lakik : *Bpest* 1954 évi *szeptember* hó *1* n.

Lehota Mária

vezető.

Fegy. 68. minta.

76733/5 — Csillag Nyomda. Budapest (1M) 912.

Elbocsátólevél.

6

Prefabricated Elements

AFTER the eight days spent with the Russians I was often driven back and forth between the Markó Street prison and the ÁVH headquarters, at times even without paper-lined goggles, sometimes handcuffed, then again with my wrists free. I stayed for a few nights in the Andrássy Street cellars, then a few nights in the Public Prosecutor's jail, then again below ground in one of the secret ÁVH villas.

During this period I came to know the most varied sections of the ÁVH. The interrogators enquired, sometimes threateningly but with conspicuous objectivity, even in a civilized manner, about my Hungarian and foreign acquaintances, my Hungarian, but particularly my Western experiences, as if their main concern were to supplement their archives with reliable and genuine information. There was no mention of László Rajk, nor of those subsequently accused in his trial, nor of the suspicions voiced against me. Only hints were dropped and questions asked that betrayed ignorance or personal inquisitiveness.

It seemed obvious that after these bypaths we would get back to the main road and would then soon reach the finishing straight. Thus, in the tension of expectancy, I did not sufficiently appreciate the objective tone, often lacking in rudeness, and was not unequivocally glad of the change of diet in the Andrássy Street cellar. Now the daily menu was no longer flour-soup in the morning and a small quantity of beans in the afternoon; breakfast was followed by lunch, usually potatoes in sour sauce and boiled beef, and in the late afternoon the gaolers handed in to their prisoners soup or vegetables. At week-ends there might be fried bacon or cheese.

The illustration on the opposite page reproduces the certificate of discharge handed to Béla Szász on his release from prison. He had served five years of a ten-year sentence, but the certificate records that he was detained for one day only (see page 214).

The prisoners were being fed so that, as Major Károlyi later expressed himself, we should be in good shape when we were exhibited to the public. For in this second phase of the *realization*–in which the experts were piecing together and polishing up the pre-fabricated elements–good care was being taken that these elements should, at least apparently, remain intact and not differ conspicuously from the propaganda photographs so often published in the past.

The Soviet foremen were now in direct control of the construction. We, the prefabricated elements, were put at the disposal of the peripheral sections of the ÁVH only temporarily, only until they had used the notes made by the Hungarian and MVD officers, to finish drawing the contours of the political trial and elaborate the most important details. Gradually we all became convinced that we were not in the hands of the ÁVH but the MVD.

After this brief transition period characterized by the objective inquiries of the ÁVH, I was once again put in a car and this time taken to a secret villa I had never seen before. The cellar was not steeped in mouldy vapour; a smell of fresh plaster emanated from every nook and corner. The walls dividing the space into cells must have been finished only a few days before. Eight iron doors, painted a greyish-green, opened on the right, and eight on the left. My cell seemed spacious compared with the burrows in which I had lived and, to my surprise, an iron bedstead with a wire-frame and a brand-new mattress stood against one of the walls. My astonishment increased when the guard handed in one cigarette and gave me a light.

'You don't deserve it,' he said, 'we all know what a stubborn chap you are.'

It seemed improbable that anyone should have informed him whether I was stubborn or obedient, so I considered his remark merely as a friendly greeting and, drawing in the smoke deeply, grinned back at him.

'I am not only stubborn, I'm hungry as well.'

'Do you want some lentils?' he asked returning my grin.

'I'd accept them gladly,' I said, 'but I won't sell my birthright for them.'

'You shut up!' he snarled at me and banged the Judas-hole shut. But a few minutes later he returned with a dixie full of lentils.

I was taken upstairs in the early afternoon of the following day. But this time I was able to glance out stealthily from behind the paper-lined spectacles. From the cellar we had to climb narrow, wooden stairs, almost like a ladder, to a cold-storage chamber. We passed shelves richly laden with fruit and the fragrance of apples tickled my nose. From the cold-storage room we proceeded through some kind of lobby into a hall, where, sitting in armchairs placed around tables I caught sight of women in gay summer frocks and men in shirtsleeves. They must have been enjoying their lunch-break and were, perhaps, stirring their coffee. I could feel them staring at me as my guards led me away holding my arms to right and left, but this sight was obviously a familiar one, for the talk did not abate and I could distinguish a few scraps of Russian here and there.

From the hall wooden steps led down to the garden. We stepped out into the open air and, for the first time since my arrest, I felt the warmth of the sun on my face. But there was no time for pleasurable enjoyment because, after a few yards, we entered the door of another villa. My attendants made me stay in the lobby. One guard remained with me, the other entered a room. While we were waiting, loud angry Russian sentences reached my ears from behind the closed door of a room, followed by the slow, hesitating, monotonous German translation of the interpreter.

After this, I was certain that I would again come face to face with the Russian Lieutenant-Colonel. Therefore I was surprised when, after they had taken off my spectacles in a small room, Major Károlyi laughed at me from behind a desk:

'Well, how are you?' he asked. 'Is Szönyi still lying?'

'If he hasn't retracted his deposition he is,' I said.

'He hasn't retracted it, but it is no longer important.' Károlyi shrugged his shoulders, then pointed to a chair facing the desk and said:

'Well, sit down.'

He paused. Then, to increase tension, rather than because he was interested in my opinion, he asked me what I thought of the spacious cell, the mattress, the bed. Did I get enough to eat? Had I received cigarettes?

'We are treating you in lordly fashion, aren't we?' he added as if he were expecting gratitude and recognition for this undeserved generosity. 'Now you see that we can be friendly and agreeable as well, can't you? Yet ... yet the Russian comrades are not at all satisfied with you ...'

'Would they be satisfied,' I asked, 'if I admitted to being a Horthy police agent and a spy? You know as well as I do, Major,' I continued, 'that these accusations are pure fiction.'

Károlyi had never tried to fool me by pretending that he believed these false accusations. He did not underestimate me to that extent. In fact, I owe him some gratitude for having so efficiently dispelled any doubts I may have had concerning the nature of the Rajk case, and thus having to a large measure contributed to my political enlightenment. His next remark was again playful and teasing rather than deceitful.

'All right, all right, but that Danish woman and that Englishman are suspicious enough. There must be something in it . . .'

I can recall every word he said, every gesture, every expression. How, suddenly, he became serious and leaned back in his chair: 'Look here,' he came down to brass-tacks at last, 'we are preparing a very important trial. We haven't had one of this kind in Hungary before. This trial is important not merely in its Hungarian context but in a world context. You must have guessed the seriousness of the affair, not only from the way the Soviet comrades interrogated you, but from the mere fact that they themselves carried out the interrogation. And because this is a political trial, we cannot use the same methods we would in a case of chicken-stealing. You must understand that. You see, Szebenyi, for instance, is much more intelligent than you.'

And then Károlyi told me that Endre Szebenyi, former Under-secretary for Home Affairs, had also been entrusted to him. Szebenyi had understood long ago that all resistance was useless; he had put himself at the disposal of his interrogators, and even made suggestions as to the charges to be brought against him. In return, he enjoyed decent treatment and when his case was judged, his help-fulness would be an alleviating circumstance. I had no way of checking Károlyi's allegations, I had no knowledge whether or not Szebenyi had co-operated, and if he had, to what extent. But one thing is certain. In one of the secondary trials connected with the Rajk-trial he was sentenced to death by hanging and the sentence was carried out. But just then neither Károlyi, nor perhaps even the Governor, Fedor Belkin, knew what the ultimate fate of Szebenyi and the other accused would be. Nor were they interested in such insignificant personal matters. Their attention was concentrated on fitting together the prefabricated elements. However, the construction still required numerous supplementary elements and supporting members.

'There will be one principal trial,' Károlyi told me 'with eight to twelve defendants. Then secondary trials. The principal trial will be public, the secondary ones held *in camera*—You may be one of the defendants in the principal trial . . .'

He paused to watch for the effect. And I tried hard to look back at him without expression, without uneasiness. Suddenly he burst out laughing, then continued:

'But maybe we shall not put you in the dock at the principal trial. In that case you would appear only as a witness. For you, naturally, this would be more advantageous. But I don't want to make any false promises to you and therefore I am telling you here and now, that afterwards we will have you sentenced at one of the secondary trials.'

The Major's last words made me prick up my ears. 'We shall have you sentenced' meant that the 'Soviet comrades' and their agents controlled the judges and decided on the sentence; and the only function of the body called 'the People's Court' was to pronounce that sentence or, in the case of *in camera* trials, record it in a secret file. It hadn't been a slip of the tongue. Károlyi's tone of voice betrayed that in saying, 'We shall have you sentenced,' he was continuing my political education; he wanted me to feel how utterly helpless I was.

'What evidence would I have to give as a witness?' I asked him, curious to know.

'All kinds,' Károlyi replied reflectively. Then he added, 'You remember, don't you, that during your student years you and a few of your fellow students published a review?'

'Not one. Three.'

'I am thinking of the one called *Virradat*. It was seized by the Public Prosecutor's department. Do you remember?'

I did remember. All the more so as the periodical had carried on its first page a symbolic prose-poem of mine of which, later, I was not in the least proud. I was even a little grateful to the Public Prosecutor for having withdrawn my poem from circulation along with the periodical, thus doing a favour not only to posterity, but to me too. However, I never found a plausible explanation for the seizure of the paper for, though it may have been somewhat muddled, it could not have been considered politically dangerous, even in Hungary, even in the days of Admiral Horthy.

'Well,' Károlyi went on, 'this *Virradat* was also distributed by Rajk, and the police detained Rajk and then recruited him as an agent. Rajk purchased his release by signing a pledge that henceforth he would report everything he learned about the Hungarian communist movement to the political section of the police. Did you know that?'

'I did not.'

'But you certainly remember that on the day following his detention, Rajk showed up at the University in a state of great excitement . . . Think back.'

'He may have been excited. It would have been natural. All of us who were connected with *Virradat* were rather nervous. But I knew nothing about Rajk's having been detained. And if he was detained and was still tense the following day, why should that prove that he had been recruited?'

'It is not your job to ask questions here, but mine. Rajk has already admitted to having been an *agent provocateur*. You know that, don't you?'

I did not deny that Colonel Farkas had shown me a document confessing this and signed by László Rajk.

'Well then, I have something else to show you.'

Károlyi placed a large file in front of me and leafed through it slowly so that I should be able to read Rajk's signature at the bottom of each typewritten page. He stopped at one:

'This will show you whether or not it is worth your while trying to protect your accomplice. Read this.'

He tapped with his index finger at a short paragraph. This was an exact replica of what Rajk admitted later at the public trial. This is how the so-called *Blue Book*, containing the minutes of the trial, quotes his words:

> The placing of spies is also related to my espionage activities. I am now thinking of those I have already mentioned: Sándor Cseresnyés, an agent of the Yugoslav intelligence, Béla Szász, an agent of the British Intelligence Service, Frigyes Major, the agent of the American intelligence agency, the CIC, Marschall, the agent of the French intelligence agency. I am no longer able to remember the exact time when I appointed them to this or that leading job. (*László Rajk and his Accomplices before the People's Court*, Szikra, Budapest, p. 58)*

'Well, what do you think of that?' Károlyi asked me with a malicious grin. 'But elsewhere Rajk explains in even greater detail why he patronized you.'

He turned the pages of the file, then put another page before me. It is true that at the trial the presiding judge had to remind Rajk of the text of this paragraph, but once reminded, the accused man

---

* As the Hungarian government has published the material of the trial also in English I have taken the quotations following from the official English version of the Blue Book. Responsibility for the quality of the translation and the occasional spelling errors rests with the Budapest translator.

recited it without a hitch and with amazing exactitude. Therefore I am again quoting Rajk's words from the Blue Book:

> The President: Did your American connections have any influence on the placing of Cseresnyés, Marschall, Major, Szász, etc?
>
> Rajk: Yes. I forgot to mention that Martin Himmler, when I talked with him at the end of 1946, also told me that, taking advantage of my influence as Minister of Home Affairs—for at that time I was already Minister of Home Affairs—I should endeavour to place in key positions people who were in their eyes reliable, that is, people following the policy of the Americans, or people who were attached to the American intelligence agencies; to place them not only in the Ministry of Home Affairs but, taking advantage of the office I held in the Hungarian Communist Party as well as the post I filled in the government, to place such elements in other parts of the state machine, too. Subsequently, partly on these instructions of Himmler, partly on another directive—that I think I had better discuss later—I placed in the Ministry of Home Affairs Sándor Cseresnyés, who was in the employ of the Yugoslav intelligence service; László Marschall, who was an agent of the French intelligence organization, the Deuxième Bureau; Frigyes Major, who was the agent of the American CIC intelligence service; and Béla Szász who was in the employ of the British Intelligence Service.' (Ibid, pp. 48–49)

'Go ahead, tell me what you think of that?' Károlyi urged.

To hide my agitation I replied, 'Not a conspicuously mixed bag. I mean as far as the casting is concerned, for otherwise all of them, except myself, fought in the Spanish Civil War on Rajk's side with the Republican army; and afterwards Marschall was given a high French distinction for meritorious service in the French resistance movement, particularly in the battle of Paris . . .'

'Who remembers the battle of Paris,' Károlyi shrugged. 'But all three of them, or rather all four, because you were also one of them, were Rajk's friends; as you can see for yourself, the confidential friends of a police-agent, conspirator and spy. Just think,' the Major raised his voice, 'and if you are not an idiot you will acknowledge that in the face of such an admission your denial isn't worth a fig. Especially as we can always bring in Szönyi as a witness. You, my dear Mr. Ministerial Counsellor, have your head firmly in the noose . . .'

I pushed my hands between the seat of the chair and my thighs because I felt them trembling.

'Look,' Károlyi continued after a brief pause, 'this is not petty larceny but a political trial.' He then pronounced the words that we so often heard repeated and which, in spite of our desperate situation, appeared so naïvely ridiculous to us: 'We want to deal the Imperialists a heavy blow. This is what you must understand. This is what you must realize. And you don't have much time left . . .'

He looked at me over his gold-rimmed spectacles, put Rajk's file in order, then had me taken back to my cell.

After Károlyi's interrogation I returned to the Markó Street prison only for a short spell; I hadn't even settled down before I was again transported to the headquarters of the ÁVH.

Though the Andrássy Street Headquarters of the ÁVH had not changed outwardly, inside it was still being reconstructed over and over again, then, like a toy children have grown tired of, it would be demolished anew and restored to its original shape. Cars no longer stopped before the main entrance or the side-entrance in Csengery Street, but drove from Csengery Street into the courtyard, one corner of which had been surrounded by a wall some twenty feet high. Opposite the gate they had erected a great wooden tower, from the top of which a fierce-eyed tommy-gunner watched the prisoners alighting from the cars. I could no longer have run into Gábor Péter at a turning in the stairs, since the prisoners were being taken up by obviously temporary but very ingenious secret routes. The changes were most noticeable and significant on the ground floor, for this is where the MVD had set up its headquarters.

The corridor leading towards the right from the Andrássy Street main entrance had been walled up, just enough room being left for a narrow iron door. The Soviet section had been newly painted, the worn furniture replaced by brand new furnishings, and the corridors were thickly carpeted. Even for ÁVH members, access to the sacred abode of the MVD was solely through the iron door. My guard knocked on this door when he led me upstairs.

Someone peeped out through the spy-hole in the narrow door. My guard must have whispered a code-word into the hole, for the door was opened to admit us. After a few steps the corridor broadened into a small lobby. Here I was made to wait. While I waited, the Russian Colonel who looked like a sergeant and the bald MVD officer with the intellectual face crossed the lobby. From one of the rooms I saw Vajda emerging, the brutal-faced young detective who had arrested me at the Ministry of Agriculture.

'This character has given me a lot of trouble,' Vajda remarked to one of his colleagues idling in the corridor. Then he turned to me: 'Are you still so stubborn?'

At that moment, Ernö Szücs, Gábor Péter's deputy entered the lobby. He motioned to me to follow him.

Szücs led me into a small room. He spoke shortly, hurriedly, about the trial in preparation. He used Károlyi's expression which I was to hear frequently thereafter, like a 'leitmotiv' in background music: 'We want to deal the Imperialists a heavy blow.' And I – Szücs added – unless I sided with the enemy, must put myself at the disposal of the Communist Party, the Soviet comrades, the ÁVH. Rajk had come to his senses, he now saw the situation quite clearly. I could convince myself of this personally, not merely on the basis of written statements. For they would again confront me with Rajk.

We proceeded into a larger room. Rajk was sitting by the opposite wall with his legs crossed. He was no longer wearing his grey summer suit, as at our first confrontation, but a brown suit, sandals and thick woollen socks. This was indeed a privilege, for the rest of us were without socks, our shoes had no laces and we were wearing the same suits in which we had been arrested. Rajk was thinner, paler than when I last saw him, but the ghastly network of wrinkles had disappeared from his face. He gave me a friendly, though somewhat embarrassed and melancholy smile. Szücs sat down at the long side of the oblong table and made me sit at the short end, then, from the papers lying before him, he read, to my surprise, a formal text of our confrontation even before it had taken place. In the text, the two persons confronted declared by way of introduction, that they were neither related to each other nor on bad terms. When the Colonel reached the end of this paragraph he looked up from the paper:

'Well, László Rajk?' he asked.

Rajk did not look at Szücs, his eyes sought mine and his hand rose in a restrained but hopeless gesture. He tried to smile, then said in a loud voice:

'*I* feel no hostility.' He pronounced this *I* emphatically, as if he wanted to stress that he had no cause to take anything amiss but would not be surprised if I were resentful.

My expression as I entered the room with the memory of the electric shocks in my muscles must have been rather gloomy. My depressing appearance was scarcely enhanced by the circumstance that I had washed my shirt at the Markó Street prison but could not put it on because it was still wet when they came to fetch me; now, in the absence of a shirt, it was my skin that peeped through the holes of my torn pullover.

I returned Rajk's look and suddenly recalled the scene in the corridor of the University when he had told me perhaps rhetorically, but without bombast, 'It's no use, there is but one solution: Lenin.' It was with these words that the young historian had set out on the road of a professional revolutionary. Now, looking into his sunken but flushed face, into his tired eyes that looked into mine, I knew beyond all doubt that Rajk had no illusions left, that he realized he had come to the end of the road.

Szücs's pencil was tapping impatiently on the table:

'And you?' he asked, 'And you?' He looked at me insistently and his shoe beat rhythmically on the floor. 'Come on, answer. Are you on bad terms with László Rajk?'

'I don't bear him any grudge,' I replied looking at Rajk, not at the Colonel.

Like Rajk's answer a few seconds before, mine did not refer to Szücs's formal question and it must have been obvious to him that we were both thinking of the statement my former fellow-student had made against me. But the Colonel took no notice of our dialogue, for our quarrel or reconciliation had no longer any influence on the set course of events.

Without further remark, Szücs began to read a previously prepared deposition. In this, Rajk mentioned briefly our university years, our subsequent meetings, but gave a more detailed account of our meetings after my return home, describing when, where and how often we had met. He declared that he had proposed my appointment to the Ministry of Foreign Affairs in the Party's organizational committee because, on the one hand, he had come to know my Trotzkyite attitude from our conversations, on the other, because according to reliable information I had been recruited by the British Intelligence Service in South America. As I had returned to Hungary as an agent of the Imperialists, he–as a fellow-agent–wanted to help me carry on my espionage activity with the greatest possible success.

At the trial, this statement was referred to by the Public Prosecutor, Gyula Alapi. Rajk, he said, had created a wide espionage network:

> Wherever possible he appointed the agents of the Imperialists, especially former Trotskyists, agent provocateurs and spies

to high position. It was thus that important offices in the Ministry of Foreign Affairs fell to Béla Szász, an agent of British intelligence. (Ibid, p. 11)

In Szücs's papers, Rajk's confession was followed by mine. As far as I remember, apart from the customary biographical details which, by the way, were accurate, the text was but a summary, prepared from the notes of the Russian Lieutenant-Colonel, of my meetings at the house of my Danish friend, with the Englishman and my conversations with him concerning my return to Hungary. As this dialogue, condensed into *oratio obliqua*, contained no evidence to prove either my recruitment or that I had been sent home by the British Secret Service, in a negative way it actually contradicted Rajk's statements. All the more so as the report did not even accuse me of attempted espionage, let alone espionage itself.

I had a side look at Szücs. He had put on weight since I last saw him. His uniform was buttoned over his quivering stomach and broad rings of fat stood out like pumped-up tyres.

As the Colonel articulated each word clearly, almost joyfully, it occurred to me as I watched his apparently unjustified self-satisfaction, that they were probably putting together these two contradictory statements to prevent me from referring to this contradiction later, or even from behaving like Hans Andersen's courtiers lost in admiration at the Emperor's new clothes. Still, I reflected, only for its internal use could even voluntaristic Soviet police-logic consider these two conflicting reports as being in agreement. If they intended to put me, too, on public trial, they could not rest content with this. The MVD could 'deal the Imperialists a blow' with the aid of my confession only if I admitted not merely that in South America I had talked about my return home with an Englishman whose name I could not even remember, but if I also confessed what espionage reports I had passed on, when, and to whom.

In that case, this confrontation with Rajk would not be an end but a beginning. But it was nothing more than the path leading to the *essentially*. Here, the Governor's men could only pause, they could not stop. They might return to Szönyi's statement concerning the mysterious Wagner, come back to Péter Hain, to Colonel Karátson. They might fling me back into the nights and dawns of the first month to mould me into a well-mannered, zealous spy. Although I foresaw with misgiving that my physical strength and my moral resistance would give out in a single day if I had to go through the same experience a second time, I was still filled with an indifferent, light-minded calm, and amused myself by maliciously calculating the weight of Szücs's quivering tyres of fat.

When at last the Colonel finished reading, he looked at us and said nonchalantly:

'Well, sign!'

Rajk walked over to the table and signed his name with a flourish on each page of the report, even those that should have been signed by me, since they contained the text put into my mouth. Szücs noticed this only when he pushed the file over to me. He glanced at Rajk reproachfully.

'Now really,' he said, 'you should know the rules better by now...'

Perhaps Rajk did. Perhaps he indicated with this indifferent hand-out of his signature that he was beyond caring, that he would sign anything; or that I should accuse him without compunction, if by doing so I could improve my own position. Perhaps he had acted without thinking. Because he no longer cared about anything, or paid any attention to what was going on around him.

We were in the month of August. Preparations for the trial progressed with frenzied haste. The press was still silent but in exclusive party-meetings, party functionaries, proud of possessing inside information, dropped a few remarks here and there about the details of the subversive activities carried on by the arrested Imperialist agents. And general secretary Mátyás Rákosi would, from time to time, give a confidential report to the members of the Central Committee concerning some unexpected turn of the investigation.

Thus, as we heard later in prison from a former member of the Central Committee, also arrested and sentenced, Mátyás Rákosi reported with serene satisfaction how spontaneously witnesses were coming forward throughout the country to give evidence against the persons arrested in the Rajk affair. There was, for instance, the former governor of the Sátoraljaújhely prison who, when he learned, somewhat belatedly, that András Szalai, deputy head of the Party's Cadres Department had been arrested, was immediately moved to inform the State Security Authority how he had trapped András Szalai when, in the last years of the war, the latter was a prisoner at Sátoraljaújhely. The former prison director testified that Szalai had become an informer, and had betrayed an attempted break-out by Yugoslav partisans and other political prisoners. This enabled the Fascist authorities to prepare in advance for the break-out and kill some sixty-five people. Thus, Szalai was not only a Yugoslav spy but also an accomplice in mass-murder. All this might have remained for ever undiscovered had the people not supported the Communist Party and had not Lajos Lindenberg, the former prison director, come forward spontaneously to give evidence.

While Rákosi was divulging this information I was tossing and turning on my narrow wooden bunk in the Andrássy Street cellar. Although it must have been long after midnight, I was unable to sleep. So, I was glad when the door opened and the guards pushed in a short, almost bald, elderly man. My new cell-mate wore a light shantung cloth suit and moved cautiously, heavily. In the lamplight everything about him looked grey, his clothing, the little hair he had left, his small eyes, even his complexion. He might have been sixty-five years old. He looked around shyly, anxiously, then sat down on the other bunk opposite mine.

'Who are you?' I asked in a low voice to start the ball rolling.

But the newcomer made no reply. He was gazing at the Judas-hole in the dark-brown cell door. When I repeated my question a little more loudly, thinking that maybe he was hard of hearing, my cell-mate shuddered, then his glance flew fearfully from the peep-hole to my face, from my face to the wall, from the wall back to the Judas-hole, and only after a while did he whisper almost unintelligibly:

'Do they let us talk here?'

'I have never asked,' I said, 'but if they put us in one cell they must assume that we won't keep our mouths shut . . .'

'I don't know . . .' the newcomer shook his head and his glance slid back to the Judas-hole.

After this I did not put my second question: 'Why are you here?' The man was scared stiff and I felt it was up to me to respect his reticence. He did not look at me, but with an experienced flick of his tongue removed his false teeth and slid them carefully into his breast-pocket. Then, without a sound, he lay down on the bunk.

By the end of the following day he had gradually thawed out. We even introduced ourselves after the morning flour-soup. My new cell-mate's name was, he told me, Lajos Lindenberg, he lived at Sátoraljaújhely where, in his time, he had been governor of the prison. Three weeks ago, on a sunny summer afternoon, a black car had stopped before his house. Three men alighted. They said they were ÁVH officers and politely requested Mr. Lajos Lindenberg to come with them. They would detain him for no more than half an hour, they only wished to ask him for some evidence. The former prison governor complied with this request without putting on his hat which, conservatively, he always wore, or taking along his over-coat, because he hoped to be back home by dinner time.

The first surprise came when the car took the road to Budapest, and the second at the Andrássy Street headquarters of the ÁVH, where they began to interrogate him about a man called András Szalai who, they alleged, had been a prisoner at Sátoraljaújhely. Although he had never yet been let down by his excellent memory, he was unable to remember that at the time in question a prisoner by the name of András Szalai had been entrusted to his care. Then the investigators put photographs before him. Again and again they showed him the picture of a man with an enormous moustache, insisting furiously that it was impossible that he should not recognize him. They made him stand facing the wall for half a day at a time, they hit him, but in vain, for he had never seen that man with the moustache and even less could he identify him as András Szalai, whom he had never seen or heard of.

Finally, however, the ingenious interrogators and the unhappy witness solved the riddle by joint effort. András Szalai had formerly been called Ervin Laendler, and Laendler had, without a doubt, served his sentence at the Sátoraljaújhely prison in 1943–44. Lind-enberg felt relieved for, to judge from the signs, the interrogators realized that their witness could not indeed have guessed that Szalai, with his Stalin-moustache, was identical with the callow youth, Laendler, who had been his prisoner.

But his relief lasted only for minutes. When it became clear that András Szalai, deputy head of the Party's Cadres Department, and Ervin Laendler, the former prisoner of the Sátoraljaújhely prison were one and the same person, the interrogators confronted Linden-berg with a new demand–to make a deposition admitting he had recruited Szalai as his informer when the latter was at Sátoraljaújhely.

Szalai-Laendler–said Lindenberg–had been a quiet well-behaved prisoner, which was why he had detailed him to the prison laundry to keep the records; he had not asked him to inform on others. He had known nothing about the planned break, either from Szalai or from any other prisoner. Had he had foreknowledge he would have tried, if only from professional pride, to prevent the attempt. He would have isolated the ring-leaders–whom Szalai was alleged to have named–investigated the matter, introduced measures of vigilance, perhaps asked for reinforcements, but he would never have left it to the military to massacre the escapers outside the prison gates.

But his attempts to explain this to the ÁVH interrogators,

Lindenberg went on, or even to the Russians, were useless. For lately it was not Hungarian but Russian MVD officers who interrogated him behind the iron door. The MVD officers made him stand facing the wall, hit him, twisted his ear, and never stopped shouting. And the interpreter, a young, heavily-built, but not exactly unprepossesing woman, with a creole complexion, constantly egged the Russian on. Was this the way to treat a witness?

'What am I to do now?' the grey little man asked. 'For if I admit that Laendler was an informer and betrayed the prisoners' plan to break out, I am a false witness, I would be guilty of a highly punishable offence which could have catastrophic consequences. And if I refuse to give evidence . . .'

Lindenberg shuddered and shrugged his shoulders wearily. His dilemma must still have been tormenting him even when he appeared before the court. He replied hesitantly in a low voice, when asked what public office he had held in 1943–44. This is how, according to the *Blue Book* his interrogation continued:

> The President: I am sure you can speak louder, obviously you did not speak so quietly in the prison! What was the consequence for the political prisoners of the fact that András Szalai informed there about some plan to escape? Do you remember that?
>
> Lindenberg: Yes.
>
> The President: Then speak about that.
>
> Lindenberg: András Szalai reported first in January 1944 that the Serbian political prisoners were whispering among themselves, and speaking about some plan of escape. András Szalai repeated this report in a more concrete form in February, 1944, when he already spoke of a break-out and escape, and quoted by name the organizers of the break-out. The break-out took place on March 21, 1944, in such a way that the Serbian political prisoners attacked and disarmed the warders and forced the gates. But only a quarter of the sentenced prisoners who were preparing to escape succeeded in getting out through the forced gates, because the troops of the pioneer formation who had been ordered to be fully prepared by Lieutenant-Colonel of the Military Court Dr. József Babos, and who were prepared, arrived unexpectedly at the prison, and detaining a large number of the prisoners preparing to break out, they pushed them back into their cells. After that they started to catch the 75 prisoners who were already outside the gates and,

pursuing them, they massacred 54 prisoners. They caught 21. These 21 they brought back to the prison, and in the meantime, on March 26, the court martial of the military court arrived and ordered 11 of these 21 to be executed. (Ibid. pp. 249–50)

Szalai readily admitted his betrayal, he even supplemented the prison director's deposition by describing his less significant but continuous activities as an informer. A special division of the People's Court in the first place sentenced the accused, András Szalai, to death. But in its painstaking solicitude it took care that society should be protected from the Sátoraljaújhely informer even after his death, and accordingly it suspended the accused, who was executed shortly after being sentenced, from the practice of his political rights and of his office for 10 years. (Ibid. p. 305)

After the public trial, Lindenberg was also brought before the court and was given a heavy sentence at an *in camera* trial. The grey little man with his grey suit, grey hair, grey face, Mátyás Rákosi's 'spontaneous' witness, never saw the hills of Sátoraljaújhely again. Death overtook him in prison.

Unlike the former prison governor, Béla Korondy, the seventh accused in the public trial, looked forward to the events to come with almost cheerful serenity. That at least was his attitude when, for a few days, he was my guest in cell No. 29.

The thirty-five-year-old Korondy with his smooth manners, smooth face and erect bearing looked young, in spite of his prematurely grey hair. His disciplined movements and his style of speech immediately betrayed the professional soldier. He came from an army family, had attended the Military Academy and married into an army family. In 1939 he was assigned to the provincial constabulary. He was not very happy about this, perhaps because he would have preferred to wear an air-force uniform; but he obeyed without protest. By 1945, he was fighting as a partisan against the Germans in one of the Hungarian units thrown into combat by the Russians during the battle of Budapest to capture the fortress on the Gellért hill. Korondy's unit, as he told me, had lost over sixty per cent of its effective in this senseless frontal attack of the steep mountainside.

This detail was not mentioned in Korondy's trial. Public prosecutor Gyula Alapi forgot to mention that it was as a reward for his meritorious service as a partisan that Korondy had been appointed an officer in the new army.

On the contrary, this is how Alapi spoke of him in the indictment:

> György Pálffy arranged for his clearance and smuggled him into the democratic army in the rank of a major. Later Pálffy, in order to strengthen László Rajk's espionage organization, transferred Korondy to the Ministry of Home Affairs where Rajk had him appointed colonel of police. Rajk gave Korondy the task of organizing from among ex-gendarmes, Horthyist officers, permanent N. C. O.s and other fascist scum a battalion on which he could rely, which would in every case be available against the Republic. (Ibid. p. 24)

At the public trial Korondy made the following statement:

> In March, 1948, I had worked in the Ministry of Home Affairs for one and a half years. László Rajk summoned me on one occasion to report to him. He asked for information on the strength of the armed police units, where they were stationed, the stage of their training and aptitude for education. When I had concluded my report he asked me emphatically, so that one could feel that this was important, whether I was willing to fulfil his personal orders and command. When I replied in the affirmative, he informed me that he was preparing an armed *putsch* against the democratic government and his intention was for me to organize a special detachment, with whose help I could arrest the members of the government, in the first place Ministers Rákosi, Farkas and Gerö. (Ibid, pp. 183–4)

According to his confession, Korondy saw Rajk only once more, in October, 1948, at the Ministry of Foreign Affairs. Rajk assured Korondy that his plans had not changed and therefore he encouraged him to try and maintain his position in the police. 'György Pálffy supplemented these instructions in April, 1949'–Korondy declared at the public trial–

> by saying that, in addition to the duties assigned to me by Rajk, it would be my task to take over the command of the armed police forces and to occupy the more important objectives in Budapest, the Hungarian Working People's Party Centre, the post office, telegraph office, the radio, railway stations and the ministries with this special armed police force. (Ibid. p. 185)

In cell No. 29, Korondy recited to me the text of this confession almost word for word, with a somewhat supercilious, somewhat ironical smile.

'But who is going to take this seriously?' I asked. 'What sort of conspiracy is this where the leaders make offhand remarks to a man who is practically a stranger, telling him to organize units for the arrest of the members of the government, and then after a whole year, during which absolutely nothing happens, adds airily that he is to assume command of the armed police force and occupy all strategic points in the capital? As if it were all only a question of his decision, as if there were no armed ÁVH and military units, not to speak of the Soviet armies, in the country . . .'

'You see,' Korondy laughed, 'that's just it. The confession is a lot of idiotic nonsense, and nobody will believe that a professional soldier would undertake a job that would seem soft-headed even to an infant in arms.'

My cell-mate then explained in detail that he had agreed to the role for which they cast him mainly because this *putsch* story was so childish that any rational person could not but doubt it; and even if anyone fell for it, it could never appear dangerous to the state. No word would be said at the trial about anyone ever having set a date for the *putsch* or taken a single step in its preparation. Besides, Béla Korondy was no leader, no moving spirit, he was little more than an underling in this idiotic attempt—for from the legal point of view this conspiracy legend could, at most, be described as merely an attempt.

I asked him what sort of sentence he expected.

'Gábor Péter told me that they would probably sentence me to five or six years' imprisonment. However, as it is a political trial and those in the know are perfectly well aware that I never conspired, I won't even have to spend half my sentence in prison. Once the storm caused by the trial has calmed down they will let me slip out by the back door. And Péter says I won't have it too bad even until then. Somewhere in the Mátra Mountains they are building a new labour camp on the Russian pattern: that's where they'll send me. We shall fell trees, spend our time in the open air and get plenty of food, like the troops. My wife will be allowed to visit me once a month. Of course, after my release, I won't be a Colonel again, perhaps not even a sergeant, but I don't mind that . . . I've had enough. I'll take a job as a chauffeur, or a stableman. Or perhaps, as they think me useful, they may send me out to a foreign country as a training instructor or . . . or . . . some such thing.'

My cell-mate's words reminded me suspiciously of László Farkas's promises to me. I could not help interrupting him.

'Do you think all these promises can be taken for gospel truth?'

'Look,' Korondy shrugged his shoulders, 'Gábor Péter calls me by my first name, treats me like a pal, jokes with me. I know, it would be stupid to overestimate this. But tell me, what point would there be in breaking their promise and hanging me? Didn't I play the sheep perfectly?'

'Indeed,' I thought to myself, 'what point would there be in despatching this nice, superficial boy into another world? To render the utterly implausible plausible by treating it with ruthless reality? Silence the doubters with a draconic verdict?' Although I did not speak, Korondy was watching me keenly, then, as if he wanted to dam the flow of my thoughts and perhaps his own, too, he rose lightly and stepped between the two bunks.

'Well, let's do gymnastics,' he said, 'whatever happens, let's do gymnastics.'

And we did. Several times a day, especially before breakfast and in the early afternoon, we whiled away the time by doing light, muscle-relaxing boxing and breathing exercises in our cellar, which stank like a crypt. Now I would count: one, two, three, now he would command: quick-time on the same spot. I think to both of us it seemed amusing rather than ghastly to regard this road leading to darkness, if only for a few moments, as a sundrenched sports-ground, and to pretend that we had no other worry than to preserve our physical flexibility for our still distant old age. However, as even these light exercises would soon make us gasp in the musty cell, soon we were sitting on our bunks again. On one occasion Korondy gazed silently before him for a while, then smiled at me:

'Could I have acted differently? Perhaps so. Perhaps not. There is no sense in thinking about it. It is too late. I have signed the statement. And whether you believe me or not, I feel relieved. Now it is all out of my hands. Therefore, I do gymnastics. Will you join me again?'

I shook my head. I felt faint, my ribs hurt, my legs were shaky. I had not yet recovered. I looked at my cell-mate. Why indeed should he brood? For he was a finished, polished, prefabricated element without a will of his own, waiting to be fitted together along with other prefabricated elements. He was again standing between the bunks, both hands on his hips, his back straight as a ram-rod. In the pause between two slow, painfully regular squatting movements, he remarked airily:

'Suppose they cheat and hang me all the same? Well, that's just my bad luck . . .'

The special division of the People's Court pronounced its verdict in the case of László Rajk and his accomplices on September 24, 1949, at a quarter to ten in the morning. The presiding judge, Dr. Péter Jankó, left out the two soldiers, addressed the other accused one by one, and then announced, 'The Special Court states that it is not competent to hear the charge against the accused György Pálffy and Béla Korondy and therefore separates their case, and directs it to the competent military court.' (Ibid. p. 306)

The military tribunal sentenced Pálffy, Korondy and several others, to death. Their plea for mercy was rejected, and the sentence promptly carried out.

7

Political Iconography

IN this *second phase of the realization*, as it gradually assumed shape and proportion, László Rajk and Béla Korondy stood as fully fashioned and polished prefabricated elements before the main architect, Lieutenant-General Fedor Belkin. Lajos Lindenberg, former prison director, had already some inkling of what purpose he was to serve when, grey and shy, he had first stumbled into my cell. A few weeks later, though with a troubled conscience, he recited in a low voice the text prepared for him. I, however, was still bubbling, an undefinable compound in the joint melting pot of the ÁVH and the MVD.

Korondy spent only a few days in cell No. 29. After he had gone, I was led again to that section of the MVD protected by the iron door. Colonel Szücs received me. He offered me a chair behind the desk and sat on top of it, with his foot dangling in the air. Only if I bent my head over the back of the chair could I see his florid face. After a few introductory sentences, Szücs broke into an almost melancholy smile:

'I think some self-criticism in indicated,' he sighed and shook his head, 'for really, we ought to have treated you differently. I am sincerely sorry for everything that has happened. If we had talked openly to you from the first, if we had explained things to you, I suppose we could have saved you a great deal of unpleasantness. But at first, of course, we acted impulsively, hastily. Please, try to understand this. Look . . .'

And, as if he had forgotten that he had told me similar things before, as if he were taking me into his confidence and revealing to me some secret kept under seven seals the Colonel recited, in part word for word, elsewhere in greater detail, the by now familiar sermon. The increasingly tense socialist-capitalist conflict, he declared, but particularly the treason committed by Tito and his accomplices, made it the duty of the Hungarian communists to strike the Imperialist powers and their Yugoslav agents 'a heavy blow'. It was their duty to unmask them, brand them, make them suspect in the eyes of every person of good will. This would benefit not only Hungarian socialist progress, but also the Soviet Union, all the people's democracies, the Western Communist Parties and even the Yugoslavs themselves. For the trial now in preparation would make it possible for other contaminated Communist Parties also to eliminate Imperialist infiltration, to separate the wheat from the tares. This is how this trial of world-wide importance, and Szücs rolled the words *worldwide importance* on his tongue with enthusiastic emphasis, would serve the sacred ideal of socialism, the whole of the communist movement, the cause of the international proletariat.

The Colonel's transports which sometimes rang sincere, sometimes false, and more especially his self-criticism, filled me with suspicion and fear, for I could not doubt that this introduction would soon be followed by a request for self-sacrifice. Listening to the phoney slogans borrowed from a leader in the Party press, my reflections and fears were overshadowed by an aesthetic aversion to the man which, I felt, made it entirely impossible for me to concoct a confession aided by Szücs or to become, in any way, a co-author with this cliché-ridden man.

During his lengthy speech, my neck-muscles grew cramped and I became tired of watching the face, the blinking little eyes, shrunken to narrow slits in the puffed face, of Gábor Péter's deputy. I fixed my glance on the Colonel's stomach bulging before my nose. The tyres of fat between the buttons of the tunic were quivering peacefully to the rhythm of Ernö Szücs's words.

'At this moment,' the Colonel went on quietly, 'I am not speaking to you as an ÁVH officer. I have been sent to you by the Party. I assure you that no-one among us, no responsible person believes that you are a spy . . .'

This was something I had not counted on. Surprised, I interrupted him, 'Then why don't you release me?'

Szücs appeared pained. 'I'm surprised at you asking that. Do you call yourself a perfect Party member? Would you say you never made mistakes? . . . Your Party life was not beyond reproach,' he suddenly snapped out.

'Why not?' I enquired, although it seemed obvious to me that this détour would in no way alter what Szücs still had to say, or the role for which I was to be cast.

'Why not? I'm surprised at your question. Didn't you constantly protest, argue, invariably resist the Party? And your private life? Didn't you leave your wife to live with another woman . . .'

'Is that the reason for my arrest and detention?'

'No, no, of course not. But you must admit that you made mistakes which you will have to put right. Or do you allege that you never made mistakes?'

No, indeed, I wouldn't have risked such an allegation, particularly now when I was beginning to see more and more clearly towards what moral horizons, towards what sort of people, the movement, into the stream of which I had thrown myself in my youth, was driving me. Szücs, interpreted my silence almost with glee.

'You see,' he cried triumphantly, 'you are silent. You can't answer. Yes, you have committed mistakes, grave mistakes. And yet the Party offers you an opportunity to atone for them all and at the same time serve the interests of the international proletariat. What's more, the Party *asks* you to do so. Do you understand what this means? *The Party asks you.* Is it customary for the Party to ask?'

Szücs watched me closely, then he repeated with emphasis:

'Thus, the Party asks you to understand the situation as numerous other communists have understood it. After all, you didn't join the movement yesterday. Do you understand now?'

I nodded. I understood. The Colonel was speaking in the name of a metaphysical notion, the Party, written and pronounced with a capital P. Still, though it was indeed not yesterday that I had joined the movement, I had never reached that level of religious ecstasy where I could personify the Party and disregard its constituent elements. What was the Party? Its supporting pillar was the bureaucrat who had summoned me to Headquarters to make me issue a communiqué denouncing an act of sabotage that had never taken place; its bricks were the Hungarian or French workers who, bent over their machines, had no inkling of what was going on in their name in a building on Andrássy Street in Budapest; and its hope for the future was perhaps the student in Bologna or in South America, engaged at that very moment in reading Marx's witty analysis of Napoleon III's *coup d'état*. However, it was not the student, not the worker, but the Party bureaucrats, László Farkas, Ernö Szücs, the Russian Lieutenant-Colonel and especially Fedor Belkin, the Governor, who acted in the name of the Party. Admitting, as we safely could do, that I had committed mistakes, how could I feel guilty towards the Nádor Street Party functionary, towards László Farkas, Ernö Szücs or the Governor? Or towards a metaphysical abstraction?

I think the Colonel's pseudo-mystical vision of the Party would have pulled me back even had I been, consciously or unconsciously, searching for some form of atonement, if for no other reason than that Szücs left my sense of humour out of consideration. It was all very well to confront me with this doll in quaint ceremonial dress personifying the Party; but it was a mistake to divest it verbally of its festive clothes by talking of the practical tasks to be performed in the name of this idol demanding human sacrifice and letting me see the wrathful little image in its ridiculous underpants! Because this is how the Colonel continued:

'We must supplement the minutes of your confrontation with Rajk. We must really give them a sharper political content. That is to say we must make them more compromising politically. I can assure you, Rajk will admit everything.'

In more than one case the various methods of awakening a sense of guilt contributed, particularly among arrested communists, to the admission of espionage and conspiracy. Some of them insisted for years afterwards that they had truly committed the fictitious crimes with which they were charged, even when they mixed with other prisoners in gaol and it could have become clear to them from daily conversation that not only they, not only certain other persons, but, at a conservative estimate, over ninety-five per cent of the political prisoners had been sentenced on the basis of purely invented charges.

At times, dissecting year by year the life of the man entrusted to their care, the interrogators would try to instil into him a sense of guilt not with reference to the party, but by laying great emphasis on some personal matter in his past. One of my cell-mates, for instance— the son of a protestant theologian turned freethinker and then communist—tried to convince me amidst innumerable *mea culpas*, that fundamentally he had deserved his punishment, not, of course, because of any espionage activity as alleged in the indictment but because of having been twice unfaithful to his wife many years before his arrest.

I, personally, never tended to this kind of mysticism and I thought my face betrayed my views. Still, after his unequivocal remarks concerning the minutes of the confrontation, the Colonel did not immediately begin on the detailed elaboration of the draft confession. He must have thought that in order to convince me beyond any doubt, it was necessary to enlighten me as to the great honour he was doing me by speaking openly, for such frank sincerity was nothing less than an indication of the Party's trust. But precisely because the Party trusted my loyalty, it asked and could ask me to make a sacrifice for socialism, for the international proletariat, and to put myself at the service of the Soviet and Hungarian comrades.

I made no reply. I believe that my silence at last awoke the Colonel to the realization that the Party's suddenly manifested confidence in me was only increasing my lack of trust and strengthening my resistance to making a false statement. It is possible that for Szücs, routine obscured the grotesque nature of the situation; appealing in the name of an avowedly materialist philosophy to some sort of immaterial religious loyalty, they were demanding self-sacrifice from the chosen victim, trying to extract a false confession from him by instilling into him a sense of guilt—and all this was done by the same tormentors who had attempted to extract the same results earlier by the application of much less subtle means.

Suddenly Szücs jumped off the table with an agility belying his weight and with this movement he descended from the exalted regions of the soul to a somewhat more rational level.

I would have to appear at the principal trial only as a witness, he declared, and even if they did sentence me afterwards, it would not be for more than two or three years. I would be restored to health by outstanding specialists, I would be given an ample diet, in healthy surroundings. They would give me books and periodicals to read and I could even write if I wished. And finally, for this, too, was possible, I would be allowed to recuperate in the Crimean peninsula, one of the most beautiful coasts in the world, before returning to normal life.

'And you will be guarded by us,' Szücs continued, pacing up and down. His tone suggested that he considered it a special favour to be, for years, in the hands of the ÁVH. And then, to explain the improbably humane nature of this treatment and to lend the rest-cure in the Crimea more verisimilitude, he added, 'Because we want to re-educate you and lead you back to the Party.'

Later, in prison, this expression became a joke, for it was used not only by Szücs and had not been invented merely for my sake. And when far from tender educational methods were applied to us, we quoted Szücs's words; later a glance sufficed to suggest them.

'Yes,' the Colonel stopped in front of me, 'it is our aim to turn you again into useful members of the Party.'

Then he rested his hands on the two corners of the desk, bent over me, and began, in a low and friendly voice, to acquaint me with the text of the draft-confession. I must once and for all admit that I had established contact between Rajk and my British superiors. But at this point we were interrupted by an investigator who came and whispered something into Szücs's ear. Thereupon he hastily explained that I would now be questioned by a Soviet comrade of the highest rank. I had better be very careful with my replies. The Colonel motioned to me to follow him, then, as we went along side by side, he whispered to me that he hoped that I would not prove my own worst enemy.

We entered the room where shortly before Szücs had confronted me with Rajk. It was now empty. Only a worn leather cigarette case lay on the long table; next to it matches and an ashtray. Szücs made me sit at the table and he took his place at right angles to me.

'Do you smoke?' he asked.

When I said yes, he pushed the ashtray closer to me and offered me the cigarette case which was filled with American Old Gold cigarettes. It was obviously not his, for the Colonel did not smoke. We sat without talking and not until I had smoked three-quarters of my cigarette did the owner of the cigarette case appear. It was Lieutenant-General Fedor Belkin. He wore the same Stalin tunic of soft silver-blue cloth that he had worn at the secret villa. He sat down diagonally opposite me, almost in the middle of the long table. He leafed through some papers, then looked at me and began to speak in Russian. Szücs interpreted.

After my personal details and the disapproving confirmation of the fact that I came from a bourgeois family, we were back again at my University days and my acquaintance with Rajk.

'When did you find out that Rajk was an agent of the Horthy police?' Belkin asked.

'I never did,' I replied.

'Remember the periodical *Virradat*?'

Yes, I remembered very well what Major Károlyi had insinuated. That Rajk had been detained for distributing the seized issue of the periodical but had purchased his freedom by signing a pledge that he would, henceforth, report to the police every move of the communists, and that—according to Károlyi—I had guessed this from Rajk's nervousness when he came to attend classes the next day. Yes, I said to Szücs, I remembered the *Virradat* very well, also its seizure, but if Rajk had been detained for it and was still nervous the following day, I could by no means draw from this the conclusion that he had been recruited by the Horthy police as an agent.

'Then how did you find it out?' Belkin asked.

The Governor wanted me as a witness to support Rajk's confession and lend some verisimilitude to Károlyi's fiction. The moment had come when I was to be promoted to co-authorship. In a few weeks' time I would stand before the court and recite the jointly invented story, or at least be expected to recite it, for it was very doubtful whether I should be able to pronounce even the first syllable. I gazed at Belkin with an expressionless face, for at times of extreme tension, some sort of defensive fuse usually blows within me, disconnecting part of the nervous system. My attention flagged, I had to suppress a yawn, my thoughts wandered, and I made no reply to the question.

'All right,' the Lieutenant-General shrugged with scornful tolerance, 'you'll remember in time. Your mind seems to work slowly.'

From his shrug and his remark, I deduced that for the time being Belkin had shelved the unanswered question, reserving it as a detail to be elaborated later; and that he did not interpret my silence as defiance of his authority. As I watched his movements I remembered another man, in every way different from the Lieutenant-General and no longer among the living, against whose authority I had so often rebelled in my youth.

I thought particularly of a quiet scene, unobscured by the passing of time. My father had summoned me to his study. He was standing in front of his desk holding an envelope in his hand. I was a young university student and had only recently been released from prison. They had sentenced me to three months imprisonment for communist activities. My father had punished himself for his failure as an educator by staying away from his friends and his club, and though he was passionately fond of hunting, he hunted only on his small estate and consistently refused any invitation, however attractive, to the large hunts in the neighbourhood. He handed me a letter.

'I thought it was addressed to me,' he said, 'that is why I opened it. I am sorry.'

As we both bore the same name, my friends never forgot to put 'Jr.' on my letters. But this letter had not been sent by some close acquaintance. It came from the Transdanubian section of the underground Communist Party to establish contact with me. This was more than obvious from the transparently conspiratorial wording. My father feared for me nothing so much as a labyrinthine illegal movement. But as it would have conflicted with his sense of honour to throw the letter into the fire, however fateful it seemed to him, he had handed the conspiratorial letter to its rightful owner. He stood pale and erect in front of his desk. The corners of his mouth, the greying, short moustache, trembled almost imperceptibly. Perhaps he had acted against his better judgment, but he had not been untrue to himself.

The memory of my father's action did not soften me; on the contrary, it inspired me with the same temper that, a few weeks before, had prevented me from asking Farkas for an interview, when

I had already begun to wonder whether it might not be more rational to admit to one or other of the charges.

The Governor was not in a hurry. He lit a cigarette, then pushed the case over to me, offering me one, too. For a time, he questioned me about the Englishman in Buenos Aires, then suddenly he asked:
'And how did he recruit you?'

To my reply that the Englishman had not recruited me, Belkin broke into hooting laughter and Szücs joined in with respectful servility.

'Of course he recruited you! Of course he recruited you!' Belkin cried, 'and even if he didn't formally recruit you, it was he who sent you home. Tell me now, on what assignment did they send you to Hungary?'

When I replied that I had neither been given nor had ever accepted any assignment from any secret service whatsoever, Belkin's laughter rose to an almost eerie whinnying, accompanied by Szücs's more discreet giggle. When, finally, the synthetic hilarity abated, we came back to Rajk. When, where, and under what conditions did we meet after my return and what had we talked about?

'And when did you blackmail Rajk?' the Lieutenant-General suddenly and dramatically asked.

This was entirely new. Perhaps it was one of the 'lesser details determined by the premise' that Szücs had mentioned in passing from the other room.

The confession expected from me took shape as the questions followed one another. Then, in order to prevent misunderstandings, as Belkin said, glancing at his papers he summed up. The story was that I had been recruited by the British secret service in Buenos Aires, and afterwards, in 1946, sent home to Hungary. In Budapest I went to see László Rajk, Minister of the Interior, a former fellow-student of mine. Already, in my student years, I had known that Rajk was an informer for the Horthy police. I blackmailed him by threatening that my superiors would publish the documents of his betrayal abroad, unless he agreed to work with me. Rajk yielded and for two years supplied me with confidential information obtained at the Ministry of the Interior, and later at the Ministry of Foreign Affairs and Party Headquarters; he also supplied me with documents which I forwarded to the British secret service.

Did Szücs think that the presence of the great man would be enough to overwhelm me and that, if the Governor himself took me in hand, I would, as if touched by a magic wand, be transformed into malleable material? Or had some technical error been committed? For Belkin was, without a doubt, questioning me on the basis of the final statement that was usually submitted to the accused only amidst conspiratorial glances indicating 'we know that not a word of this is true', after he had already signed a confession admitting he had been a spy or a conspirator.

Whatever the reasons, Szücs's method had not worked with me. As I learned later in prison, it had been successful in several cases but perhaps the Colonel had become tired and had in my case employed his usual tricks sloppily, unimaginatively. He had failed to fit them to my personality. On the one hand he had said too little, on the other, too much. He talked of the Party's request, the Party's confidence, appealing to a mystical faith, the existence of which he could only suppose; but he had said too much when, in the MVD section behind the iron door, he had conjured up the picture of a rest-cure in the Crimean sunshine.

After outlining the confession they had elaborated for me, the Lieutenant-General conferred in Russian with Szücs. Then Szücs addressed me with portentous severity:

'The Lieutenant-General wants to give you a last opportunity to come to your senses and save yourself from the worst. We shall once more repeat the questions. Give short and sensible answers. And be very careful!' he added in a different tone, as if to indicate that the warning was personal.

At this moment I could no longer decide which to dread, which to fear more: the consequences of a confession, or the consequences of my refusal to confess? I had neither time, nor strength for sober reflection. I could only trust my instincts.

The questions followed each other in quick succession: Did you know that Rajk was a police agent? Were you recruited by the British secret service? Did you blackmail Rajk? Did you recruit Rajk for the British secret service?

I was obeying no moral command, nor was I driven by anger when, stubbornly, I gave a negative reply to every question. Somehow I knew beyond all doubt that whether it would be helpful or harmful to me, I should never be able to do other than speak the truth at the trial. Just as my father was unable to burn my letter. For no-one can step over his own shadow.

Belkin jumped up in a rage, flung down the sheaf of papers he was holding, snatched the leather case filled with Old Gold cigarettes from under my nose and shouted in Russian for a minute and a half. All that Szücs translated for me from the involved sentences was:

'This is not a Trotskyist meeting, this is not the place for provocation . . .' and with this, the Colonel pushed me from the room. That was my last meeting with Lieutenant-General Belkin, Commander-in-Chief of the South-East MVD. Years later I looked for his name in the archives of various foreign newspapers but could find nothing about him. It was rumoured in Hungary that after the East German uprising in 1953, the Lieutenant-General fell from favour and disappeared. Later, the Soviet press spoke of him as an accomplice of Beria and Abakumov. Rumour had it that Belkin was executed along with them. If there is justice in the world, they first offered him an Old Gold cigarette.

After what had happened in the MVD section I supposed that they would try to make me agree to the text of the confession by physical means, by tortures more refined than those employed during the first period; or perhaps they would try to blackmail me by arresting members of my family or kidnapping my son – as they had repeatedly threatened. Compared to this nightmare it appeared merciful to me if they would only fulfil Farkas's threats and, discarding obsolete formalities, put a full stop to the last line of my unfinished deposition by shooting me in the back of the head.

But in the cellars of Andrássy Street, nothing happened as prisoners expected. 'The secret police is always incalculable', was one of the ÁVH precepts, and accordingly its prisoners were kept permanently on tenterhooks. I waited in vain to be questioned again or transferred somewhere else. Nobody spoke to me. I spent my days in the tiniest of all the cells, the last in one of the side corridors, where Cardinal Mindszenty had scratched his name into the wall during his imprisonment there, and surrounded it with the radiating rays of Jesus' heart. Nothing happened and, what is more, until my sentence was pronounced, nobody ever laid a finger on me.

I would gladly believe that Belkin was not a man bent on vengeance. But it is also true that there was so little time left before the principal trial that had they submitted me to hard physical pressure they could not have let me appear before the audience and foreign correspondents admitted to the trial. Nor was the Lieutenant-General convinced that I would not create, at this public performance, a painful and irremediable scandal. So he chose a stop-gap arrangement and entrusted the most essential part of my role to an American citizen of Hungarian origin, the absent Lieutenant-Colonel Kovach, without, of course, first asking the Lieutenant-Colonel's consent.

According to the *Blue Book* Rajk stated at the trial that he had filled a 'high function' in the Communist Party and in 1945 was appointed secretary of the Budapest Party organization. Then he goes on:

> Not long after I had received this assignment from the Party leadership, I was visited by a man named Kovach who was a member of the American military mission. This was around August–September, 1945. He informed me that he had received a message from Sombor-Schweinitzer, who was in the American zone, through which he discovered that I had worked for the Horthy police. Being in possession of this information Kovach ordered me to place myself at the disposal of the American intelligence service. If I did not carry this out they would denounce me to the Communist Party leadership. Of course I agreed to do this. Kovach asked for political information about the Hungarian internal political situation. (Ibid. p. 45)

According to the new version it was not the British but the Americans who blackmailed Rajk, the threat was not that they would publish the documents of his betrayal abroad, but that they would bring the facts to the knowledge of the Hungarian Party leadership; but these small modifications did not make much difference to the accused. However, as various people told me six years later, it had not escaped the attention of the readers of the *Blue Book*, nor of those attending the trial, that Gyula Alapi, the Public Prosecutor, first did me the honour of calling me 'an agent of the British Intelligence Service sent home from South America' (*László Rajk and his accomplices before the People's Court*, Szikra, Budapest, p. 11), only to describe me, a few minutes later, as a notorious 'American spy' (Ibid. p.21).

The editorial board called together to elaborate the text of the trial could not bring itself to discard a few ideas they considered ingenious, as, for example, that Szönyi maintained contact with his superiors abroad by means of messengers. As, during the first weeks, they had not succeeded in making me admit that I had brought a message to Péter from the mysterious Wagner, and then handed Wagner's letter to Szönyi, they divided my doings between the absent László Bartók and the arrested Iván Földi. 'In 1946'–Szönyi stated during his examination–'that special courier who brought me the message by word of mouth that "Péter should get in touch with Wagner's acquaintance from France", that is with Rajk, was László Bartók, a former diplomat with the rank of counsellor in the Hungarian Ministry of Foreign Affairs. (Ibid. p. 153). In the trial it was Field, not Wagner who sent a letter from Switzerland. This is what Iván Földi stated in his deposition: 'From Switzerland I returned again to Budapest in May, 1946. I handed over to Szönyi a letter of Field in a sealed envelope which I had brought with me' (Ibid. p. 241).

And this is how Szönyi described the contents of the alleged letter so as to keep me in the picture, too:

> When Iván Földi came to Budapest from Geneva for a few days in May, 1946, he brought me a sealed letter from Field in which the names of three American spies were mentioned, Béla Szász, György Ádám and Iván Máté, who were already organized agents of the American intelligence service and he told me about that. Later on, knowing that Béla Szász and György Ádám were American spies I placed them in important jobs, in the case of Béla Szász on the special instructions of Rajk. (Ibid. p. 152)

When, in the last year of our imprisonment, we were given books to read, we obtained from the prison library the *Blue Book* of the Rajk trial. In this it was Szönyi's questioning that threw the clearest light on what was not exactly a side-issue in the trial: the Party purge, and particularly a certain trend within it. The producers of the trial put Szönyi in the spot-light as the symbol of a category, for his confession was made up in such a way as to throw suspicion not only on himself, not only on those in the dock with him, but on all those who had returned home from the West, especially the intellectuals.

Szönyi's confession insinuated that all those who had lived in the West, or shown an interest in Western culture, were the agents, or at least the potential agents, of one or another of the Imperialist powers.

From Szönyi I at last obtained a reply to the question that had for long preoccupied me, although it had no bearing on the identity of Noel Field or of Wagner, about whom Gábor Péter had questioned me during that first hour of my arrest and his men for weeks following, in a rather unfriendly manner.

All this emerged clearly from Szönyi's account of the preliminaries of his return home:

> In the summer of 1944, towards the end of the war, in its last year, it had become obvious that a part of the East European and Central European countries would be liberated by the Soviet troops. At that time the American intelligence service,

under the leadership of Allan Dulles, began to concentrate on the task of bringing into its organization spies from the political émigrés there, especially from the left-wing communist groups. The purpose of this was to infiltrate these people into the territories liberated by the Soviet troops, to carry out underground activity against the Communist Parties there. It was in the course of this activity that I came into contact with the American spy organization. The chief helpmate and closest collaborator of Allan Dulles in his work of organizing spies from among the political émigrés was Noel H. Field, who was officially the head of the Unitarian relief organization called the Unitarian Service Committee. In reality he was a direct collaborator of Dulles in the spy organization. (Ibid. p. 146–7)

After that there is a lot about Allen Dulles (the *Blue Book* spelled his name everywhere as 'Allan'), and there is a great deal about the Yugoslav, Czech, Polish political refugees who had also been recruited by the American secret service. Szönyi continues:

I met Dulles regularly until my return home in January, 1945. My formal enrolment into the American spy organization took place at the end of November, 1944, in Berne. At this meeting Dulles explained to me at length his political conception for the period after the war and told me that the Communist Parties would obviously become government parties in a whole series of Eastern European countries which would be liberated by Soviet troops. So support for an American orientation and the American collaboration policy should be carried on first of all within the Communist Party. (Ibid. p. 148)

Finally, Szönyi concludes this part of his confession as follows: 'Later I met Dulles more than once. I agreed with him that after our return home we would remain in contact with each other, and I would use in this contact the cover-name "Péter" and he the cover-name "Wagner".' (Ibid. p. 148)

More than four years later, turning the pages of the *Blue Book* in my prison cell, I at last understood the question Gábor Péter had asked me at the T-shaped table, I understood what that alleged password: 'Wagner's message to Péter . . .' meant. But my conscience did not bother me, not even when I remembered Szücs's wasted efforts, for after all, I had put no spoke in their wheel; they had found understudies to play my role, a prisoner in the Andrássy

Street cellars and someone living beyond their reach abroad. But the most important role, the one written for László Rajk, could be played by no one but László Rajk himself.

During the first phase of his arrest, as was shown by the deep furrows cutting across his face, which I observed at our first confrontation, his interrogators had treated this former underground communist and former minister just as ruthlessly as his fellow-prisoners; perhaps he had been submitted to even more cruel tortures. But in the end, Rajk accepted the golden bridge offered to his self-respect: that it was not to escape torture that he finally yielded, but to make a sacrifice for socialism and to serve his party. It was János Kádár, then Minister of the Interior, who sought to persuade Rajk with the same arguments Colonel Szücs had used to convince me.

Evidence of the conversations between Rajk and Kádár became known only in 1956. In 1949 Secretary-General Mátyás Rákosi still took credit for the 'unmasking of the Rajk gang'. To arouse the sympathy of his audience, he described the 'sleepless nights' he had spent until at last, fitting together the mosaics, he had become convinced of the guilt of László Rajk and his accomplices. Thus, it was only natural, that in 1956 at the time of the 'thaw' when public opinion began to assert itself, it should have made Rákosi responsible not only for the Rajk affair but also for a series of other show-trials that had demanded numerous victims. Therefore, the Central Committee of the Communist Party, regardless of the political shade of some of its members, felt it wrong that Rákosi should still be standing at the helm, and one group thought of putting János Kádár in Rákosi's place. Because within a year of the Rajk trial, Kádár had also been arrested and condemned, and certain members of the Central Committee would have liked to gloss over their own past by hiding it behind Kádár's prison years.

But–to prove that the new nominee was no more innocent in the preparation of the show-trials than the present Secretary General–at a session of the Central Committee Rákosi played back a tape-recording of the dialogue between the detained Rajk and Minister of the Interior, János Kádár.

Thus the members of the Central Committee heard with their own ears how the new Minister of the Interior explained to the ex-Minister that he must give up his stubborn resistance, put himself at the disposal of the Party and help to condemn Tito's heresy.

No-one in the Party leadership believed that Rajk was guilty, Kádár emphasized, and they would admire him even more if he made the sacrifice. Wasn't it true that he had often risked his life in the underground movement, in the International Brigade fighting in the Spanish civil war, and in the anti-Nazi resistance movement? Now it was not his life that was demanded of him, only his moral suicide. For after the trial, even should he be condemned to death, he would not be executed, merely spirited away. They would send him to the Crimea, together with his family, and later he would be entrusted somewhere else, under another name, with an important position suitable to his abilities.

Rajk gave little credit to these promises, he lined up counter-arguments, debated, rebelled. But if we enquire into his motives, why, though hesitatingly and struggling with himself, he agreed in the end to be presented by his comrades as a monster, it seems that his dilemma was decided by his loyalty to the cause, his loyalty to his own past and to the idealized communist party, and not to the hope that they might spare his life if he proved his willingness to co-operate. According to one of his former cell-mates, it was this somewhat self-deluding loyalty that compelled Rajk to accept the star role in the trial.

László Rajk, known in the communist underground for his unconditional sincerity, must have overcome his own fierce resistance before, at the public trial, he declared with resigned indifference that he had only carried out 'spy work' in the communist movement and had informed on his comrades (*László Rajk and his Accomplices before the People's Court*, Szikra, Budapest, p. 35), had thwarted the strike of the building workers 'with deliberate premeditation' (Ibid. p. 37), had participated in the Spanish civil war, where he was wounded three times, as an agent of the Budapest political police, and, as he said:

> I went to Spain with the double assignment, on the one hand to find out the names of those in the Rákosi Battalion–this was the name of the Hungarian unit–and on the other hand through political disruption to bring about the reduction of the military efficiency of the Rákosi Battalion. (Ibid. p. 38)

It must have turned his stomach to relate as he did his subsequent political career, for he confesses that after the Spanish civil war he was the informer of Pétain's '2-ième Bureau' at the internment camps of Gurs and Vernet (Ibid. p. 40), returned to Hungary with the help of the Gestapo (Ibid. p. 42) to be interned again but only so as 'not to be suspected' of being a police agent (Ibid. p. 43). The risks he took in the anti-Nazi resistance movement were again intended to allay suspicion, for, in reality, he worked as an informer, and he was arrested mistakenly because, as he said: '. . . I was arrested by the military counter-intelligence who did not know that I was an organized agent of the Hungarian police, and as a consequence of the war situation I was immediately sent to Sopronköhida a few days after my arrest' (Ibid. p. 44). Strangely enough, he was not released. On the contrary, when the Hungarian fascists were compelled to evacuate Sopronköhida on the western frontier, they moved their more important prisoners, among them Rajk, in a three-weeks' forced march to Germany. Rajk could return to Hungary only after Hitler's final defeat, where he was soon blackmailed by Lieutenant-Colonel Kovach and recruited 'for the American intelligence services' (Ibid. p. 45). He was ordered by Martin Himmler, another American intelligence officer, to take advantage of his power as Minister of the Interior, for at the time Rajk was already Minister of the Interior, to place in leading positions, in the key-posts of the state machinery '. . . people who were in their eyes reliable, that is, people following the policy of the Americans, or people who were attached to the American intelligence agencies' (Ibid. p. 48).

Considered from both the human and the political angle, this portrait appears comically improbable. For, as there is no book so bad that it is devoid of something good, there is no man so degenerate that there should be nothing humane, nothing winning in his life. It was precisely this abundance of detail, this condensed wealth of villainies, that must have aroused the greatest doubts. It is obvious that less would have been more effective. Especially, when Lieutenant-General Belkin's workshops produced a series of portraits, that of the Albanian Koczi Xoxe, the Hungarian Rajk, the Bulgarian Kostov, the Czech Slánsky, that not only resembled one another to an amazing degree, but resembled, astonishingly, the over-gilded, over-decorated ikons of the weary unimaginative Byzantine painter-artisans.

But these stiff and lifeless ikons were characteristic not only of the Byzantine taste of Lieutenant-General Belkin and Marshal Stalin's political school of painting but, being intended not so much for export as for domestic use, they were to proclaim, in the lingo of political iconography, by the improbability of their over-ornamentation, that in Moscow, the centre of the concentric magnetic fields of the European communist world, not the slightest breach of discipline would be tolerated.

The initiated at once understood this sinister lingo. The un-initiated were scared stiff by the ear-splitting din it created; then they noted the increasing severity of the organizational measures, the vigilance, work-discipline, political indoctrination, the decrease in the number of small freedoms and pleasures, and finally, from the ceremony of ritual murder, they at last grasped what the high priests intended them to know.

It was probably to enlighten the more ignorant, that Belkin referred back to the Moscow trials and made the men in the dock at the Rajk trial admit that they were Trotskyites. For according to the Stalinist chain of logic there can be no honest counter-opinion to the wisdom emanating from the Moscow core of the concentric circles. Anyone representing an antagonistic opinion must necessarily be of bad faith, that is, a Trotskyite; the Trotskyites were traitors and, in countries where the communists were not in power, that is, where the police were not communist but perhaps even anti-communist (as Rajk had to recite at the trial) '. . . in general the Trotskyists always and everywhere, internationally, worked in close contact with the police' (Ibid. p. 40).

What could be more natural, therefore, than to find that the Yugoslav political leaders, who had been highly esteemed in Moscow until they opposed Stalin's authoritarian arguments, turned out, after the break, to have always been Trotskyites, and that in the Vernet internment camp the Yugoslav members of the International Brigade had been agents of the French police: 'It became clear to me that these Yugoslavs were, in fact, the organized men of the Deuxième Bureau, and were carrying out its instructions just as I was' (Ibid. p. 40), said Rajk at the public trial. What is more, when Rajk spent a holiday in Yugoslavia and met the Yugoslav Minister of the Interior, Rankovich, in Abbazia, it became clear to him: '. . . that not only Rankovich, Vukmanovich, Milich and others who had been in Spain, pursued a Trotskyist policy and maintained connection with the American intelligence service but also Tito himself, the Prime Minister of the Yugoslav government' (Ibid. p. 52). It was when summing up this and similar statements (Pálffy, the Yugoslav Brankov, Szönyi) that the public prosecutor declared: 'This trial has exposed the Titoites, the great majority of the present members of the Yugoslav government in their role of allies of the American Imperialists and of common agents of the imperialist intelligence organizations' (Ibid. p. 265).

The Public Prosecutor, Alapi, was simplifying. He dropped the adjective 'Trotskyist' which, according to Muscovite political thought, engendered causal interdependence between ideological opposition and the serving of foreign powers. Thus while Alapi evaded any kind of ideological argument, on the other hand he denied that the struggle between Belgrade and Moscow was, fundamentally, one of principle. With this simplification Alapi attempted to trace the essence of the trial back to the religiously ancient and traditionally intelligible primitive antagonism between capitalism and socialism, between reaction and progress, and in the last resort between good and evil.

Communist ideology had, for decades, proclaimed the irreconcilable conflict between socialism and capitalism. Although during the war there had been a *treuga dei* on the open propaganda front, speakers at secret or private communist meetings, such at least was my experience in South America, depicted the Western allies as enemies capable of any trickery at any time, and stressed that it was the task of the communists during the ideological armistice to secure the greatest possible number of strategic positions within the fortresses of the allied capitalist front, since the final show-down, the ultimate settlement was unavoidable.

The public prosecutor ascribes the same train of thought and action to the other side when he declares:

> For it becomes evident from the material of the trial that the American intelligence services were already getting ready during the war against Hitler for the fight against the forces of socialism and democracy. They did this not only by diplomatic and political methods but with the base means of internally disorganizing the democratic forces and revolutionary workers' parties. Behind Rankovich there are the shadows of Mr. Field and Mr. Dulles. (Ibid. p. 269)

Belkin did not turn the point of the confessions directly against the West, and even the shadow of Allen Dulles conjured up by them must be considered as nothing but an instrument to blacken the Yugoslavs. This is how the public prosecutor proclaimed the primary and true aim of the trial, its 'international significance' as he put it:

> It is true and right that the Hungarian People's Court, passing sentence on László Rajk and his gang of conspirators, should also pass sentence, in a political and moral sense, on the

traitors of Yugoslavia, the criminal gang of Tito, Rankovich, Kardelj and Djilas. The international significance of this trial lies particularly in the fact that we are passing sentence on the Yugoslav deserters and traitors to democracy and socialism. (Ibid. p. 264–5)

According to the editors of the text these traitors and deserters had never even intended to bring about any form of socialism. For this is what, according to Rajk's confession, Rankovich had said:

> ... that neither Tito nor the rest of the members of the Yugoslav government wanted a people's democratic régime even after the Liberation, and through it the building of socialism in Yugoslavia. If they as a government were still compelled to take such revolutionary measures which in essence and de facto began to lead towards the liquidation of capitalism, this was not because they wanted to carry out this programme in earnest, but because they were compelled to do so under pressure from the Yugoslav working masses. (Ibid. p. 62)

In order to heap even more coals on the heads of the Yugoslavs, Governor Belkin did not shrink from the logically as well as technically impossible accusation that the Western Powers had handed their espionage organizations over to Tito, so much did they trust him, so closely did they co-operate with him. Rajk is made to say:

> At the same time Martin Himmler told me that in all probability this would be my last talk with him and with the representatives of the American intelligence agencies in general, for they would hand over their whole network to the Yugoslavs, and in the future I would get instructions for further work through Yugoslav channels. (Ibid. p. 48)

These tasks incumbent no longer upon the Western Imperialists but upon Tito, were the following: first–Rajk said:

> they wanted to ensure their full right to command armed forces, that is, the army and the police ... Keeping in view, of course, the final aim of shaping a bloc of states, Tito demanded such a foreign policy, and its guarantees from Hungary, as would always be in harmony with the foreign policy of Yugoslavia, that is, that her foreign relations, too, should be subordinated to the Yugoslav government. (Ibid. p. 74–5)

By the end of September, 1949, when this indictment was heard, the plans ascribed to the Yugoslavs in Hungary had long since been carried out by the Soviet Union, naturally to her own benefit. Hence the Philippic oration of the Public Prosecutor was not intended merely to win the laurels so easy to gain and so easy to lose in the people's democracies, but also to serve as a thinly-veiled threat. A threat to all those who observed that the Prosecutor's statements applied not to Yugoslavia but to the Soviet Union, not to Rajk and his colleagues, but to the party functionaries sent back from Moscow to Hungary; for this is what Alapi said:

> It is also obvious, honoured People's Court, that the conspiracy of Rajk and his company was aimed to sell Hungarian independence and to liquidate national sovereignty. This gang was formed to put Hungary under a foreign yoke, to make our fatherland a foreign colony, to form its government from foreign spies and agents and to create in the place of an autonomous and independent Hungary a system which would have carried out the orders of agents, dancing to the tune played abroad, and which would betray Hungarian national interests. (Ibid. p. 262)

The party leaders sent home from the Soviet Union were, naturally, champions of Hungarian independence, they represented national interests and did not dance to 'the tune played abroad', and that was why the Yugoslavs told Rajk:

> ... that Tito was absolutely determined that at the time of the coup d'état, at the same time as the coup d'état, the Hungarian government would have to be arrested and three of its members, Rákosi, Gerö and Farkas, would immediately have to be killed during the first action. (Ibid. p. 73)

In fact, Rákosi, Gerö and Farkas all returned to Hungary in the wake of the Soviet army. And the collaboration or working relationship of two of them—Gerö and Farkas—with the Russian secret police, was so close and of such long standing that even the least well-informed were aware of it, from Spain to Hungary. In addition, most communists who returned from the Soviet Union, such as Rákosi, Gerö and Farkas, kept two passports in their desks, one Russian and one Hungarian. This was proved in 1956, when numerous Muscovites fled the country with Soviet passports in their pockets. By choosing these men as the selected victims of assassination, the editorial board working on the text of the confessions intended not only to surround them with a somewhat ambiguous halo; they also wanted to make it quite clear in Soviet liturgical jargon that Rákosi, Gerö, Farkas and others of their kind represented the true faith in contrast to the heretics. The trial was to be the party's crusade against the heretics.

The social-democratic parties were let off lightly for the present. Indeed, one of the secondary aims was to ascribe the failures of the people's democratic system in Hungary to the subversive activities of the accused. Foreshadowing new trials and a large-scale mustering of forces and likely manœuvres in the crusade were also those parts of the confessions which, according to Alapi, showed that:

> ... the destructive work of the traitors and spies [was] conducted not only in our country, but in all the countries of the people's democracy ... from Albania to Poland and from Rumania to Czechoslovakia (Ibid. p. 269). What is more: Tito and his clique, hand in hand with the imperialist intelligence services, carried on their work of dissolution not only in every people's democratic country but also in those capitalist countries which have strong labour movements, communist parties with a strong influence on the broad masses. (Ibid. p. 256)

In other words, Tito's heresy was threatening the harmony of Moscow's magnetic circles over the entire range of their power fields, that is, over the whole world. And this not merely by giving fresh impetus to the centrifugal forces in the fluctuating play of centrifugal and centripetal forces, but also by the threat that Belgrade might become a new core, that new magnetic circles might develop around it, which would cut across, perhaps even disrupt, the concentric Muscovite power fields.

This was such an important stake that the leaders of the Soviet Union felt compelled to take the risk inherent in the improbability of the accusations and confessions that followed each other in the Rajk trial and its successors, both in Hungary and in other countries in the Soviet orbit.

Soviet and people's democratic propaganda shrugged off with superior irony the observations and corrections voiced outside the concentric circles; of course they denied everything, because, for the time being, they could not be reached by the all-revealing magic wand of the communist police, compelling them to tell the truth.

So this was how the official daily of the Hungarian Communist Party replied to Allen Dulles's statement published in the New York Times: 'Following the notorious imperialist method, Mr. Dulles attempted to deny everything in the course of an interview equivalent to an admission' (*Szabad Nép*, September 14, 1949).

However, in the outer areas of the Communist Party's circles, the question whether or not to believe the impossible allegations separated the faithful from the unfaithful, as nitric acid separates gold from waste. For the indictment, the confessions, the very ceremony of the trials with their demand for human sacrifice, and the message emanating from the ceremony, appealed not to reason, but to faith, to the logic ascribed to Tertullian: *credo, quia absurdum est*, the religious humility of 'I believe—because it is absurd'. As for the luke-warm and the hesitant in the outer circle, the Party would be content if they accepted Tertullian only in Nietzsche's malicious re-formulation *credo, quia absurdus sum*—I believe because I am absurd, because I am a simpleton, because I know nothing about higher politics.

The general attitude in those Party-circles less remote from higher politics and lying somewhere in the middle, followed a considerably more modern line than that of Tertullian. To illustrate this mentality we must reach back if not to the second, to the eleventh century and its eminent scholar, Anselm of Canterbury, the father of the ontological method. Anselm used the subjective idea of God to prove God's objective existence, thus deducing reality from faith. *Credo, ut intelligam*—he wrote—'I believe in order to understand'. In the middle circles of the Hungarian Communist Party, the general attitude was at least to try to believe in the party, in order to be able to understand its actions. It was therefore subjective faith that induced them to accept the allegations made in the Rajk trial as objective reality.

Within the inner circles, some individuals were compelled to judge certain parts of the trial's material as improbable and other parts, since they were familiar with the facts, as purely fictitious. Yet, subjectively, they, too, trusted and believed in the pragmatic wisdom of the party and therefore in the objective guilt of Rajk and his fellow-accused; they would never have assumed that the party could sacrifice innocent men. They regarded it as an almost formal question of terminology, whether Rajk was sentenced for effective crimes or merely for crimes formulated to fit momentary political expedience.

Thus, in the concentric circles of the party, the trial's message, appealing as it did to faith, did not as a rule fail to strike home, although the various degrees of faith, from the blind devotion demanded by Tertullian, to confidence in the party's practical adroitness, not only differed in depth and quality but were interwoven with innumerable individual motives, fears, and opportunist considerations. So much so that the majority of the party members were unable, even years later, after they had been completely disillusioned, to untangle the motives of their former gullibility with convincing objectivity.

Some communists already had doubts as early as 1949. When I speak of Communists, I do not mean the heterogeneous Hungarian Workers' Party of one million members, but the truly convinced partisans of the proclaimed ideals. Any wavering and doubt among them was due less to the crusade conducted against Yugoslav heresy than to the shape this crusade took in Hungary where it was intended to prevent the emergence of trends of thought resembling that of the Yugoslavs and to bring about the preventive liquidation of all elements susceptible to, or suspected of, heresy. To this category belonged the communist intellectuals who had returned from the West, the Hungarian volunteers of the Spanish civil war, and the 'old guard' of the underground Hungarian communist movement. The doubters could hardly believe of those arrested, who were often their friends, their superiors, even their personal heroes, that they were already police agents when participating in the underground movement, had risked their lives in Spain while working as informers, and had then, after 1946, enrolled as agents of foreign espionage organizations.

A strange situation arose. The innermost circle of the party, the Muscovites and the ÁVH leaders would, for once, have been justified in proclaiming that they were 'spiritually of one and the same mind with the overwhelming majority of Hungarians'. For the initiates of the party gave as little credence to the texts recited at the Rajk trial as the anti-communists whose lack of faith automatically immunized them against the ceremonial fanfares of the trial.

But while the Muscovite party leaders, although from different motives, were just as cautious as the millions outside the party not to betray their disbelief publicly, the ÁVH did not pretend. Not to its prisoners and victims at least. Even ÁVH officers who had taken no part in the preparation of the trial liked, at times, to boast of their inside information. We could not get rid of these investigators, even after we had been condemned. They visited the prisons almost every month and questioned us about persons and events. Often they were accompanied by one of their younger colleagues in order that the apprentice could observe the methods of interrogation.

My cell-mate, György Heltai, was once faced with such a pair when he was being interrogated at the Vác penitentiary, and this brief scene throws a favourable light on the praiseworthy frankness of the ÁVH.

On this occasion, the pupil, a young woman, was sitting beside the experienced interrogator. The girl performed the administrative tasks, she recorded the prisoner's personal details and asked him how many years he had been sentenced to and why.

'To ten years, on the pretext that I was a spy.'

'What do you mean by "on the pretext?" Are you suggesting that you were not a spy?'

Heltai shrugged his shoulders and replied in an indifferent voice: 'I was never a spy.'

Whereupon the young woman jumped up from her chair beside herself with fury, gave the prisoner a good dressing-down, and finally announced loudly and with great dignity:

'The court of the People's Democracy would never sentence an innocent man to ten years.'

Soon afterwards the experienced interrogator sent the girl from the room on some errand and turned to the prisoner with an explanatory, almost apologetic murmur:

'The comrade doesn't understand yet. The comrade hasn't been with the organization very long . . .'

The initiates of the organization ate from the tree of knowledge and therefore they were not dependent on faith. But whether an initiate believed or not that he understood the implications of the Rajk trial, and even if the wheels of his mind turned sluggishly, the measures introduced after the trial left him in no doubt. For it could not remain a secret for long, either in Hungary or abroad, that the threefold aim of the Rajk trial–the crusade against the fully developed Yugoslav heresy, the prevention of an eventual heretical movement in Hungary, which led to the decimation and compromising of the so-called 'communists of Western orientation' and the 'old guard', and the intimidation of the people in neighbouring countries by the ceremony of blood sacrifice–served the final Russian seizure of power, assured the smooth operation of the power-transmission and the steering gear.

Among the political leaders of the satellite countries most loyal to Moscow, the general secretary of the Hungarian Workers' Party was the most zealous in guessing Stalin's plans and foreseeing his wishes. He had good reason for his zeal. For Stalin did not like Rákosi and, for some time, had not trusted him.

Thus it was presumably not on direct orders from Moscow, but as a proof of the relative independence of the Hungarian communists in the period immediately following the end of the war, that the Budapest propagandists wove a web of legend around Rákosi's person. They made it appear as if Rákosi really had been the leader of the 1919 Hungarian proletarian dictatorship and as if, while serving his sentence in Admiral Horthy's days, he had directed the Hungarian communist underground movement from his cell in the prison of Vác.

These yarns made the people of Budapest smile. Even the most uninformed remembered that Béla Kún had headed the Hungarian Soviet Republic, Béla Kún who disappeared at the time of the Trotsky trials in Moscow never to reappear, and whose very memory had been erased from the history of the Hungarian party according to the rules and regulations of Soviet etiquette. It was not until years after Stalin's death that his name was mentioned again, when in 1956, on the seventieth anniversary of Béla Kún's birth, Pravda published an article on the Dictator of the Hungarian Soviet republic. Yet, the suppression of Béla Kún's role did not alter the fact that in 1919 Rákosi had played only second fiddle, and the editors of the illustrated memorial album published on the thirtieth anniversary of the proletarian dictatorship were wasting their time when they searched for photographs showing Rákosi in company with such well-known leaders of the Hungarian Soviet republic as had not been executed in Moscow. To trusted friends, communist ex-prisoners in Vác Penitentiary described Rákosi as a bossy fellow-prisoner who put his physical comfort above everything else, and who, if indeed he had cherished any such ambitions, had been in no position to direct the Hungarian underground movement. Not only because he was not sufficiently familiar with the situation but also because he was deprived of contact with the world outside the prison walls.

Though the legends were untrue, the unanimous account of several Muscovite Hungarians appeared reliable. According to this report, when the Comintern sent Rákosi back to Hungary in the 1920s to do underground work and he was subsequently arrested by the Hungarian police, Rákosi, to help his own position, had given damning evidence against his comrades. This, at least, is what Béla Kún, at the time still a high-ranking functionary of the Comintern, alleged of him. It is possible that Kún, a notorious intriguer, only invented this accusation and supported it with invented evidence, in order to rid himself of a potential rival. He succeeded in convincing Stalin, because it was on direct orders from Stalin that Comintern suspended Rákosi's party membership.

In the mid-thirties, Rákosi had almost served his entire sentence, but new proceedings were started against him in Budapest for acts committed during the 1919 Hungarian Soviet Republic in which he could have had no share, and he was sentenced a second time. Such verdicts were unusual in Hungarian court practices even between the two world wars. Therefore, Rákosi's trial gave an opportunity to the Secretary of the Hungarian communist faction in Moscow to submit a proposal to Stalin. He suggested that Rákosi's party membership be restored and that an international movement be launched to obtain his release. After the Trotsky trials, Stalin was ready to accept the recommendation, for Rákosi's trial and the court sentence sanctioning the illegality of the procedure, seemed to offer a convenient means of distracting the attention of Western public opinion, particularly that of possible waverers among the fellow-travellers, from the Moscow sentences.

The 'Save Rákosi' movement raised the Vác prisoner to the rank of a martyr and made his name known throughout Europe, and his continued imprisonment became a source of embarassment to the Hungarian government. After the signing of the Russo-German treaty, the Hungarians therefore started negotiations with Moscow. It was agreed that the Soviet Union would return to Hungary the flags of the 1848–9 War of Independence–captured by the Russians in 1849 when Czar Nicolas I helped the Hapsburgs to defeat the Hungarian struggle for liberty–and Budapest would release Mátyás Rákosi and allow his departure for Moscow.

That was how Rákosi returned to Moscow before the outbreak of the Second World War. True, he was given an office in the Kremlin, but he received no important function. What is more, as several Muscovite Hungarians told us in prison, Stalin had more than once made derogatory remarks about Rákosi and had repeatedly called him a 'British agent'. This insinuation was based on the circumstance that before the First World War, Rákosi had spent some time in England, liked to talk about his experiences there and did not restrict himself merely to hostile remarks or ritual oaths about that country. The Hungarian communists in Moscow were therefore surprised when, after the war, the Kremlin appointed Rákosi Head of the Hungarian Communist Party. Now we know the history of the next fifteen years it is easier to find an explanation for this choice in the fact that Stalin intended to rely not so much on the Hungarian Communist Party as on the presence of the Soviet army and on the party within the Party organized by the MVD: the Hungarian secret police. Therefore, and because Rákosi had been raised to a hero by the movement launched for his release, Moscow was disinclined to waste the capital invested in this propaganda; indeed, it was intent on exploiting it when Stalin placed Rákosi in the foreground.

Rákosi was aware of the insecurity of his position and therefore, in the years following 1945, he not only faithfully fulfilled every command from Moscow but strove to outdo with his zeal all the other leaders of the People's Democracies. In 1948, at the conferences of the Cominform, it was Rákosi who attacked Tito most sharply. He went even further. At a time when differences had not yet reached breaking-point, he did not shrink from provoking the Yugoslavs and denouncing them to the Kremlin.

With four years of unrelenting officiousness, but particularly with his untiring zeal in the vilification of heretics, Rákosi succeeded at last in dispelling Stalin's suspicions and without protest from Moscow he tagged on to his name in the Hungarian party press the Homeric adjective, 'Comrade-Stalin's-best-Hungarian-disciple'. He participated actively in the preparation of the Rajk trial and afterwards in the elaboration of the confessions. He maintained permanent telephone contact not only with the leaders of the ÁVH but at times even with the specialists operating in the interrogating rooms. Often he would give the interrogators direct instructions; and his imagination, his ideas on how to add colour to detail, enriched Lieutenant-General Belkin's political iconography. The Governor listened to the advice of the General Secretary of the Hungarian Workers' Party; and thus Rákosi had a decisive say, not only in the details, but also as to the persons to be arrested and the roles they were to play. As far as the principal accused was concerned, he could only make suggestions, for in this question even Belkin did not have the last word, but Stalin himself. Before reporting to Stalin, Belkin turned over in his mind Rákosi's and Gábor Péter's views. At the conference of these three, the initiated explained later, it was debated whether they should not suggest Imre Nagy or János Kádár, instead of Rajk, as head of the gang of Imperialist spies and Tito agents.

Everything seems to indicate that Moscow's deliberations about who to put in the dock as principal defendant had been sober, tinged by neither sentimentality nor anger. The main consideration was not who was most susceptible to heresy, but who was most likely to resist Stalin's directives, and should, therefore, be the first to be liquidated as a preventive measure. Most heavily weighed in the balance was who was the most suitable person to serve as an instrument of the crusade against heresy, who could be presented to the world, with some measure of verisimilitude, as a traitor to Moscow's cause.

Those who had returned from Moscow – although several of them ended up in prison after the secondary secret trials – were unsuitable. By passing sentence publicly on a Hungarian Muscovite, the Kremlin would admit the failure of its indoctrination and acknowledge that heresy was possible in the Soviet Union. At the same time, it would have been difficult to connect with western espionage organizations people who had spent decades isolated in Russia. If it did so, the Kremlin, by suggesting that the West had penetrated so deeply into its political positions, would be creating an impression of weakness.

The choice could only fall on a person who had not matured into a communist leader in Moscow and who, therefore, could be punished as an enemy of the Moscow-centric *Weltanschauung* in his own person, concretely, and also symbolically, as a measure of intimidation, aimed at several categories of people.

The Western press, although unintentionally, helped the promoters of the trial in the selection of the principal defendant. It gave them an idea. As early as 1948, serious newspapers both in Europe and America were publishing reports of a conflict between Rákosi and Rajk, of inter-faction squabbles within the party. Rajk was described as the representative of some sort of national communism, and Rákosi as the Quisling of Muscovite communism. It is not inconceivable that after the first, purely fictitious rumours, it was the Kremlin itself, or its representatives in Hungary who fomented the legend concerning the inner struggles of the Hungarian Communist Party, although it is far from certain that their plans were then already laid. In reality, there could have been no inter-faction squabbling within the Hungarian party, if only because Rajk's weight in the party was far less significant than outsiders who judged him by his position in the state administration could have guessed;

he had no possiblity of assembling any important group around his own person.

The leaders who returned from Moscow did not regard Rajk as their equal. Ernö Gerö remarked to one of his close collaborators, depreciatingly but without malice, that in spite of his honesty and militant communist past, Rajk was too inexperienced for a party leader.

Rajk went to the Soviet Union merely as a visitor; he was unfamiliar with Kremlin intrigue and seemed an unsuitable candidate for initiation. But contrary to Western beliefs, not even his closest relations, friends or confidential collaborators had any idea that Rajk had ever cherished any kind of national communist ideas, that he had represented such a trend within the party or tried to organize such a faction, or clashed with Rákosi on any significant question.

The truth is that within the international movement, Rajk considered himself a Hungarian communist and in this he no doubt differed from the Comintern technicians of Hungarian descent. For the Comintern instructors regarded their native country also as a field of operation, one among many, more favourable than Belgium, Scandinavia, Spain or Outer Mongolia only because they used its language with greater ease than if they had learned it from books, though, after their long absence, many of them spoke their mother tongue with a somewhat foreign accent, alien syntax and a halting vocabulary.

The articles published in the West on the conflict between Rajk and Rákosi, and the halo round Rajk's head resplendent in national colours and polished bright by propaganda, made the communist Minister the ideal choice to play the star role in the trial, filling the bill from both the domestic and foreign viewpoint.

In 1945, the Hungarian Communist Party still needed a leader whom it could present to the world as a communist hero of the Hungarian Resistance Movement against Hitler and the Hungarian fascists, though compared with that in other countries this movement was rather insignificant. The majority of the leaders who returned from Moscow, including Rákosi, Révai and Farkas, had never ventured nearer to the fighting front than the Soviet radio bunkers of the POW camps. In 1949, after the Cominform resolution concerning Tito, Rajk's participation in the Resistance, hitherto celebrated as a national merit, became an inducement to accuse the former volunteer of the International Brigade in Spain of nationalist deviation.

And yet, Rajk trusted the Russians unreservedly, almost naïvely, and, in contrast to the Comintern functionaries, he was not afraid of them. When he had suggestions to make in his own sphere of activity or when he gave orders, it never occurred to him that, even if Moscow disagreed with his ideas or actions, they would doubt his loyalty to the party. Nor is it probable that apart from the general suspicion with which the Russians looked upon the Hungarian communists, whether they had lived in the West or not,* they regarded Rajk with any particular wariness: not even when, as Minister of the Interior, he had interfered with the Party's organizational affairs.

Rajk wanted to re-organize the party groups of his Ministry. This move appeared eminently rational, but could not be carried out without the knowledge and approval of Mátyás Rákosi, Secretary General of the Party. If, therefore, this measure proved a mistake the responsibility for it was at least divided, or rather, according to standards of communist practice, it devolved in the first place on the Secretary General. Thus, when later Rajk alone was blamed by the Central Committee for the re-organization of the party groups of the Ministry of the Interior and, by way of punishment, was transferred to the Ministry of Foreign Affairs, Rákosi used the re-organization of the Party groups only as a pretext. The interpretation given to this re-organization at the trial betrayed to those even slightly familiar with the rules of procedure in the Communist Party, that at least in this respect the accusations voiced against Rajk were fictitious. For László Rajk, playing a secondary role within the Party leadership, had never been in a position to introduce such measures independently.

Therefore, it seems certain that Belkin intended the text recited at the trial by Rajk concerning the reshuffling of the Party groups of the Ministry of the Interior and the Police, not merely to compromise the Yugoslavs and convince the uninitiated, but also to mislead the uninformed Western observers concerning the internal structure of the Hungarian Communist Party and the Communist Parties of the satellite states in general, the sphere of authority of their leaders and the Soviet chain of command. For this is what the former Minister of the Interior said:

Finally one more directive arrived from Tito and Rankovich in the second half of 1947, that is, after the meeting at Kelebia. Efforts should be made to withdraw the whole of the police and

* The trial of János Kádár and his associates, staged secretly about eighteen months after the Rajk trial, was conducted against such Hungarian communists who had never lived either in Moscow or the West.

the army, as the armed forces, from the influence of the Communist Party and in general, from the political influence of the People's Democracy, and to place them more and more under right-wing political influence. One of the ways of doing this—justified in the message—was that I should suspend the political activities of all Party branches within the police and, in fact, in this way kill two birds with one stone. First: I would withdraw the police from the political influence of the People's Democracy, and more than that, from the political influence and control of the Communist Party. In the second place, as Minister of Home Affairs, I could become without Party control the all-powerful master and leader of the police organization. (Ibid. p. 58)

Re-organization of the Party group of the Ministry of the Interior extended only to its officials and the numerically as well as influentially insignificant police forces (criminal, traffic, etc.) but not to the political police which at that time was called ÁVO (Államvédelmi Osztály, State Security Department). Therefore it in no way jeopardized Moscow's direct line of police control. Nor could it have done so, as the ÁVO was only formally subordinated to the Minister of the Interior, and later when it was proclaimed an independent body and its name was changed to ÁVH (Államvédelmi Hatóság, or State Security Authority) it was again only formally responsible to the Council of Ministers, for in reality the Hungarian political police was, from the moment of its inception, directed by the Russians.

For a while, an MVD officer of Hungarian origin who used the name Kovács, was assigned to assist Gábor Péter as deputy head of the ÁVO. In 1948 Kovács went to Moscow, supposedly to have a gastric ulcer treated, but he never again returned to Hungary. It was rumoured in Budapest that he had died in a Soviet hospital. Kovács was replaced by Ernö Szücs who, while in exile in the Soviet Union, had also been in the service of the MVD. The MVD leaders of the Hungarian secret police, men like Kovács and Szücs, could naturally maintain unhindered contact with their superiors in Moscow, all the more so, as the collaboration between the MVD and the Hungarian political police was no secret to the Minister of the Interior. The criticism voiced in the Central Committee against the Party group re-organization as a violation of the party line worried and pained Rajk. But as his transfer to the Ministry of Foreign Affairs was accompanied by palliative compliments, he did not regard it as a fall from favour.

It may be that during the preparations for the trial, János Kádár and the expert persuaders succeeded in awakening a sense of guilt in this faithful communist by reproaching him again and again for his infringement of the Party line, by convincing him that he had something to atone for and suggesting that to prove his loyalty to the Party, he should undertake the role designed for him.

While László Rajk was alive and in power, many of his opponents fell victim to his fanatical, ruthless, and sometimes even cruel loyalty to the Party, and for this he was called to account in the interrogating chambers. But a few years after his execution, his death, which he accepted because of that very same mystic party-loyalty, harmed nothing other than the object of that loyalty: the Communist Party. It was precisely in their faith and loyalty to the Party that the consequences of the Rajk-trial shook tens of thousands of convinced communists.

8

The People Judge

THE first day of the public hearing in the Rajk affair was set for September 16th, 1949. The newspapers published the text of the indictment in full or in excerpts. They spoke of 'the murderous plans of Rajk and Tito' which were 'thwarted by the vigilance of the Hungarian Workers' Party, Mátyás Rákosi and our People's Democracy' (*Független Magyarország*, September 12th, 1949). A flood of leading articles blared forth such and similar slogans: 'He who attacks the people's fatherland will pay dearly' (*Szabad Nép*, September 13th, 1949). Blitz-meetings were held in factories and offices, both in the capital and throughout the country. The party press reported on the general indignation under giant headings: 'Angyalföld's message is: Next it will be Tito's turn!'; 'Red Csepel's reply: Greater love still for Comrade Rákosi'; 'In the name of all mothers'–says Mrs. Gellérthegyi at the blitz-meeting of the fitting-shop of the Auxiliary Telephone Central–'I send the Tito-clique, the imperialists and their agents the burning hatred of all mothers' (*Szabad Nép*, September 13th, 1949).

While the Communist Party celebrated its 'victory achieved by the unmasking of the gang of spies' (*Szabad Nép*, September 14th, 1949) the MVD section behind its iron doors at 60 Andrássy Street had been for some time bathed in an idyllic atmosphere. At the end of August and early in September the premises had been transformed as if by magic into a cosy, intimate pastry-shop where the Soviet and Hungarian security-men plied their selected victims with pastry, fruit and even alcoholic beverages. The rubber truncheons, 'the people's educators', reminders of the painful events of the last few months, had disappeared. The cruelly gloomy MVD and ÁVH faces smiled encouragingly, charmingly, and the interrogating rooms, these new scenes of police jollity, were heavy with the nauseating smell of fresh fruit, beer, coffee, sweets and male sweat.

This MVD pastry-shop was the scene of the *third and last phase of the realization* where the plastering, decorating and polishing of the building erected from the prefabricated elements were completed: where the principal, public trial was prepared.

I knew nothing of these changes when I crossed the threshold of the iron door. I was wondering, uneasily, about the possible consequences of my interrogation by Belkin, for I had not been here since Szücs had pushed me so vindictively from the Russian Lieutenant-General's room. My worries were not dispelled when, in one of the rooms, I came face to face with Major Károlyi, smiling at me with his habitual, somewhat ironical air of good humour. He offered me a seat. He was in his shirt-sleeves, leaning heavily on his desk; from time to time, he wiped his perspiring forehead with his handkerchief.

'Well,' he said after a few introductory words, 'you will play your part in the public hearing of the great trial.'

'Do you intend to use me as a witness?' I asked.

'Yes and no,' Károlyi replied, 'for though you may not appear in person, you will, as I said before, play your part.'

'I don't understand,' I said, amazed, 'all the less so as you don't even have a statement from me.'

Károlyi must have found my remark inordinately amusing, for he laughed not only loudly but, this time, with apparent sincerity:

'You leave that to us. We may have no statement from you, but we have plenty from the others and you are mentioned in them. You are a lucky man. For whether or not you come forward as a witness at the public trial, we shall, for the moment—and let me emphasize, *only* for the moment—treat you as a witness. Though you don't deserve it,' he added after a short pause. 'However, we are not ungenerous.'

With this he pushed a tray loaded with pastries before me, along with a plate and a spoon:

'Have some?'

Then he offered me fruit and black coffee.

'You may sit here for a while,' he said, rising. 'After the cellar, it will do you good to breathe a little fresh air.'

He got up wearily from his desk and left. One yawning ÁVH-man remained in the room. Immediately I stopped eating he offered me a cigarette. Then he pushed more pastry, more fruit towards me. Károlyi returned in a little over a quarter of an hour.

'Are you alone?' he asked, then, when I glanced somewhat stupidly first at him then at the detective, he added, laughing, 'I mean in your cell.'

The Major knew, of course, that I was on my own and therefore he continued without waiting for an answer:

'Well, you'll get a cell-mate now. It's better than being alone, isn't it?'

My new cell-mate was called Dr. Lajos Bokor. He had once served as a police captain, but in the middle of the '30s he had established himself as a practising lawyer in Budapest. He was related to the Rajk family and when László Rajk was arrested for communist activities, Bokor went to the political police to make some enquiries. At first, this was all the nearly sixty-year-old lawyer told me, together with a number of excited, confused stories. A few days before, he said, sounds of street-fighting, of violent demonstrations, the hum of many aeroplanes, had penetrated his cell; at the same time, the streets resounded with the shouts of excited newsboys announcing their headlines. He could clearly distinguish what they were saying: Rákosi had been overthrown, a military government had seized power. Very soon—Lajos Bokor drew the promising conclusion from his hallucinations—we should be free.

When, after a few days, his nervous tension abated and he could no longer hear the aircraft or newsboys, he told me with calm objectivity what he was going to say at the trial where he was to appear as a witness. His deposition would be simple and brief. When, in 1932, Horthy's police detained László Rajk for distributing communist leaflets, Lajos Bokor, at the request of his anxious family, went to see Imre Hetényi, then deputy chief of police. Hetényi had Rajk brought to his room and put a typed declaration before him, according to which Rajk promised to serve the police in the capacity of informer. If he agreed and signed the declaration, the police would immediately release him, Hetényi said. Rajk yielded and put his name to the paper in the presence of Lajos Bokor and detective inspector Borszéki.

I did not pump Bokor for details, it would have been useless to do so. My cell-mate talked with pleasure about his orchard, but he evaded my question whether the scene shot in Hetényi's room contained even a grain of truth. I tried to understand his attitude as dictated by psychological self-defence, for he enjoyed self-forgetfully, almost childishly, the pleasures of the pastry-shop and the relaxed atmosphere. He appeared to trust unconditionally the pledge, made under oath, by the Russian Lieutenant-General. Belkin had promised Lajos Bokor that he would be allowed to return to his wife on the day of the trial, by evening at the latest.

There was little I could tell Károlyi when he enquired about my cell-mate. 'His nervous condition is not too good,' I declared, 'in my opinion he needs medical treatment.'

'There's nothing wrong with him,' the Major waved his hand,

'besides, all I am interested in is whether or not he will repeat his testimony at the public trial. What do you think?'

I shrugged my shoulders and murmured a commonplace: how was I to know? I couldn't see into the man's brain. But I considered it my duty to inform my cell-mate of the Major's question. The effect was surprising. Before answering, Bokor explored the walls of the cell, the bunks, the door, not for the first time since his arrival but more thoroughly than ever before, to make sure there was no microphone, then he spoke excitedly into my ear. He, too, had been questioned about me, he whispered, and he begged me, in heaven's name, to be his ally. I was to tell Károlyi emphatically that he would maintain his testimony, that he would repeat the contents of the deposition word for word.

Bokor's agitation showed me more clearly than anything else could have done that the scene to which the former police captain was to testify at the trial was pure invention. Some involuntary movement must have betrayed my thoughts, although I made no reply. My cell-mate began to plead with me. He begged me to understand how dire the consequences would be for him if they no longer trusted him. They might not release him after the trial even if they were satisfied with his evidence. He would supply me with plenty of material, should they ask me about him again, material that held no danger for him and was generally known, anyway. But I must stress again and again that he had no intention whatsoever of retracting his confession. As he did not want to mislead me, he could not but admit that he considered my situation much graver than his own. There was little he could do for me. But he promised that should he go free, he would take a message to my family, and a present to my little son—as if it had been sent by me.

I conveyed to Károlyi my cell-mate's message, or rather messages, and Bokor presumably also conveyed mine: that I would under no circumstances admit to even the most moderate details of the statement attributed to me. This may have been why I became a less and less frequent guest at the pastry-shop and, as I was proving hopeless even as a reserve-witness, the Major began to neglect me and left me to his underlings if, by chance, I was occasionally taken up to that heaven of cakes and fruit. It is not impossible that the astute Károlyi saw through our little game, although Lajos Bokor probably respected our agreement as scrupulously as I did, and betrayed our alliance neither to the secret police nor, as far as I know, to his cell-mates later.

Yet this alliance created an ambiguous atmosphere of caution between us rather than one of friendship. We both resisted the promptings of our isolation and interdependence which would, in different circumstances, have inspired talkativeness. This was, with the exception of Érdi, the second and last time that I and a fellow prisoner infringed prison etiquette, and failed to call each other by our first names.

The accused and the witnesses rehearsed their statements in the scented atmosphere of pastry, coffee and fruit, while the Hungarian and Russian secret police went on busily training the stars as well as the secondary actors with the painstaking care of conscientious stage directors. Not only the text, but also movement and gesture, were analysed in great detail. The bald, intellectual-looking MVD officer demonstrated to Bokor, a lawyer who had witnessed many a stormy trial, how to bow to the judge in order that the audience should regard him as a free, self-assured man and not a humble, intimidated prisoner from the cellar.

After such preparations, the Russians smiled, for now they were always smiling, a slip or blunder was unimaginable. Though even slips of the tongue were carefully planned, as once upon a time in the Trostky trials. Just as Karl Radek's apparently involuntary slip of the tongue cast suspicion on General Tukhachevsky, there would be someone in Budapest, too, to make a similar mistake. And indeed, a casual phrase spoken by the witness, Endre Szebeny, cost Colonel András Villányi – listening to the broadcast testimony at home – his life.

Later, I often pumped my fellow prisoners about the various episodes of the last phase of the *realization*. It was not so much the reasons for the gullibility shown by the accused and the witnesses that preoccupied me for, having no way out, it was understandable that they should take refuge in an optimism inspired by their gaolers. What concerned me was rather the change – not simply feigned – in the attitude of the secret police. For in pauses between rehearsals the MVD and ÁVH officers confided in their prisoners with an open-heartedness bordering on the dangerous. They discussed their private affairs with the prisoners, talked about their young days and their love affairs and boasted of their professional successes.

Thus, Gyula Prinz, who had been a detective in the pre-war police, but who at the time of the trial was an ÁVH Inspector, explained with great pride that he was the only Hungarian policeman whose ideas had been adopted and applied in the Soviet Union.

Prinz described in detail and with obvious relish the method devised by him to win married couples with children to act as 'B. men', (Bizalmi ember–i.e. confidential men)–as the ÁVH euphemistically liked to call its agents.

'Jonny' Prinz explained his methods with gusto: 'The son of the selected couple sets out for school. At a street corner he is accosted by a friendly, confidence-inspiring stranger, "Jonny, I am a friend of your daddy's, I am passing your school, I'll give you a lift in my car." The boy accepts the lift and then fails to return home after school hours. It turns out that neither his teachers nor his schoolmates have seen him. The police know nothing of his whereabouts. No hospital has admitted him. In vain the distracted parents run from pillar to post, Jonny has vanished without trace. A day goes by, perhaps two, and then a pleasant-looking young man appears at the parents' home to inform them that their child will be returned to them within a few hours. On one simple condition, easy to fulfill: in future they will have to perform certain services for the ÁVH in their circle of friends or at their place of work. Should the couple refuse to agree, the young man makes no threats. He takes his leave. After a few days of anguish, he returns and repeats his offer.' There was no parent, Prinz boasted, who did not, in the end, undertake the duties of a 'B. man' which, by the way, is considered a privileged position in a People's Democracy, for now, 'everything is different, everything has acquired another meaning from what it had in the rotting bourgeois societies,' said Prinz.

The imprudence of such revelations was, of course, diminished by the fact that the fate in store for their prisoners was no secret to the secret police; they knew that after the public trial, the witnesses would without exception learn at *in camera* trials whether the inner concentric circles intended them for the gallows or for imprisonment. And where they were not out for the prisoner's blood, it made little difference whether the court sentenced him to six years, ten years or life, he would be sentenced to silence and unable to make suitable remarks in an unsuitable place. Thus, the police put more confidence in their prisoners' discretion than in maintaining their professional reticence. At last the members of the party within the party had an opportunity to break the oppressive silence imposed upon them, and moreover, in the presence of men from whom they had nothing to fear and with whom they were on close terms. The faked confessions created an intimate feeling of co-authorship between a security man and his prisoner, a sense of complicity.

Almost every ÁVH officer, even those who in this *third phase of the realization* had become so identified with their part in this false reality that they almost believed in it, developed this kind of bizarre relationship with the witness he had prepared for the trial. He came to love him, as a craftsman loves his handiwork; he looked upon his creation with tender pride. Gradually, this tenderness came to generate not only talkativeness but even humanitarian impulses, a temptation against which the ÁVH officers of the inner circle had until now proved themselves totally immune. One or another of the secret police sometimes became so emotional that he even made his prisoner feel sorry for him, as he actually courted his victim's sympathy. None the less, these frequently grotesque and irregular ardours neither delayed the process of preparation for the trial, nor endangered its success. They may even have had the opposite effect.

That, at least, is what the results suggest. For, when, after all the preparations, the trials finally began, everyone confessed smoothly, without a hitch. As though they were all volunteers for the gallows. It was this very perfection that awakened the suspicion of objective observers. They were amazed at the unnatural readiness of the defendants to admit every charge and to forgo even the mildest, most modest, attempt at self-defence. The terminology employed by the accused was also striking, because they all applied the same pejorative expressions and adjectives to themselves as the Public Prosecutor and the party press applied to them. It was not Hungarian they spoke, but an international language, the phraseology of the communist seminar booklets, leading articles and pamphlets from which a multitude of political filters and chemicals had removed every individual colour, taste and shade.

The extracts from confessions I came across in the official *Blue Book* were almost without exception word for word identical with those I had heard from my cell-mates weeks before the trial. Then, for one day, I could raise Lajos Bokor as a kind of periscope above the level of my underground cell and look, through his eyes, into the background of the courtroom and behind the judge's platform, into a room invisible to the audience.

At the suggestion of his interrogator, Lajos Bokor wrote a letter to his wife in which he asked for his navy blue suit, a matching tie, a white shirt, black shoes and socks. At dawn on September 20th, the day when the witnesses were being questioned, Lajos Bokor was shaved. He took off his wrinkled sports jacket and trousers and tied them into a bundle. He would no longer need them for, even if they brought him back here after the hearing, he would not change, but would return home in his navy blue suit. Bokor didn't sit down, he drank his white coffee excitedly, (for the past five days, since the beginning of the trial, they had poured white coffee into his dixie instead of the usual flour soup) joking that next morning he would have breakfast in a room where there was a door knob even on the inside of the door; then he declared seriously that he would not forget to take a present to my son Michael. We took leave of one another more warmly than usual, because it was possible that we would never meet again, that he would be released without coming back to the underground cell.

Late in the afternoon, Bokor returned. He said that they had taken him in a car to Magdolna street, the trade union headquarters of the iron and steel workers. The trial took place in the large auditorium of this building. First, they led Bokor into a largish room where the witnesses were made to sit in a circle with their faces to the wall. They were offered sandwiches, cake, coffee and soda water.

'Well,' Bokor's interrogator, Ervin Faludi said, 'this is your last day. You will dine at home tonight.'

Before the hearing started, Lajos Bokor and two women were led from the room and told to stand at the entrance of the courtroom. The women were given handbags to hold. The three witnesses were surrounded by some fifty ÁVH men and women. To the public and the invited journalists, this group must have appeared as though accidentally formed from voluntary witnesses, all the more so as they were soon to see Lajos Bokor as well as the two women before the judge. Apart from those in the know, not many people could have guessed that Bokor and the women had not come here from their homes, with a formal summons in their pocket or handbag, but under strong escort from the Andrássy Street cellars, and that since their disappearance their families hadn't even heard from them.

A few minutes before the beginning of the hearing, a squat man with curly grey hair appeared in the corridor. He was wearing a well-cut, double-breasted navy blue suit. When he reached the group standing at the entrance, he broke into a friendly smile and then, as if unexpectedly coming upon an acquaintance, he waved to Bokor as if in surprised greeting.

'Ah, Herr Advokat . . .' he cried enthusiastically in German, then he raised his hand once more, a little stiffly.

Bokor smiled back from the ring of the ÁVH-men, and the living ring smiled with him, for the squat, curly-haired man was none other than Fedor Belkin, the Governor.

Dr. Péter Jankó, the presiding judge, summoned the 'Herr Advokat', Lajos Bokor, as first witness before the People's Court. Bokor remembered the teachings of the bald MVD officer, he did not bow like an eighteenth-century muzhik, and in his smooth, well-oiled deposition he said neither more nor less than what was prescribed for him, the untruths in which he had been painstakingly rehearsed. When he was led back into the room where the witnesses were still sitting eating, with their faces to the wall, his interrogator congratulated him and assured him once more that he had deserved his release which would soon take place.

It was after such preliminaries that Bokor was brought back to the cellar. He paced up and down the cell with increasing impatience. He refused dinner, saying that he would have his at home, sitting at his own table. The guard nodded, with an air of understanding, but persuaded Bokor to take the dixie all the same. Hours went by, then at last the cell door flew open. The same guard came in, swinging a bundle, Bokor's brown jacket and trousers, which he threw on to the floor.

'Change your clothes,' he said.

'Yes, but . . .' my cell-mate protested, 'I am to be released tonight . . . the Lieutenant-General promised me personally . . .'

'I know, I know,' the guard replied mildly, 'if he promised he'll keep his promise. But now you must change.'

For a while they argued the point, till our guard grew tired of the farce and cut off Bokor's protests in a threatening voice:

'You change right now, do you get me? You can ask for a hearing tomorrow.'

Next day Bokor did indeed ask for a hearing, and the next and the the next. In vain. He did not get it. Not only hours, but days and weeks, almost two months went by until, in November, he was led before Colonel Décsi.

The trial, Colonel Décsi declared, had created a greater sensation than expected, therefore Bokor must not take it amiss that they had not released him; on the contrary, they would have to keep him a little longer in seclusion. But in appreciation of his readiness to help, they were giving him the opportunity to choose for himself between two possibilities. They would either intern him or sentence him for failure to lodge information against Rajk. Internment was for six months but unless it was lifted by a very involved process, it was automatically renewed for another six months and so on. Failure to lodge information was punishable by, at most, one year's imprisonment though, in Bokor's case, they would refrain from demanding the maximum sentence. Thus it would seem the best course for him would be to choose prison rather than internment. This would be all the more advisable as Bokor had by now done almost six months and–this was something the Colonel could guarantee–he would receive privileged treatment in prison, would be given excellent food, cigarettes and fruit and, what was more, his wife would be allowed to visit him.

Bokor thanked Décsi for his benevolence and chose prison, because he figured that they might still put him on trial for withholding information even after he was released from the internment camp. The Colonel immediately dictated a deposition and a few days later my cell-mate was taken away. I learned later that it was not, after all, for his failure to lodge information that he was sentenced, but on some fictitious charge, and not to one, but to eight years' imprisonment. He was last seen by his fellow prisoners in the yard of the Vác penitentiary, during the few brief minutes allowed for exercise. Bokor suddenly stepped out of line. In vain did the guard shout at him, Bokor set out towards one of the yard gates, at first with hesitant steps, then tottering, as if he were a little drunk. Halfway to the gate he collapsed and never regained consciousness. He died in the prison hospital of Vác.

After Bokor's departure, I spent over a month in the cellar, then I, too, was transferred to the ÁVH section of the Markó Street prison. To my amazement, the food we were given surpassed in quality anything the majority of the country's population could afford. Soon, I had an even more agreeable surprise when, at the end of December, I was given a cell-mate who was an old acquaintance of mine. We talked almost uninterruptedly for twice twenty-four hours, so that on the afternoon of the third day, I fell asleep. When I awoke my friend was standing at the foot of my bed gazing rigidly, with tears in his eyes, at my still black-and-blue toe-nails. I feigned sleep so as not to catch him betraying emotion. He pulled the blanket softly over my feet. But at that very moment, I had to stop pretending and rise quickly from the bed because my ears had caught the signal of our prison-telegraph. It came from the prisoner in the cell next to ours.

Those who were not familiar with Morse-signals resorted to a well-known, primitive system of prison telegraph. One knock stood for *a*, two for *b*, three for *c*, and so on, increasing the number of knocks all the way to *z*. It was a lengthy but precise method of conveying information and it required little practice. Our neighbour had learned the sentences passed in the principal trial and the first of the secondary trials in the Rajk affair, and was now passing on the information. As any attempt by prisoners to break silence and communicate with each other was severely punished, our neighbour was careful to tap out the letters quietly and cautiously on the radiator, stopping whenever he thought he heard a movement in the corridor. When, at times, the signals became blurred, we would repeat and query names and words. Thus, with interruptions long and short, it took us hours before we got the message telegraphed from a distance of two feet.

–Rajk: death, Pálffy: death, Brankov: life sentence, Szönyi: death, Szalai: death, Ognenovich: nine years, Korondy: death, Justus: life sentence, Németh: death, Marschall: death, Deszkás: death . . .

When the transmission was over, my friend ran twice up and down the cell, then stopped in front of me and peered into my face. We gazed at each other silently. My cell-mate broke into unnatural, whinnying laughter and clutched at his throat as if he were feeling the pressure of an invisible rope.

A few weeks later I was again alone, comforted only by the prison-telegraph and a few books. For in the *last phase of the realization* we were given reading-matter. True, the choice was rather modest and the guards, as if obeying service regulations, almost invariably handed in the last volume of any extended work first, and the first volume last. Still, the printed word brightened the cell and peopled it with friendly beings. Especially, when we were fortunate enough to spend our time with Anatole France, Thomas Mann or Leo Tolstoy and not with the mass-produced war novels of the Soviet writers. Yet it is not to these authors but to Mr. Davies, former U.S. Ambassador to Moscow, and to his involuntary humour, that I am most indebted for entertainment. I look back with gratitude upon his *Mission to Moscow*. Being familiar with the *realization* of the Rajk affair, I found it not merely amusing but also instructive to read how, sitting in his diplomatic box, Mr. Davies witnessed and believed in the Moscow Trotsky trials.

After four or five months, hardly any books were left in the 70–80 volume library of the ÁVH section that all of us had not read over and over again. So, to pass the time, and also to prevent ourselves from worrying, most of us resorted to games based on memory and imagination. I myself elaborated the action of long novels, or set my mind to work on the question of colour television and three-dimensional films. I designed whole towns and sent my imagination on trips all over the world, but mainly I engraved upon my memory consistently and stubbornly everything that had happened to me since my arrest. I tried to fix every word spoken as upon a sound track, to catch every movement, every gesture on the film reel of my mind, however hopeless it appeared that I would ever be able to play back that sound track or that film.

Several times a day, at fixed hours, I would do gymnastics. 'Let it not be my fault,' I said to myself, 'if I never see the world outside again.' At the same time I would occupy myself with variations of the cosmic games played by Thomas Mann's hero, Hans Castorp. For such abstractions no environment could be more inspiring than a prison cell. And if, though naturally only for a while, we succeed in ridding ourselves of the frighteningly false proportions of an anthropo-centric, or rather egocentric, outlook, if with the eye of the sun we can see the ocean as a drop of water, and with the eye of the universe the sun as a geometrical point without extension, death appears merely as the gentler sister of life, a different but easily bearable condition. I thought it only proper to prepare myself for this change of condition, as the prison telegraph went on tapping out messages concerning new secondary trials, new death sentences.

Thus, side by side with gymnastics to improve my physical condition, I continued my escapist mental games. Sometimes the results were disquieting but sometimes, more and more often, I played on with malicious glee, thus freeing myself from the power of a ruthless, giant international organization. Doing so calmed my anxieties because I imagined that as the weeks and months went by, I could hope with increasing justification that those passing sentence on me would have no reason to gloat over my weakness; and that when, in the end, I had to face the ultimate change of condition, my dead father would have had no reason to blush for me.

In our cells, as in the Andrássy Street cellar, the light was left on all night and as we were never allowed into the yard, only two events broke the week's monotony: the appearance of the ÁVH barber and when, late on Friday evenings, we were led singly and almost surreptitiously to the shower-room. Comparable to these pleasures was the gleaning of information by spying. In the corners of our Judas-windows, decades of continuous use had worn holes into the thick iron doors. Although the angle was difficult, we were able to peer out at the opposite gallery and see the door of one, or perhaps two cells. Our guards would, from time to time, fill up these crevices from the outside, but by using a bristle torn from a broom head I could, with a few hours' cautious labour remove or pierce the filling, and watch, for instance, when they took away for his trial Árpád Szakasits – former Secretary General of the Hungarian Social Democratic Party, dressed in a dark suit and an open collar. At the moment of my arrest he was still president of the Republic.

Every time I was transported back to the Andrássy Street cellar, the change interrupted the often unreal, apparently peaceful rhythm of life to which I grew accustomed in the Markó Street prison, but it also shook my peace of mind which I hoped had been stabilized. They would keep me there for days, sometimes for weeks, questioning me about myself and others. In the spring of 1950, I was again charged with having been a police informer and interrogated about Péter Hain, and, particularly, about the military attaché in Paris, Colonel Karátson.

Though my interrogator did not use a rubber truncheon, he would, just as Farkas used to in the old days, tear up my notes in which I described how I met Karátson and what we had talked about, and threaten me with extremely unfriendly methods if I didn't write the truth on the fresh sheet of paper put down before me. After I had scribbled in this way eight identical depositions, my interrogator declared that his patience was exhausted, that I would now be locked in a cell from which few people had emerged alive and there I would stay until I was ready to confess, or until my confession was no longer needed, because from the cell they could send me straight down for cremation.

The cell was indeed rather oppressive. Subsoil water had seeped through its floor forming small lakes varying from one to three inches deep. Only at the threshold and under the bunk did two muddy little concrete islands emerge from the water. In a few hours my clothes were saturated with damp and I was shivering from head to foot. I stamped my feet on the concrete islands or squatted on the bunk with my legs drawn up. In this way I celebrated the first anniversary of my arrest. But I did not take the threats of the ÁVH officer too seriously and I had no intention of making a confession. I was not mistaken: after having shivered, sat petrified and gasped for air in the icy mist for over three weeks, I was returned, without a word of explanation, to the steam-heated cell of the Markó Street prison.

My first concern was to find out who inhabited the cells next to mine. I received no reply from the cell on my right, but from the left someone answered my knocking and introduced himself as Miklós Szücs. I was flabbergasted, because Miklós Szücs was the brother of the deputy head of the ÁVH. But in the war, while

Ernö Szücs had fled to the Soviet Union, Miklós had spent the war years in England, to become after the war London correspondent of the official Hungarian Party organ, *Szabad Nép*, and later head of the Foreign Ministry's London Information Bureau. In 1949, he was recalled, then arrested and accused of having been a British spy. In his case, no physical methods of persuasion had been applied. Perhaps it was this circumstance that still made him hope for an objective investigation, or perhaps he counted on his brother's prestige when, through the wall, he spoke of himself as a faithful communist. He declared he had full confidence in the party and that he had no doubt his innocence would soon be proved and he would be released.

Any argument, any contradiction seemed senseless, and what is more, cruel, so this conversation was not continued, but every single day we played a game of chess. The guards did not prevent us from moulding chess figures from bread; I sat next to the wall, Szücs lay down on his bed on the other side and we would convey our moves to each other by means of low knocks. The guards suspected us but never caught us in the act and so, like two old-age pensioners confirmed in their habits, every morning at nine-thirty, we would sit down to our chessboard. We went on playing chess through the spring, through the summer, until, sometime in August, Szücs was removed.

Strangely enough he was partly right, because they released him in the autumn. But he had but a few days in which to celebrate the triumph of his faith in the party, for he was shortly rearrested. And this time there was no mercy. When an acquaintance saw him in the ÁVH cellars, he was being dragged along by two investigators because he could no longer walk. Half-conscious, he kept repeating, 'Don't touch me, don't touch me, I'll sign anything.' He could no longer count on his brother for it was precisely against the Colonel that they were trying to obtain damning evidence from Miklós Szücs. His release had been nothing but a trap set for his brother which enabled the ÁVH to ask Ernö Szücs why Miklós had made no admission during the months of his first arrest? And why, when he was rearrested, he admitted his crimes within a few days when the investigation was not in the hands of the Colonel? The reason was clear. Obviously they were birds of the same feather, both agents of foreign Imperialist powers.

Not even in 1956 did it become clear why the deputy head of the ÁVH had lost the confidence of his Russian and Hungarian superiors. But, side by side with a number of fanciful stories, there circulated two plausible accounts concerning the closing scenes of Colonel Szücs's career. According to one of these the Colonel committed suicide when he learned of his impending arrest; according to the other he had been beaten to death by ÁVH investigators. What is certain is that no prisoner came across the Szücs brothers in prison, and neither of them emerged in 1956 when all prison doors, even the secret ones, were thrown open. Thus, it is more than probable that neither survived the Colonel's fall from favour and that both the London and the Moscow Szücs met the same fate.

By the time they took away my chess partner the ÁVH had, behind closed doors, finished with most of the secondary trials in the Rajk affair. The accused had been divided into groups: the soldiers were the first to go to the gallows or to prison, followed by officials of the Ministry of the Interior and former volunteers of the Spanish civil war; and finally at separate trials those prisoners were sentenced who had returned to Hungary from France, Switzerland and England. However, there were a few, like myself, who did not fit even into these very broad categories. We were, therefore, swept together indiscriminately, like crumbs from an abundant feast.

This is how I came to figure in the same trial with the writer György Pálóczi-Horváth, with István Stolte whom the Russians had kidnapped in Vienna and then smuggled into Hungary to use as a key witness against Rajk, with György Heltai, former head of the Foreign Ministry's political department, with János Marton, former head of the Ministry of Industry's industrial-political department and finally with György Ádám, the economist.

I knew them all and was on friendly terms with most of them, but only in György Ádám's statement was there mention of me as a Trotskyite with whom Ádám had nevertheless maintained 'social relations'. My own deposition contained little more, though the wording was made highly suggestive, than that I had collaborated in Buenos Aires during the war with the committee promoting the Allied war effort, and had, before my return home, carried on a long conversation with a certain Englishman. There was no mention of my having been a police informer, no suspicion of my having passed on espionage material. An objective judge would have acquitted me, not for lack of evidence, but for lack of any punishable offence, and in any Western country the prosecutor would simply have dropped the charges. But such considerations furnished only moral satisfaction when I remembered the zealous efforts of László

Farkas and other interrogators, for, after my spell in the dripping dungeon, it had become abundantly clear to me that the sentence would not correspond to the degree of the crime I confessed to, and that it was of little interest whether the defendant damned himself more or less convincingly.

For the sake of security, the Public Prosecutor, Gyula Alapi, questioned me–in sharp contradiction with the spirit and letter of the law–not in his office but in prison, and what is more, in the centre of a threatening ring of ÁVH-men. He castigated Rajk and most of the veteran communists as police spies. Therefore, although my deposition did not refer to this, he questioned me too, perhaps only from habit, as if he took it as proven that before the war I, too, was in the Horthy police service. The overzeal of the Public Prosecutor incensed me to such a degreee that I replied to this with an energetic but very impolite 'No'. The ÁVH-men exchanged glances but soon led me away.

I returned to the Markó Street prison and awaited developments. Nothing happened until several days later when I was led to another cell. Behind a small prison table sat Presiding Judge Jónás who, in the presence of Ervin Faludi, an ÁVH lieutenant, read out my indictment at top speed. This, of course, was also contrary to the regulations of the code of criminal procedure according to which the indictment should be handed over to the accused person in writing. I hardly listened to the text; only one sentence awakened my interest; for this sentence implied, though indirectly, that while I was working in the underground communist movement, I had helped the pre-war police to persecute the communists.

I see now, as indeed I saw then, that it was really petty hair-splitting, an apparently senseless *idée fixe* for me to pick on such insignificant details. Yet I decided that on this front I would not retreat, I would not yield. Let them make of me a British spy if they wished, but I would not tolerate being called a police informer. I felt that I could not relinquish this miserable little fortress because complete submission would break me psychologically; it would render me helpless, not so much in the present as in the future, in the years to come.

I was sitting ruminating in my cell when a young ÁVH officer appeared. He did not introduce himself, but as time went on I gathered his name was Tamás Gerö. He talked intelligently and behaved agreeably, for his job was to calm us down, keep us quiet, and, with an eye to a smooth, undisturbed trial, create an atmosphere of complicity with us. As I was familiar with this police technique, it was no surprise when Gerö made no pretence of believing the charges brought against me but handed me a typewritten copy of my deposition asking me kindly to learn the text by heart, if possible word for word, as he did not imagine I could remember every silly detail of the hotch-potch as it stood.

I skimmed through the text and declared, with surprise, that it coincided with the original I had signed. But Gerö did not take offence, he did not shut me up, but made himself comfortable on my bunk. I mentioned how Alapi had tried to sneak into the indictment the insinuation that I was a police spy and I said that if this should come up at my hearing in the form of a statement, or if the Prosecutor or the judge should put it to me in the form of an insinuation, I could assure them that they would not have a smooth trial.

Gerö laughed so hard that he fell back on my bed. I should pay no attention, he said, using a considerably stronger and earthier expression, to what the Prosecutor was gabbling about in his indictment; the ÁVH, or rather he, himself, would talk to the judge. He could guarantee in advance that the presiding judge would ignore the Prosecutor's meddling. This took care of the official business between us. Gerö caught sight of my chess figures made of bread, they reminded him of Stephan Zweig's story about the chess-player and our conversation took a more cheerful and agreeable, at times almost an intellectual turn.

After this, the young ÁVH officer visited me and my fellow-accused every day. He brought cigarettes, asked us what we wanted, had our shoes repaired and ragged clothes ironed or exchanged for others, sent in a barber to cut our hair, and on November 29, 1950, he made us line up in the gallery before the cells.

Apart from the defendants, the judges, the Clerk of the Court, Alapi, the Public Prosecutor and the appointed defence counsels, there was no-one in court except a few ÁVH officers. The interrogation went off without a hitch and the sentences to which I had objected in my indictment were left out. Tamás Gerö had kept his promise. Not a single witness was called and, apart from their own confessions, no evidence was submitted against the accused.

As far as I know, only in a single case in one of the secondary trials was material proof submitted to the court; this was in the trial of Ottó Horváth. Horváth belonged to the middle-class stratum of the Hungarian minority living on Yugoslav territory, but had joined the Communist Party in early youth. Between the two world wars he had spent two years in prison for communist activity. During the war he joined Tito's guerrillas and performed liaison duties between the Yugoslavs and the Hungarian resistance movement. Regardless of risk, he repeatedly crossed the border between the two countries and, to be able to move about freely in Hungary, he used forged Gestapo papers. After 1945, he remained in Hungary at the request of the Budapest Institute of the Working-Class Movement, and wrote an account of his adventures. The Institute exhibited the forged Gestapo papers among the relics of the Hungarian Resistance movement. Horváth joined the Hungarian police, obtained the rank of colonel and, as he was bilingual in both Serbo-Croatian and Hungarian, he often interpreted for the Hungarian and Yugoslav police authorities or for other important functionaries in confidential matters. After the anti-Tito Cominform resolution, Horváth, who knew who had conferred with the Yugoslavs, where and about what, became an uncomfortable, perhaps even dangerous witness. It was to this he owed his arrest in the Rajk affair. The ÁVH took the forged Gestapo papers from the glass cabinet of the Institute of the Working-Class Movement, submitted them to the Court as genuine, and on the basis of this material proof, Horváth was sentenced to death as a traitor, an accomplice of the German National Socialists, and agent of the Gestapo. His clemency plea was rejected. The sentence was carried out.

The absence of evidence in our trial did not worry the Public Prosecutor, not even for the sake of appearances did he try to prove the charges. Instead, he made abundant use of his zoological vocabulary in selecting apt epithets for the accused. In extenuation I must stress that Alapi was merely acting as a translator. There was no need for him to seek recourse to his own inventiveness; all he did was to render into Hungarian the words of Vishinsky, the Public Prosecutor at the Moscow Trotzky trials. As an aggravating circumstance and a flagrant offence against copyright, it must be recorded that Alapi failed to acknowledge the name of the original author.

This omission on the part of the Public Prosecutor was not put right by the official defence counsels; on the contrary, most of them vied with Alapi in the passion of their indictments. The more modest ones condemned their clients in a few plain sentences; my own could but stammer out a single sentence, asking the Court to take into consideration that I had already spent a year and a half in preliminary detention and that I had a young son. My defence counsel perspired freely, although the room was unheated; he was quite obviously painfully embarrassed, for we knew each other and had formerly met frequently at parties. When, in 1955, we met again, he told me that when he was appointed, they did not tell him who he was to defend or in what sort of case. Only a few minutes before the beginning of the hearing did the ÁVH-men show him my record and indictment; they stood beside him while he read it, then immediately took it away from him. What could he have done?

Indeed, nobody could have done anything. Not even the Prosecutor, not even the judge. For even while the defence counsels were speaking, an ÁVH-man stepped up to the judge's dais and handed over a file to the presiding judge. I watched carefully and when Jónás opened the file I was able to see what it contained. No documents, no sheaf of papers, only a single quarto sheet of paper was in the file. This scene preoccupied us for a while. There were various guesses as to what the ÁVH-man may have wanted to convey to the presiding judge when the hearing was almost over and the People's Court was about to retire to deliberate. I have never, to this day, been able to rid myself of the conviction that the slip of paper contained the typewritten sentences passed by the party within the party, as a thoughtful guide to the outer circle—the independent court of justice.

A year and a half earlier a similar sheet of paper with Mihály Farkas's signature on it inaugurated the arrest of some two hundred and twenty men and women. Now, at last, the *realization* was nearing its end. The People's judges rose, then, after a brief pause during which we just had time to smoke a cigarette, Jónás, the presiding judge, proclaimed the verdict of the People's Court. It sentenced István Stolte to life imprisonment, György Pálóczi-Horváth to fifteen years, János Marton to twelve, and the remaining three of us to ten years in prison. Thus in the scales of the people's democratic justice it mattered little whether the charges were of substantial or insubstantial nature, for they had meted out to me, on almost no evidence, ten years in prison: as a punishment for wartime espionage, into the bargain, though during the war I resided in a neutral country and the People's Democracy—against which, according to the indictment, I had spied—did not as yet exist.

Our trial was one of the last of the secondary trials in the Rajk affair. The head of the ÁVH could now proudly proclaim: 'I have understood and executed the command, and have accomplished its *realization*.' But the party press omitted to publish a single word concerning the secretly conducted trials; it did not even mention the names of the spies it had rendered harmless. Although at the time of the principal trial the official Party organ, *Szabad Nép*, announced in an editorial: *The People Judge*, the party leaders tactfully spared the people's feelings and did not disclose the information who had been sentenced, or why, or what the sentences were. Even after the trial their closest relatives were given no information concerning the fate of those arrested. Of me it was rumoured in Budapest that I had been deported to the Soviet Union and shot. After a while everybody stopped asking questions. The people soon forgot that it had passed sentence at all. And we? We disappeared without trace.

9

Which is Mine?

THEY took our group to the so-called solitary confinement section of the Vác penitentiary. The six of us were crowded into a tiny cell, fit to accommodate at most two prisoners, though when this wing of the prison was built at the turn of the century, the cell, approximately two yards wide and three yards long, was intended for a single prisoner.

Three straw mattresses, placed on top of each other, were stretched under the window; our predecessors had slept them flat and had squashed the once fragrant straw into mouldy, dusty chaff. After 'lights out' we would spread these mattresses crosswise for the six of us to settle down on for the night. We could only lie on our sides, with our legs stretched out straight. If one of us turned on his back in his sleep, he rolled his neighbours over like a row of standing dominoes.

Tables and chairs were probably regarded as bourgeois, sybaritic luxuries in the socialist prison of Vác, so the authorities omitted to put any kind of furniture in our cell. A table or something to sit on would have been useful, though the lack of cupboard or a shelf did not particularly disturb us, as everything we possessed had been taken away; they did not even leave us that cherished gift from Tamás Gerö's days: our toothbrushes.

Every morning and evening they handed in a pail of water. We drank from it, used it to rinse our dixies and measured it out with a mug, in order to keep a little of it for the ceremonial rather than effective morning ablutions. In the corner by the door stood the *kibli*–a massive iron can with a lid. This served as a receptacle for the dirty water and was at the same time our lavatory. Once a day, in the late afternoon, it would be emptied by the prisoners acting as orderlies. This depressing piece of equipment compelled us to be unwilling but intimate witnesses of each other's bodily functions. Later, during the summer months, when the sun, beating down on the building, turned the cell into a suffocating oven, the intrusive presence of the *kibli* oppressed me, and I think the others, too, as a cruel supplementary punishment. I say 'I think', not because I doubt the susceptibilities of my cell-mates but because mutual tact prevented this supplementary punishment from being mentioned among us.

Not even this oppressive environment could dispel the sense of euphoria that filled us during our first days at Vác. After months of solitude we were excited by each other's company but even more by the fact that we had survived and that this was no day-dream but a palpable reality, that was proved by the presence of reliable comrades, their physical proximity and animal warmth. Thus, none of us worried about our worn frieze clothes smelling of sweat nor the fact that we were left unshaven for weeks on end and spent months without once being allowed exercise. We whiled away the time talking and playing parlour games. It was early spring before we were led out on our first walk, many of us after two years' imprisonment.

On each floor the inhabitants of the cells to the right and left of the entrance were let out into the yard separately, to walk round in single file, keeping a distance of five to seven yards from each other. Obeying a constantly reiterated command, we circled the yard with our hands behind our backs, our heads bent, and when the guard shouted: 'Fascist mass-murderers right wheel', we turned sharply in the angles of the oblong prison yard.

The guards were kept in ignorance of our names and the little wooden plaques hanging from our frieze uniforms did not betray our identity. There were hardly any former Hungarian fascists among us. But in the political arithmetic of our gaolers, the pre-1945 and post-1945 Parliamentary Speaker, the general who had turned against the Nazis with his army, the post-war Minister of Construction, the Smallholder and Social Democratic Member of Parliament, the Franciscan abbot and the former communist intellectual were all reduced to the common denominator of *fascist mass-murderer*. However obediently the prisoners, answering to the collective noun 'fascist mass-murderers', walked the yard with their chins touching their breasts and making sharp turns, the armed guards would invariably compete with each other in shouting the most obscene oaths. Most of the time we could hear them only through the window, for after circling the yard for five to seven minutes, we were herded back into our cells; unfortunately, on most days the yard was silent—I say unfortunately, because on those days, not only were we deprived of the pleasure of the swearing competition, but also of the brief airing.

Any attempt at talking during our stroll was severely punished.

Retribution, as also in the case of anyone being caught talking in the shower, was dark-cell, underground punitive cell, deprivation of food. But as they made four to five prisoners stand under a single shower, not even the chief prison warder, the eagle-eyed Sergeant Mocsáry, could see through the veil of steam. Thus, after every bath, the prisoners returned to their cells laden with encouraging rumours. They learned, for example, that a revolution had broken out in the Soviet Union and simultaneously, American parachutists had occupied Albania; two weeks later, the number of overseas divisions standing on the southern border of Hungary ready to attack, in alliance with the Yugoslavs, had increased from forty to sixty. Two weeks later Moscow, in a threatened position, had begun negotiations with the West and in Budapest preliminary conversations were being carried on with a view to the formation of a democratic government. It is still a mystery to me by whom and from where these wishful rumours were launched, but there is no doubt that many prisoners drew strength for years from this hope of approaching freedom. In vain did facts contradict the prophecies, in vain did the passing of months exceed the ever-deferred date of our expected release, the hopeful did not lose faith but, quoting ever new rumours, continued to fix new dates for their longed-for freedom.

Soon after our first exercise, there was a change in our status. We were moved from the ground floor to the floor above and were made external members of the workers' state. Although we were not allowed to leave our cells, we were provided with useful activity. Our task was to unwind the broken or cut yarn from used spindles, tie together the pieces, often not more than two or three yards long, and rewind them on spools of different sizes with the help of a primitive contraption. We received no wages for this work, not even a toothbrush or toothpaste as a reward. But sometimes, perhaps every seven or eight months, we would find a scrap of old newspaper among the spindles; this was our only reward, and also our only intellectual nourishment. For we were never allowed books to read.

Then György Pálóczi-Horváth and György Ádám were transferred to other cells. Only four of us remained. The rattle of our winding wheel was very rarely interrupted by interrogation at ÁVH headquarters or fruitless enquiries in the prison to find out who had made knocking signals to whom, who had looked out of the window; and even less frequently by a three-day session in the dark cell. Approximately every three months, in the middle of the night, we would be awakened by the distant tramp of heavy feet.

The nervous turned pale: 'They are taking us to Russia!' they would whisper while we lined up outside the duty officer's room. But we would find only a sergeant or sub-lieutenant sitting behind the table, busy completing some sort of prison statistics. He would ask, for instance, what our last address had been or what languages we spoke. Unless these nightly alarms were deliberately intended to heighten tension, it would be difficult to explain why they chose the hours of darkness and rest to collect statistical information. Naturally, we prisoners attached great significance to everything that happened; when our last addresses were recorded we felt certain that our families were going to be told about our whereabouts, and when we were asked what languages we knew, we hoped we would be given translation work. A month went by, two months, the self-deluding dreams went up in smoke, nothing changed, we continued knotting and winding our yarn and starving.

From our first to our last day at Vác, we starved in the plainest and simplest meaning of the word. The soup was water of a strange colour; the mash was a thin soup. And when they gave us noodles or, on Sundays, a stew, a man of medium appetite might, perhaps, have taken the edge off his hunger with four or five portions. The fare we had received at the Markó Street prison lived in our memory as a heavenly delight. At Vác our food was totally innocent of fat or oil; we never got fruit or any kind of salad; only early in 1952 did they occasionally distribute small quantities of sauerkraut. Although we moved as little as possible, all of us, but particularly the older prisoners, were visibly losing weight. Once, when they weighed us, merely out of objective curiosity, prisoners who formerly weighed 160–170 lbs. no longer weighed even 100 lbs.

Even though I was now accustomed to such emaciations, my attention was held one day in the shower-room by the spectacular picture presented by one fellow-prisoner who was over six foot tall. He reminded one of pictures taken in German concentration camps. Not only his ribs, but every bone in his body seemed about to pierce through his skin. He tottered out for exercise less and less frequently, and then he stayed away altogether. We learned that they had taken him to the prison infirmary and that was where he left empty for ever his prison boots. He was a mild-faced priest by the name of Gergely Tornyos. After an interrogation, perhaps because they caught me looking out of the window, I was separated from the others and put for a while into Gergely Tornyos's deserted cell. On the floor, close to the straw mattress, I discovered his cheap, wire-framed spectacles, all that was left of him.

Other faces, known only to me by sight, also disappeared as time went by, but the majority of prisoners blessed, out of self-defence, with a salutary blindness, failed to notice in themselves the signs of slow but progressive decay, and casting rational thinking to the winds they trusted in an imminent amelioration of their lot. Yet, when in the second half of April, 1952, we were once more awakened at night by the thud of heavy feet, it did not occur to us that the noise might herald a change in our circumstances. No use getting worked up, we shrugged, they would ask our mothers' maiden names for the tenth time, or enquire about our university degrees. But this time, while our hobnailed boots clattered along the gang-ways we saw, as we looked down to the ground floor, the shiny epaulettes of a collection of highranking ÁVH officers.

They took our personal details, then made us wait for a consider-able time until, at last, canvas-covered military lorries lined up in the yard. They told us to sit on the floor of the lorries with our legs crossed, packed together in dense rows to prevent us from moving. The last row was chained together and behind us ÁVH-men with tommy-guns stood guard. They were evacuating us from the Vác penitentiary.

On the journey, we listened to the breathing of the sleeping town and the city noises that by now seemed alien and unnatural to us. Every time we stopped, the motorized ÁVH-men ordered to escort us would exchange a few words with our armed guards and light up the interior of the lorry with the bright beam of their torches. We could not see out of the lorry. Only when we heard the sound of shunting engines and the clatter of wheels did my friend Heltai declare, after having peeped out through a crack in the canvas, that we were standing in the Rákos shunting-yards. We waited there quite a while. Nobody said a word but when, at last, the lorry drove on, a sigh of relief swept through the rows: 'They are not taking us to Russia, after all!'

The day was not yet breaking when we reached the so-called National Prison at Köbánya, the *Gyüjtö*. Here they divided our group of four and put us into two double cells, but a few days later, in the course of a re-organization, I was separated from the last of my fellow-defendants. I was detailed to work in the prison button-shop. After a year and a half of preliminary detention and almost a year and a half at Vác, I could now familiarize myself with a new stratum of prison society, with a new facet of prison life.

The buttons were made from synthetic material and animal bone and horn, and by antediluvian instruments and methods. First, the boiled bones and horn were cut into thin slices with the help of a circular saw, and the sheets of synthetic material soaked in formalin, then all three were cut into discs of the desired size. The next stage of the process was the shaping of the discs on primitive lathes, after which came the drilling of the holes. The drilling process was followed by polishing and finally by inspection and selection.

When we were marched down on the first morning the civilian foreman glanced along the lines and then sent the taller ones among us to the circular saw or the polishing shop. I owed my selection for the polishing shop not to my technical skill but to my height. They sat us down in front of a high-speed buffing-wheel and put a metal tool resembling a cylindrical electric torch into our hands. This tool was provided with a head revolving in a ball-race in which a changeable wooden inlay was fitted with an indentation corresponding to the size of the button cut into it. We placed the button in this indentation, then pressed the tool on to the wheel which was coated with polishing paste. The buffing-wheel, travelling at two thousand revolutions a minute, spun the head of the tool round and round, and if the process was successful, we dropped a shiny button into the box placed on our right.

All this seemed ingenious, even brilliantly simple when the foreman explained it. But the work demanded not only skill but also physical strength. For, if one did not hold the tool sufficiently firmly, the whizzing wheel would tear it from one's hand; and if one did not press it down with the required force on the wheel, the button would fall dull and unpolished into the box. The head of the tool would spin only if it touched the wheel at a right angle, and when it did, the button would often jump out. We soon discovered that it would take us not days but weeks, before we learned the tricks of the trade.

The foreman, a blustering though apparently benevolent elderly working-man, was almost affable in his dealings with us; he gave us four cigarettes each. If we did our work properly, he said, and accomplished 70 per cent of the prescribed norm, they would not only double our food rations but would credit our account with a sum proportionate to our work with which, each month, we could purchase tobacco, toothbrush, toothpaste or even food. But until then they would give us cigarettes every day. Therefore, we had better get down to it and do our best, for it was worth while.

We were allowed to eat our midday meal in the yard. Beaming

with happiness we would drift together in small groups with our dixies in our hands and greet friends and strangers alike. Our guards walked up and down among us in silence and we sniffed the fresh air as though reborn, turning our faces towards the weak but friendly sunshine. We found the fare of the *Gyüjtö* not only more tasty than the food at the Vác, but also more plentiful; and after the four walls of the solitary confinement section and the imposed motionlessness, this brief but informal session in the yard was pure heaven and the after-dinner cigarette an unearthly delight. Only for our companions who did not work did we feel sorry. They were now striding up and down in their cells, compelled to turn after every fifth step; they probably could not even imagine what it was like to take twenty steps in one direction, as we could if we wanted to.

For a few days the distribution of cigarettes continued. Then they skipped two days, resumed the distribution for two days, then stopped it altogether. The foreman spread his arms:

'There aren't any,' he said, 'there's nothing I can do about it. Work hard and get that 70 per cent. Believe me, it is not my fault, not my fault at all,' he repeated apologetically and offered some of us his own cigarettes.

The entire procedure betrayed not the mentality of the well-intentioned foreman, but that of the ÁVH specialists. First, to remind them of their past freedom, they had given the workers in the button-shop a whiff of the half-forgotten taste of tobacco. They had reawakened in them the craving for nicotine in order to deprive them of it suddenly and, at the same time, to hold out the doubtful pleasure of smoking as a bait for the prisoners to fulfill the prescribed work-norm. This was not easy. After the first few weeks, even the most skilful of us did not attain 25–30 per cent. Yet, the scramble for cigarettes had begun.

The slaves of the button-shop and nicotine not only drove themselves to ever-greater effort but some, though only a small minority, stooped to tricking their fellow-prisoners by trying to snatch for themselves the more malleable materials and the better tools. Thus, by driving their prisoners into a craving for cigarettes, the ÁVH specialists pursued a double aim: on the one hand to raise the output, on the other, to create strife and discord among the prisoners.

Although in the first month few of us were able to exceed the magic 70 per cent target, in the second month 80, then 90, and finally only over 100 per cent entitled the fortunate to the purchase of a few packs of cigarettes and a tiny quantity of margarine, sugar, onions or bread.

The prison leadership resorted also to other, more conservative means to increase our output. They lengthened the hours of work. We rose at five o'clock, were in the button-shop by six and returned to our cells only after eleven o'clock at night. If we deduct the two half-hour breaks for meals, we spent eighteen hours a day at the work-bench. As a result, many of us broke down, one after the other, and the accident rate, always very high, rose even higher. The exhausted, undernourished prisoners would cut off their fingers at the lathe, totter into the circular saw, drill holes in their nails instead of the button, and our ankles swelled enormously. I was not greatly surprised, therefore, when one day, on my way to work, everything turned black in front of my eyes and I rolled down the stairs. My comrades helped me back to the cell. Sergeant Sándorfi, the inspector of our wing of the prison, Departmental Head, to give him his official title, inspected me from my pale hollow cheeks to the pillars that served me as legs and delivered his considered professional opinion:

'This is where your guts will rot . . . and pretty soon, at that.'

A few days later, to refute this prophecy I dragged myself to my feet and took my place in the line, because the four walls of my cell suffocated me even more nauseatingly than the button-shop. The old foreman took a look at me, meditated a little while and then, because in the meantime he had assigned someone else to my machine, detailed me to join the button inspectors.

I found myself next to an old acquaintance, a Social Democratic journalist. When, at night, towards eleven, the buttons were but a vibrating blur before our eyes and the guard quitted the workshop, we devoted a few agreeable moments to conversation. I expressed my amazement at the original way in which the ÁVH prison leadership had developed and carried out the basic principle of Marxist socialism, 'the liquidation of man's exploitation by man', by slowly but surely liquidating the exploited themselves, with the help of an eighteen-hour working day. My friend enlarged on my trend of thought and pointed out the unlimited capacity for development in the progressive ÁVH capitalism—as he called it—then, taking each other up, we drew a utopian picture of a society without exploitation created by ÁVH methods. At this moment we paid little attention to our production target, but appreciated mutually and with great hilarity, our world-saving ideas. Suddenly we heard someone shout at us:

'What's so funny?'

It was not the guard, however, but a young man in prison uniform who had stopped at our table. A cigarette dangled from his lip and his brand-new tunic was a different colour from ours.

'Get on with your work,' he said lowering his voice but in a tone of command.

This young man was Ferenc Vándor, once a major in the ÁVH. He had taken part in the preparation of the Rajk trial but then, for reasons unknown to us, he too had been sent to this educational institution to be 'led back to the party'. The prison director, Antal Bánkuti, had appointed Vándor overseer of the button shop, and the former ÁVH major did everything in his power to regain the confidence of the Party within the Party. Once Vándor had familiarized himself with the organizational methods and the work process, the elderly foreman disappeared overnight. We soon discovered that Vándor represented the interests of the owners much more effectively and ruthlessly than his diminutive working-class predecessor and never stooped so low as to share any of his abundant supply of cigarettes with the prisoners.

They provided Vándor with two aides-de-camp, a pair of former ÁVH officers, who had been jailed for offences of a financial nature. The aides-de-camp showed less zeal than their superior, but they were just as afraid of him as we insignificant mortals in the button-shop. Even the uniformed ÁVH guards feared Vándor because they knew that he reported everything directly to the prison governor.

However, this police-solidarity manifested itself not only among the present and former ÁVH officers but also side-stepped any apparently ideological obstacle, too. All confidential posts were filled with former officers of various police organizations from various eras, regardless of what régime or régimes they had served. One such confidential job was that of the orderlies, but particularly that of their commander, the chief orderly. The latter was boss of the wing under his command; he distributed the food, locked and opened the cells and detailed his fellow prisoners to different jobs, such as scrubbing corridors, coal heaving or whitewashing. Thus it came about that in one wing of the prison (which was built in the shape of a three pointed star) a pre-1945 military investigator was appointed chief orderly; in another, two members of Szálasi's Arrow-Cross political police, and in our wing, a former German SS sergeant.

The warders called this six and a half footer by his pet name, Hansi, and tactfully looked away when Hansi, distributing stew, ladled out two dixiefuls of meat for himself and then bestowed on us three or four nut-sized morsels of meat. On this fare, the ex-SS sergeant grew fat enough to burst, while the workers in the button shop were slowly fading away. Hansi could also give himself the pleasure of dislodging with a blow the cap of my former school-mate, Dr. Ferenc Matheovits, M.P., a member of the Barankovics Party, when the latter did not take it off with the speed demanded by the SS. But as the victim protested at the attack, next day, while we slaved away in the shop, Hansi turned Matheovits's cell upside-down and then denounced him for being insufficiently clean and orderly. Section-leader Sándorfi believed, not the former deputy, but the SS sergeant and the evidence of his own eyes, and Matheovits was severely punished. When not employed in provoking such scenes, Hansi was allowed to write his memoirs in idyllic peace. One of our fellow-prisoners afterwards translated this distinguished work from German into Hungarian; he told me that Hansi had participated in the deportation of the Nagyvárad Jews, and that in addition, the blood of at least 180 persons burdened his conscience. When in his memoirs he listed his murders, the former SS sergeant showed far greater modesty, tact and refinement, than he did when distributing the daily ration in the prison.

It was not only in the prison proper that officers of former police organizations lorded it over their fellow-prisoners, but also in the shower house, which was commanded by a pre-1945 political investigator, and in the button-shop where a detective inspector inherited from Horthy's political police by Szálasi performed the tasks of chief orderly, though due to Vándor's presence his authority was limited. In prison, of course, the 'worker-peasant alliance', the 'leading role of the working class' and 'international proletarian solidarity' were never mentioned but the facts, taking the place of the propaganda slogans, proclaimed with amazing frankness the national and even international unity and solidarity of the power-enforcement organizations and demonstrated unequivocally whom the party within the party recognized as its blood-relations.

The workers in the button-shop were perceptibly losing their strength. More and more of them died and before long the prison leadership was faced with a painful alternative: either to renounce its original method of 'liquidating man's exploitation by man' by liquidating the exploited, or to give up the production drive. Seeing the general exhaustion, even Vándor could no longer ignore the alternative and it is to be presumed that he used his influence to obtain a shortening of the working hours. Outside orders for buttons must also have decreased because after a while we were allowed to put down our tools in the late afternoon, instead of the middle of the night.

Now, when at last we could think of something else besides the moment when we would be able to stretch out on our straw mattresses, we slowly began to build up a somewhat irregular messenger service with our fellow-prisoners working in the laundry, the carpenter's shop and the furnace-room, and even with the other wings of the prison. The messengers brought not only greetings and messages, but from the more abundantly supplied places of work, as for instance the furnace-room, bread and sometimes even cigarettes. One of my cell-mates, Robi S., maintained almost regular contact with his father who was lodged in another wing of the prison. Several times a week he would receive news about his father's state of health and was able to send him portions of the *Gyüjtö's* quaintest delicacy.

Robi worked in the so-called bone-boiling shop. The raw material for the bone buttons, mainly horse bones, were stored in a pit covered with boards. In early summer, a foul, sickening stench of carrion hovered over the pit and if the wind was adverse it even penetrated the neighbouring cells. Before the bones were sent up for processing, Robi and his companions would boil them so that they were relatively clean white shins, hip-bones and shoulder-bones that the circular saw cut into slices.

It did not escape the attention of the famished prisoners clustered around the cauldron that the fat, boiling off the bones, formed a thick layer on top of the water. Robi was inspired with an epoch-making idea. Carefully avoiding the filth, he ladled the hot islands of grease into his dixie and when this mess had cooled into a jelly, he spread it, like butter, on his bread. It was some of this gastronomical delicacy that he sent his father who shared it with his cell-mates, all elderly gentlemen incapable of work; and the old men conveyed their enthusiastic gratitude for the generous gift. Kind-hearted and comradely as he was, Robi also offered some titbits to me and our third cell-mate, Péter Gy., Canon of Kalocsa, and he was struck dumb with amazement when we both refused his offer with friendly tact. He explained that in the purgatory of the cauldron all bacilli perished and that we should forget the pit and the stench that rose from it, for, after all, we never thought of the smell of the pig-sty when eating ham at home, did we?

We obstinately refused to be persuaded and neither of us partook of this unusual delicacy; we refused even to taste it. Robi shrugged his shoulders, then grew suddenly angry and went for us both. He warned us threatingly that in prison fastidiousness was a sin and could bring about one's downfall. Although he returned to the subject repeatedly, depicting in detail the fateful consequences of our choosiness, he never succeeded in convincing us. But later, when conditions worsened, on matters of far greater importance we always agreed.

Unpleasant changes generally broke upon us unexpectedly, just as we had begun to relax a little or live in the expectation of better things. Now once again, a new era began with promise. It may have been the very same day that our cell-mate, the Canon, was removed from our cell that they sent the workers of the button-shop to the warehouse, where we were given worn but well-cut military trousers. There were probably economic reasons behind the distribution of these khaki-coloured garments; perhaps they were still one grade too good to be thrown away. We felt almost elegant in them. After the stiff frieze cloth and the broad-striped coarse linen, the worn military trousers seemed worthy indeed of gentlemen. We put our collection of pieces of string and small rags into our pockets and walked with a swagger, as if we were going a-wooing. But not for long.

A day or two later, shortly after the lunch break, they made us line up in the button-shop yard. Then the prison commander himself appeared with a large retinue. He ordered us to take off our trousers there and then. Within a few seconds we were standing in our underwear in the prison yard. The sight must have been rather amusing, for several members of the retinue were unable to suppress their laughter. The commander made us wait for a few minutes, then he delivered a brief but threatening speech, saying that he would soon show us where we got off. Next, some prisoners carrying large baskets appeared on the scene, gathered up the military trousers and distributed our old striped prison uniforms. We were at a loss to account for such behaviour, nothing untoward had happened in the button-shop, and we understood even less why we were directed to return to our cells, instead of our places of work.

Robi and I were still wondering about the possible reasons for this unusual event when we became aware of the opening of doors, the stamping of feet and short, sharp reports. Then groans and screams reached our ears.

'Execution,' Robi declared, adding with cool soldierly competence, 'they are using rifles with silencers.'

'There must be political upheavals outside,' he went on, 'perhaps a war has broken out, and as there's no time to evacuate us, they're making short work of us.' It seemed a very long time before our cell was unlocked. An ÁVH-man, with bloodshot eyes, livid with anger, stood panting on the threshold.

'Outside!' he bawled.

From the gangway outside the cells we could look down. An iron grill ran along the centre of the ground floor covering and protecting the main pipes let into the floor. Regulations said we were to walk this grill in Indian file, in case our boots should leave a mark on the shiny, polished floor. Now our fellow prisoners were running along this same grill at a distance of perhaps ten feet from each other, while some twenty ÁVH-men stood on both sides of it. They were swinging their leather belts, bringing the buckles down on the heads, shoulders and backs of the prisoners as they passed. The blows made short, sharp cracks, almost like shots. It was these sounds we had heard in our cell. Robi raised his hand to his lips, I saw that he, too, drew a breath of relief. I whispered to him:

'Let's not run.'

'Just what I was going to say,' he whispered back.

So we did not run, but sauntered along the grill, unhurried, as if we were going for a walk. This surprised our guards so much that they encouraged us to greater speed mainly by kicks and almost forgot why they were holding their belts in their hand. Robi received only one hard blow on his skull; the skin broke and blood ran down his face, but the injury was not serious. Those who betrayed their fear by raising their arms to protect their faces came off worst. Frightened eyes attracted the ÁVH-men as a magnet attracts iron filings. The undisguised terror and suffering of the victims made the effort of swinging the belt worth while. On this afternoon, so reminiscent of the gauntlet-running of a previous era, more than one of our companions spat out a few teeth, lay sprawled on his mattress for days and carried, for months, the scars from the leather belt and the buckle.

That day we were given no dinner, the next day no breakfast or lunch, but on the third day we were lined up again and led to the button-shop. The warders appeared more brutal than usual and Vándor more taciturn, but not until night did we experience a new alarm. We woke after midnight to the sound of cries, thumps and bangs. The guards were going from cell to cell, sweeping the dixies from the table, ransacking the mattresses, beating up and kicking the prisoners one by one. These assaults were repeated several nights on end and lasted each time for about one and a half hours. But not all the guards enjoyed this nightly overtime. One or two of them—while their companions wrought havoc in the neighbouring cells – kicked our dixies about making a great deal of noise, but did not trample on our mattresses and one said almost apologetically, in a low voice:

'Go back to bed, rest as long as you can . . .' Then he would thump the wall with his boot to make the guard in the next cell believe we were getting it in the neck.

As our messenger service had ceased functioning, it was a long time before we found out to what we owed the collective punishment. The khaki drill trousers had given one of our fellow-prisoners a bold idea. He was working in the furnace room as a stoker and somehow or other he succeeded in climbing on to the cardan-shaft of a coal lorry. As the guards at the gate inspected the inside of the lorry but did not look underneath, our fellow-prisoner, a former frontier guard, escaped from the prison. Moreover, as we learned later, he even got across the minefield. We all wished him luck, although the gauntlet-running marked the beginning of the *kurtavas* era.

Originally the *kurtavas* was a handcuff attached to a short iron chain. In the Austro-Hungarian army, insubordinate soldiers used to be shackled with this contraption. The ÁVH brought this hundred-year-old army punishment up to date. In the *Gyüjtö*, they used a looped chain instead of a handcuff and pulled it so tight that it cut into the flesh. With this they bound the prisoner's right hand to his left ankle and his left hand to his right ankle. Whereupon Sergeant Pintér, the foremost *kurtavas* specialist, would take hold of the two ends of the chain, place his boot on the prisoner's foot and exerting all his strength, bunch both hands and feet together like the open end of a sack. In the old days, the soldiers of the Austro-Hungarian army were kept in *kurtavas* for two hours at the most. But here, too, the ÁVH introduced innovations by fixing the maximum punishment at six hours. During that time the guards kept watch to make sure the prisoners sat on the ground-floor grill with their legs stretched straight out and if any attempted to pull his knees up to ease to some extent the unbearable strain on his back muscles, the warders, always devoted to carrying out their duties meticulously, would trample on his shin to straighten out the line of leg and thigh.

The workers in the button factory rarely gave cause for punishment. But our jailers were under no obligation to wait for an excuse, because, at bottom, the intention was not to punish minor or major offences but to turn us, in our physical captivity, into slaves of permanent fear and anxiety. They were obviously following orders when every day, with painful regularity, they noted down the numbers of eight or ten button-shop workers who would be told next evening to how many hours of *kurtavas* the prison command had sentenced them. A man would be sitting quietly over his work when suddenly the sergeant would yell at him:

'Why don't you get on with it?'

No answer was equivalent to a confession, and a reply equivalent to insolence, so the prisoner's number was added to the list. But should it happen that, by roll-call, there were insufficient candidates for the *kurtavas*, the sergeant would walk along our gloomy lines until his glance alighted on one or another of our faces.

'What are you laughing at?' he would yell at the chosen man.

'I wasn't laughing,' the prisoner would reply and, indeed, he had little cause for mirth.

'Don't lie to me, you bastard. What is your number?'

This cat-and-mouse game became a permanent feature of our prison life and each night, eight or ten prisoners were put into *kurtavas*. The groans and cries of the tormented kept not only our wing, but the other two as well, awake from nine in the evening until three in the morning. We all had our turn. I was sentenced to the maximum, six hours. The two men next to me fainted; one was brought to with the help of cold water but the other had to be taken away because he did not regain consciousness, even when they emptied several pails over him. In the meantime, I followed the generally accepted routine of the prisoners, and pulled my knees up however much it hurt and however often they pressed them back; for in this way, one's limbs did not atrophy as did those of some of our fellow-prisoners who limped even six months later. Some were left crippled for life.

We no longer rejoiced at being able to take twenty steps instead of five in any one direction and we thought almost nostalgically of our cells at Vác. We were in the middle of summer, but tension had not abated; on the contrary, the prison authorities found occasion to stage a new and spectacular show.

One day, around the middle of July, at lunch time, our noses were assailed by a smell of sewage in the yard. During soup distribution, we established that the stench came from the cauldron containing our second course: rotten cabbage. Many prisoners did not queue up for their portions while others poured the slop down the lavatory. The guards must have reported the matter, for around three o'clock we were ordered to line up.

The so-called 'operative group' working in the prison consisted of plain-clothes investigators. One of them climbed up the few steps leading to the prison bakery and stood facing us. Had I met this handsome young man in the street, I should probably have thought that he was a student, an intellectual. He gazed at us darkly and ordered those who had not accepted their portions of cabbage to step forward.

About twenty of us stepped forward. The investigator shouted that there were more than that, those who poured their food down the lavatory should also step forward. This time nobody moved. Thereupon Cabbage–for henceforth he was known by this nickname–ordered us to do frog-hops. We jumped around the yard with our hands on our hips, our ankles close together, in a squatting position. The older prisoners collapsed in the first round, the younger ones stood three. But after the frog-hops, it was the same twenty or so prisoners who stepped forward, and even after a few more rounds their number remained unchanged, though from the amount of refuse that blocked the lavatories, it seemed clear that not twenty or twenty-five but at least two hundred prisoners had refused or otherwise disposed of their cabbage. Let those who knew that one or another of their companions did not eat his cabbage step forward, the investigator commanded. Nobody moved. Cabbage looked helplessly at the mute human wall. His well-chiselled features were now contorted with anger and he was bathed in sweat. He shook all over. He shouted incoherent threats in a choking voice, then ran off as if pursued.

The next afternoon, we were again ordered to line up in the yard. The prison governor, Bánkúti, appeared with his retinue but we looked in vain for Cabbage among the officers and investigators accompanying him. Bánkúti repeated the challenge of the previous day; again, the same twenty prisoners stepped forward.

'Then I shall tell you who refused their portions and also who poured theirs away,' Bánkúti declared, pulling a piece of paper from his pocket. 'What do you know about today?'

'We have become a member state of the Soviet Union,' my neighbour whispered.

'What is more, with unanimous enthusiasm,' I whispered back.

'Today,' Bánkúti cried, 'there is a dictatorship of the proletariat in Hungary. I am going to show you what dictatorship of the proletariat means.'

And he did. He read a few numbers from the paper in his hand. The prisoners called stepped up to him, one after the other. Bánkúti asked each what his father did, what he did, and usually also why he had been sentenced. Then, according to the replies, with the refined classification of propaganda pamphlets, he called them capitalist exploiters, social democratic traitors to the working class, mass-murderers, peasant-tormentors, or Trotskyite spies; then he kicked those nearest him in the belly, laid about him a bit with his rubber truncheon and his officers did likewise. After this came running the gauntlet. The prisoner ran along the inner-prison-corridor between two rows of twenty truncheon-swinging ÁVH-men. Only the dull thud of the truncheons and the clatter of the dropped dixies was heard in the yard.

Vándor was standing by the wall of the button-shop not among us, but facing us, at a respectful distance behind the commander's retinue. Bánkúti went on reading numbers from the paper in his hand. At times he would turn back to Vándor:

'How does he work?'

And Vándor would characterize his fellow-prisoners with soldierly briefness: 'He produces a lot of waste–he is a mediocre worker–he fiddles his wages.' None of us doubted that the former ÁVH major was consulted in the preparation of the list.

The next prisoner to step forward before Bánkúti was a young man in his mid-twenties.

'Your father's occupation?'

'Peasant.'

'How many acres does he have?'

'Three.'

'What's your occupation?'

'Franciscan monk.'

Neither capitalist exploiter, nor social democratic traitor, mass-murdering general, Trotskyist spy. For a while the prison commander stood undecided, staring at the monk, then he broke into shrieking abuse:

'Get it into your head that here I am God, I am Lucifer!'

After this, no matter who stood before him, Bánkúti, as if he had gone completely mad, went on repeating in increasingly hoarse tones: 'I am God here, I am Lucifer!' Reaching the end of the list and recovering a little self-composure, he delivered a brief address in which he declared that he had the right to have us hanged when-ever he felt like it; he was in a position to throw our families into prison and we had better bear this in mind. For this was his last warning.

This is how the second gauntlet-running within three months

ended, to be remembered in the unwritten records of the prison, with the braggadocio of all chronicles, as the cabbage-revolution.

Expert opinion in Central European prisons and barracks always held that as soon as discipline, at whatever level, becomes monotonous routine, the threat of indolence, slothfulness and even a relaxation of discipline will necessarily and inevitably follow. It was to prevent such a situation from arising that they introduced, from time to time, in the Austro-Hungarian army as well as in the Hungarian army between the two world wars, disciplinary exercises, a sort of collective punishment by meting out disproportionate retaliation at times for some insignificant offence, at times only as a matter of principle, and without any special reason. It was to no small degree to these traditional considerations that we owed the era of the *kurtavas* and the cabbage-revolution. A few weeks after Bánkúti's big scene, the shackling became infrequent, only to be resumed again at regular intervals. In addition, new and intimidating measures were constantly being introduced. Thus, for instance, the daily, hitherto superficial search in the button-shop became stricter.

When we had finished our work we were made to line up in the yard with our boots in our hands, waiting for our guards to paw us all over, then inspect our boots to see whether we hadn't hidden something under the string or in the toe. The search became particularly painful in the late autumn and in winter, when we stood barefoot on the wet gravel, or sometimes in snow or on ice. But it was painful on milder days, too, when we were under the command of the green-eyed, elderly sergeant. For, after having inspected our boots inside and out, he would throw them with surprising accuracy at our bare feet, aiming the iron-shod heel to hit our toe-nails.

But even the green-eyed sergeant was less zealous in his target practice when he happened to be by himself. The cruelty of our guards always abated as soon as they were safe from the supervision of their superiors or had no other ÁVH-man watching them, or when they had to deal with prisoners singly, not in groups or couples. The prison leadership must have been aware of this, even if it had no knowledge of particular instances. I think I am not far from the truth when I assert that the chainings, running the gauntlet and other excesses served not only to terrorize the prisoners, but also to discipline the discipliners, and intimidate the guards. Any ÁVH-man who did not swing his truncheon with requisite fierceness and demonstrative hatred was in danger of becoming suspect in the eyes of his superiors; then again, when face to face with his victims, he had no reason to suppose that they liked him; on the contrary, he had good cause to fear some kind of retaliation or at least a desire for revenge; so occasionally, one of the guards, yielding to some hysterical fear, would suddenly attack a prisoner. But in the majority of cases, an ÁVH guard would become more human when only a few people were present, and even more so when he found himself alone with a prisoner. At such times the guard did not have to fear that a colleague would denounce him or that the prisoner would attempt some desperate coup. Thus, in an intimate man-to-man setting, the ÁVH-man would indirectly dissociate himself from the brutality of his companions by becoming more humane and speaking a few mild words; he would, even, at times, risk plain speaking to extract himself from the universal responsibility for the reign of terror.

For the same psychological reasons, in the solitary confinement cells, where a guard would be in contact with only one or two prisoners, the tone used was less brutal than in the crowded workshops. And yet everyone preferred the humiliations of the button-shop to being locked up in the quietest, most polite section of the *Gyüjtö*, the *Kisfogház* or little prison. Apart from the female prisoners, the little prison housed only the strictly isolated prisoners and those sentenced to death. Whenever we delivered buttons to the *Kisfogház*, where the women sewed them on to cards, my companions drew my attention to a modest but ghastly feature of the yard: some concrete pits covered with sheet-iron. It was in these that they stood the gallows on execution days.

The scaffold was a massive upright wooden block about nine feet high. Wooden wedges were hammered on each side of it to keep it upright and fix it firmly in the pit; then the rope was thrown over the top.

The victim's two wrists were tied to his left thigh, then they put the so-called *állazó*, or chinstrap over his head, locking his lips and immobilizing his chin in case he should disturb the prison calm with his cries. The man about to be executed was made to stand on a footstool at the foot of the scaffold, then they put the rope around his neck. The assistant hangman standing behind the scaffold pulled the rope running through a series of pulleys and simultaneously, the chief hangman would kick the footstool from under the victim's feet and at the same time turn his chin sharply to one side, thus separating the head from the spinal column and breaking the thread of his life. The fact that the executed man's two wrists were bound to his left thigh left the heart area free. This is where the physician tore open the dead man's last shirt, to insert his stethoscope and certify death. This is how the prisoners sentenced to death and then pardoned and sent to work in the button-shop described the hangings. In the death cells they had inhabited, they could not only hear the dull thuds of the hammer fixing the wooden wedges in place and the whining and creaking of the rows of pulleys but, at unguarded moments they could glance out of the window to observe what was in store for them. Some of them had spent eighteen months in the death-cell before having their sentences commuted to life imprisonment. A former army officer who afterwards became foreman of the hole-drillers in the button-shop had already limped out to the scaffold with his wrists tied to his thigh, and the rope was already around his neck, before, amidst trumpeting laughter, they read to him the decree commuting, by an act of clemency, the death sentence to life imprisonment.

On execution mornings, they did not allow us to go to the button-shop, but locked and bolted the doors of our cells. When at last we were lined up for work, we could watch Dr. Benedek waddle past with his black satchel, on his way from the *Kisfogház* where he had just torn open the shirt of an executed prisoner. Naturally, we had to stand to attention. Pretending not to see us, the handlebar-moustached Dr. Benedek walked on, gloomily waggling his gargantuan behind.

In the autumn of 1952, we saluted Dr. Benedek more and more frequently, as the executions increased in number. They would hang three men at a time, so the prisoners entrusted with the removal of the bodies told us, and on one occasion they executed eight simultaneously. These were said to be Rákosi's eight body-guards who had in some way fallen short of the requirements of communist vigilance. At the end of 1952 the head of the ÁVH, Gábor Péter, was also arrested, then Károlyi, who had taken Ernö Szücs's place when the latter was imprisoned: Colonel Gyula Décsi, appointed Minister of Justice after the Rajk trial and Antal Bánkúti, the governor of the *Gyüjtö*. It was not to his prison activities that Bánkúti owed this distinction; he joined the gallery of notabilities in something of an extramural capacity, because he had once been a sort of confidential messenger or batman to Gábor Péter. Nor were these prominent members of the ÁVH arrested for having refused to stage another show-trial but, as an ironic twist of fate, to become themselves the defendants in another show-trial. Stalin was still alive and the heads of the MVD wished to link up Gábor Péter's trial with the Zionist show-trial in Russia in which most of the accused were Jews. The Russian trial was shelved on Stalin's death. The provincial Budapest variant of the Moscow gala-performance did take place, but not as a Zionist trial as originally planned.

After Bánkúti's removal, the *kurtavas* sessions were dropped altogether and on Sunday mornings, an orderly actually appeared with a wooden tray of books. At first, each cell was allotted a single book and we took it in turns to read it aloud to each other, but later we succeeded in obtaining two or even three books. In the course of various regroupments, I had long been separated from Robi and now shared the straw mattresses of our cell with three other prisoners, an airforce officer, a social democratic steel-worker and a college lecturer. It was during this period that I was granted one of the greatest joys of my prison life: early in 1953, after three and a half years of captivity, I was at last able to buy the long-desired tooth-brush and tooth-paste and I even had enough money over to buy forty cigarettes as, for the first and last time, my output attained 117 per cent. This was due not so much to my efforts as to Laci B., the prisoner who acted as clerk in the button-shop; he distributed the work and recorded the output, always cleverly, and at times courageously helping us as much as he could.

In this improved atmosphere, we were able to restore our messenger service and I received news from the fellow-accused in my trial. They were working in the translating bureau and were doing their utmost to have me transferred there, too; they had brought my knowledge of languages and familiarity with technical matters to the attention of the authorities—on no account was I to contradict them. I was somewhat anxious lest my lack of technical knowledge should bring trouble upon my friends but I was given no opportunity to contradict them, for no-one examined me or put a single question to me before, in the spring of 1953, I was transferred to the building nicknamed *Kisszálló* or the Little Hostel.

A year before, when they were laying the foundations of the Little Hostel and putting up its walls, I had been among those detailed to carry bricks and remove rubble. Never did I dream then that the prisoners' translating and technical bureau would develop into such a paradise. The rooms reminded one of a workers' hostel or barracks rather than of the cells at Vác or the *Gyüjtö*. Though the panes were of frosted glass, the windows, of normal size and shape, let in a generous amount of light; the rooms were centrally heated and had wash-basins with running water; the lavatory attached to each room, but divided from it by a wall and a door, awoke half-forgotten memories of a civilized way of life. The double-decker iron bed-steads boasted good quality mattresses instead of the usual flat straw sacks. The new lodger found a standard light-coloured office chair and table waiting for him, and in the corridors the sound of his footsteps was deadened by carpeting.

In importance as well as in number, the translators lagged far behind the technicians. In the engineering office, university professors and experts of European fame designed factories, bridges, telephone exchanges, and checked the plans of the state planning offices. Hungarian and foreign language technical books, European and American technical magazines, were put at their disposal and, as staff, dozens of young prisoners who were engineers and designers.

The translators translated not only technical works but also political ones not published in Hungarian but of importance to the ÁVH; sometimes we even translated detective novels. Side by side with Winston Churchill's memoirs, we translated crime and espionage stories by Peter Cheyney and others. These served a double purpose. On the one hand, they familiarized junior ÁVH-men with the rotten civilization of the West without their having to take the trouble to go and see for themselves; on the other hand, the espionage stories fertilized the imagination of the authors of show-trials. This is how the truly curious situation arose that variations on fictitious themes became the basic reality of faked depositions and court proceedings; 'reality' of course, only in the excessively liberal, secret police and party interpretation of that word. This does not mean that the ÁVH was unconcerned with a more everyday reality as well. My first job bore witness to the fact.

I was isolated from the other prisoners along with a cell-mate who knew Serbian. We were allowed no contact with the other translators and even our walks—because in the *Kisszálló* we could go for a walk every day—we took alone. Our job was to take excerpts and make an inventory of articles published in the Yugoslav weeklies and dailies, in particular *Borba* and *Politika*. Our table was piled high with neatly-bound volumes, including the 1952 volume then only a few months old. As I knew no Serbian, my work was restricted to correcting and typing my companion's rough translations. Even after our working hours, until far into the night, we would feverishly search through these periodicals, fascinated by the review they presented to us of the past few years. There was abundant comment on works on Stalin and Stalinism published in Yugoslavia and the West, in which excerpts were quoted and there was, to our great amusement, a large number of caricatures and jokes making fun of the Russian dictator.

Only one transparent fact cast a shadow over our amusement. Why should we, of all people, be entrusted with these publications so severely banned in Hungary? Presumably not with the purpose of keeping us informed concerning the course of political developments in the way they kept the experts and scientists of the technical bureau informed of the most recent discoveries in their field, but rather because we were more reliable than any outside translator. We had no opportunity to tell anyone about what we read, we had been sentenced to silence and there was little danger that we should ever again be in a position to open our mouths.

Our future appeared no more promising even when we learned of Stalin's death. In the *Kisszálló*, everything went on as before. In fact things got worse. The distribution of cigarettes became more irregular, then it stopped altogether. And in this prison-paradise, just as in the button-shop, we saw life from the worm's-eye-view of our everyday existence and grew tired of the never-realized prophecies of improvement; so we hit the keys of our typewriters apathetically rather than hopefully. What is more, the effort of typing was becoming increasingly painful to me because, towards my fourth week at the *Kisszálló*, I was beginning to have severe pains in my chest and back.

Without bothering to examine me, the medical orderly pronounced his diagnosis: rheumatism. It seemed a reasonable one, for in the button-shop I had spent the winter close to a broken window, in a strong draught, so that the joints of my fingers and toes had swollen to the size of walnuts. The sergeant gave me aspirin; there was little else he could do, for in the winter of 1952–3 the living sick were not allowed into the prison infirmary; it was open only to the dead.

The arrival of corpses was heralded by security measures. The doors were locked and everyone was ordered to stay put. Wheels sounded in the yard. My companions cautiously pushed open half an inch the window overlooking it and peeped out. A closed, black horse-drawn carriage stood to the right of the building. Some ÁVH-men let down one side of the carriage, climbed in, and with the toe of their boots kicked down two or three naked, emaciated corpses. Fortunately, the victims were no longer in a position to feel embarrassed by the undignified thud with which they hit the ground, nor could they show anger when two hefty prisoners grabbed them by the ankles and dragged them off to the hospital dissecting room.

The year 1953 brought considerable changes. Not only were the still living admitted to the infirmary but outside the prison walls many more important things were happening. A Hungarian Party and government delegation was summoned to Moscow. In addition to Rákosi, Gerö and István Dobi, President of the Praesidium, and a number of highranking Party functionaries, Deputy Premier Imre Nagy was also invited. It is from his memoirs and verbal disclosures that the details of the conference in the Kremlin became known.

The Russian speakers at the conference—Malenkov, Beria, Molotov, Khrushchev, Mikoyan and Kaganovich—stated flatly that Rákosi and his disciples had driven Hungary to the brink of catastrophe; Mikoyan described Rákosi and Gerö's economic measures as 'adventurer politics' while Beria and Khrushchev called for urgent political and personal changes. One result of Moscow's criticism was that Rákosi, although allowed to retain his post as First Secretary of the Communist Party, had to resign the Premiership, which was taken over by Imre Nagy. Thus, with the approval of the Kremlin, Imre Nagy announced his programme on July 4th, 1953, a programme which, apart from being a turning-point in economic, political and cultural fields, set the government the task of restoring legality and individual rights. The new Prime Minister took his programme seriously. On July 26th he issued an amnesty and gradually over 100,000 political internees (Hungary's population did not amount to 10 million in those days) were released from behind the barbed wire fences of the internment camps.

The turn of the political prisoners had not yet arrived. Rákosi was still undisputed master of the Party machinery and the most important arteries of the government offices. Presumably egged on or even supported by a faction of the Moscow political committee, he strove to hinder and often to prevent Imre Nagy's economic measures as well as his political reforms and his proposed release of the prisoners sentenced in the show-trials. A life-and-death struggle began between Mátyás Rákosi and Imre Nagy. We prisoners, of course, knew nothing of all this. We did not even know that the internment camps had been thrown open and an amnesty granted. Using the language of the *Gyüjtö's* gaolers, we still called the cemetery that bordered the prison the 'amnesty-garden' and from there the wind wafted us not news but, in spring, the scent of acacia-blossom and throughout the year, whenever they were burying an eminent party member, the strains of Chopin's funeral march.

But in November, István Lehota made his appearance at the *Kisszálló*, accompanied by a glittering retinue of high-ranking ÁVH officers. It was this same Lehota who had acted as janitor at the villa of the T-shaped table, accompanied the arrested men to the lavatory, and helped, in my case, to fill my mouth with salt. In recognition of which meritorious conduct, he was first appointed commander of the Vác penitentiary, and, then, after Bánkúti's departure, took over the direction of the *Gyüjtö*. Lehota announced that we could write our families a sixteen-line postcard, our relatives would be informed when they could visit us, and, at Christmas, they would be allowed to send us a food parcel.

The ice was broken. My companions were bathed in happiness. For myself, I was somewhat anxious at the idea of visitors because my health was going from bad to worse. I had lost a great deal of weight, my pains increased and I was spending my nights racked with fever, unable to sleep. As I thought that it would badly upset and grieve my mother to see me in this condition, I asked them to send the visiting permit to my brother. I had no knowledge that a short while before my brother, Ferenc, had also been thrown into prison. As head of a large technical enterprise he had been arrested on some fictitious sabotage charge and only after long months of preliminary detention did they suddenly and without any explanation, during Imre Nagy's Premiership, stop proceedings against him.

Our meeting was an exact replica of Leo Tolstoy's description of a prison visit in *Resurrection*–according to him the shame of Czarist Russia. It seems that in Russia this procedure was handed down from the Czars to the Communist dictators, from father to son, one might say, and Hungary adopted it as an achievement of the progressive Soviet prison system. The prisoners and their guards stood in a cage entirely enclosed with wire-netting, while their visitors were drawn up, on the other side of the netting, behind an iron railing, at a distance of four feet from the cage. Everyone tried to bridge the gap by shouting and in the babel of voices it was difficult to make out one another's words. My brother showed me the most recent picture of my son. In the four and a half years since I had last seen him, he had grown into a schoolboy; had we met in the street I would probably not have recognized him. Amidst the earsplitting din I thought wistfully of Tolstoy's Prince Nehludov who, in the sometimes mercifully corrupt Czarist Russia, was able to arrange for a quieter, more intimate tête à tête.

I spent Christmas in the infirmary. Dr. Benedek had been replaced as ÁVH prison doctor by a former dentist, Dr. Ervin Szabó. I was put into No. 14 ward, housing twenty-four patients. Among them were two old generals, an aged social democratic worker and two former Ministers who, like myself, were officially suffering from rheumatism. Three of them were no longer able to sit up or even turn over in bed without help. One of my fellow-rheumatics told me he had been reading a prison library book, a novel translated from the Russian. The action took place in a Soviet health resort and described the latest discovery of Soviet medical science. This was some kind of electric treatment which cured even the most severe rheumatic cases in a few days. Dr. Benedek, who had presumably also read the book, had started using this method. The patients had been undergoing treatment for weeks but unfortunately, there was as yet no sign of improvement.

The treatment was directed by a female staff sergeant whose words of command would have made the most foul-mouthed of troopers blush. At times, the prison infirmary guards would assemble around us and they found the writhing of the electrified old men so wildly entertaining that they would make the stout stoker of the hospital furnace sit on the patients' backs, seize the therapeutic instrument which had a metal roller, and, shaking with laughter, would apply it to the soles of the patients' feet. The reactions varied from helpless giggles to groans of agony. They tried to make me submit to this procedure, but when they increased the voltage I prised myself loose from under the stoker's bottom and stood up. I had not forgotten the electric-shock treatment in the villa of the T-shaped table. The female staff sergeant glared at me:

'All right,' she said like a child whose toy a naughty playmate has broken, 'you'll be sorry for that.'

A few days later Dr. Ervin Szabó walked quickly through our ward. When he reached my bed, the sergeant at his heels stopped him. He pointed to me, 'This man pushed the comrade medical staff sergeant during his treatment.'

Whether Dr. Szabó believed him, I can't say. But he was more afraid of the sergeant and the female staff sergeant than were even the most abject of the prisoners. So, although he could see that every afternoon my temperature was over a 100° Fahrenheit, he tore up my fever chart and had me ejected there and then from the infirmary.

A few weeks later I had to be readmitted. Swellings developed on my back that grew larger all the time. Now, at last, they had me X-rayed. The diagnosis was tuberculosis of the spine. In prison, this diagnosis was more or less equivalent to a death sentence. My head sat awry on my neck, I could scarcely sit or stand and even when I was flat on my back, I was racked with such pains that sleep was impossible. During the night I would count the chimes of the hospital clock and felt lucky when I could snatch thirty minutes' sleep after lunch. The prison infirmary did not rise to the luxury of sedatives apart from such things as aspirin; I was given antibiotics, but at irregular intervals, because the guards had a habit of smuggling out in their high boots, together with the lancets, forceps and scissors belonging to the surgery, any drugs that could be sold on the black market. Yet the more hopeless my situation appeared, the more I resolved to survive, if only to spite them.

It was getting on towards spring when my friend Heltai visited me in the infirmary. He had pretended to be ill and submitted to a highly disagreeable course of injections, just to spend some time with me and my neighbour in the next bed, the old professor of medicine. We still haven't cleared up whether he came to comfort and encourage us or to take a last farewell. But he, too, confirmed the rumours circulating in the wards, that from time to time batches of prisoners were being transported to ÁVH headquarters; and some were even being permitted to see lawyers, because their cases were being reopened.

After a second X-ray examination, my diagnosis was modified: the X-ray picture of my back showed tuberculosis of the ribs only, not of the spine. Cavities of half an inch and one inch were measured on three of my ribs. I listened to the advice of my neighbour, the professor of medicine, rather than to that of the dentist. Following the Professor's instructions, I ate everything they put before me, whether I felt like it or not, and as soon as the weather turned milder, opened the window and exposed my back to the sun. By late spring I had put on a few pounds, found it a little easier to move and the thermometer, although it still indicated a slight fever, did not jump over 100° in the evenings.

Once or twice a month we would straighten out the legs of a couple of our fellow-prisoners – they were not always the aged – and tie up their chins, then the orderlies would grab the corners of the dead prisoner's last sheet and carry him in it down to the dissecting theatre. Meanwhile the others, whether they were able to use their limbs or not, were busy scribbling or dictating to their companions pleas for clemency or for a re-trial. But it was not on these memoranda, whether elegantly or primitively worded, that our fate depended, but solely on the outcome of the battle raging between Mátyás Rákosi and Imre Nagy.

About this time the conflict was nearing its turning point. The

Communist Party had formed a committee of three, designating Imre Nagy, Ernö Gerö amd Mátyás Rákosi as its members. The task of this committee was to consider the case of the political prisoners and decide whether the re-trials should also be extended to those sentenced in the Rajk Affair. Rákosi fought tooth and nail against this extension, for in 1949 he had taken all the credit for the unmasking of Trotskyite traitors and spies. But he was defeated. Ernö Gerö sided with Imre Nagy in favour of the re-trials. It may well be that he did so only in the hope that Rákosi might fall and he would take his place, but he may have received direct orders from his Moscow superiors to side with Nagy. In those days, the directives handed down by the Kremlin to the Hungarian Party leaders were not synchronized; most of the Hungarian leaders were bound by political and personal ties of dependency to a variety of Soviet statesmen or Party factions. Thus, splits in the inner Soviet circles inspired secret intrigue and raised open conflict in the Hungarian Communist Party, too. Whatever the reason, Imre Nagy with Ernö Gerö's help won this round and the re-trials were extended to the Rajk affair. But Rákosi was still on the war-path; whenever and wherever he had found an opportunity to do so, he obstructed and delayed the processes of revision.

'Indeed, it wasn't easy,' Imre Nagy said musingly when, early in 1956, we stood talking while his grandchildren and my son were tobogganing down the slopes of Pasarét.

At the time Nagy said this, Rákosi was again in the saddle; Imre Nagy had not only been forced to resign his Premiership, but had been condemned by the Central Committee of the Communist Party for 'rightist deviation' and Rákosi had succeeded in having him expelled, not merely from the Political Committee but also from the Party. Had all this happened a year and a half earlier, we prisoners would certainly not have been transferred in May, 1954, to the new Fö-Street headquarters of the ÁVH. Because it was in May that our guard entered the ward and spelled my number out from a sheet of paper. '474-D-893,' he said.

We travelled in the coffin. This was the prison nickname for the prison van, the inside of which had been divided into small cubicles that could be locked one by one. In the cubicles we could not stand upright and breathing was difficult. At ÁVH headquarters we were put into dark, but clean, well-ventilated cells, furnished with bed, table and chair, not in the cellar, but on one of the upper floors. Soon I was led before a young ÁVH officer. He introduced himself as Lieutenant Kása, for, miraculously, this time, an ÁVH officer actually introduced himself. He produced my deposition and went through it point by point, asking me what was true and what was not. Later he had me transferred from my cell to a bright room and gave orders that I should receive butter and cheese, in addition to the already by no means stingy diet; within a few days, he produced a new deposition for me.

Sometimes he would support my statements with proof. For instance, he took from a safe photostats of the reports prepared on me in the '30s by the police agents of my home town, the memoranda sent to Budapest by the Szombathely authorities and their letters concerning every move I made. It was with the aid of these documents that Lieutenant Kása refuted the charge that I had been a police spy under Horthy, disproving it even to me, as though, in the course of time, I had come to believe it myself. I remarked that these documents had been in the hands of the ÁVH five years earlier, indeed ever since 1945, and yet they had persisted in trying to prove the contrary. Except for a delicate smile, Lieutenant Kása made no reply, then he declared that he would check my statements but in the meantime would have me taken back to hospital. In a week or two, he would come and see me and would bring with him the completed deposition.

In the prison infirmary I was isolated from the others and not allowed to see any of my companions. Weeks went by, then months; not until the end of August did Lieutenant Kása reappear. He placed a gigantic sheaf of documents before me; I was to read them and if I agreed with the contents, put my name to them. The thick wad of typed pages refuted not only the deposition prepared in the trial and which contained hardly any damning evidence, but also the statements in the *Blue Book* that referred to me. The Lieutenant informed me amicably that in two or three weeks they would hear my case anew, and I could have every confidence in the outcome.

Experience had taught me to expect a wait of several months rather than several weeks, but this time I was mistaken. Although I was not yet brought before the court, a few days after the Lieutenant's visit, several of us were transported to the Fö Street headquarters of the ÁVH. No sooner did we reach the building than they led us into a large room containing a display of new shirts and underwear, suits and shoes. Obeying instructions, we discarded our prison uniform and, wasting little time on selection, dressed quickly from top to toe.

When we were ready Lehota came in. After having been commander of the Vác penitentiary and the *Gyüjtö*, he had now risen to be director of ÁVH headquarters. He handed each of us our discharge papers. Mine, which I brought with me as an amusing souvenir when I left Hungary, states that I was detained on August 31st, 1954 and discharged the following day, on September 1st, 1954. Thus, according to this document, I had spent a single night in ÁVH hands. A long night, it had seemed to me. I did not stop to wonder about the mentality of these confirmed hypocrites, nor about the strange relativity of their notion of time, for soon we were taken before a gloomy individual who said he was the State Prosecutor. He placed a sheet of paper before me, the text of which declared that everything that had happened to me should be regarded as a state secret and that should I reveal any of it, I would render myself liable to ten years imprisonment. I signed the document without hesitation, though never for a moment did I take the threat seriously.

Then, as befits a well-mannered hotel porter, Lehota accompanied us, three at a time, to the ground floor. When we reached the iron gate, he bowed to us and offered his hand. I was not only surprised but also embarrassed by this turn of affairs, though not sufficiently to respond to Lehota's friendly gesture. And yet, this was the moment when the circle was complete. The first day of my prison life, the closing of the first iron door behind my back, was linked with Lehota and so now was the opening of the last iron door.

During those few weeks when the possibility of release was no longer the creation of an overheated brain, I had begun to fear that when, at last, I walked out of prison, I would lose my self-control and be carried away by ridiculous, tearful emotions. I was wrong. All three of us prisoners walked out into the street with almost wooden faces, as if we had just left our club; we exchanged a few commonplace observations and looked around for a taxi. We had to walk quite a distance before we found a cab-rank. Here we took leave of one another. Each of us carried a bundle under one arm, a small bag of granulated sugar, our collection of bits of string and rags, and a few cigarettes.

My bundle, my pallor and ill-fitting clothing immediately made clear to the taxi-driver where I had come from. He asked no questions – I was not the first of the kind he had come across – but started a quiet, friendly conversation. I went to endless trouble before I could get him to accept the fare, one fifth of the wages I had earned during five years of captivity. After taking leave of the friendly taxi-driver, I was held up by an unfriendly, locked door on the fifth floor of the Üllöi Street block of flats. My mother, who had daily awaited my return for five years, had gone to see my brother in the provincial town where he worked.

I stood bewildered in the corridor beside the empty dustbin. And here I was discovered by the tenants. A neighbour ran down to the janitor for a master-key, opened the front door, and I stepped into my mother's room. I politely put my dirty bundle on the floor and sat down in the ancient armchair inherited from my great-grand-parents.

Soon the doorbell rang and at short intervals the neighbours marched in. In antique silver jugs or plain earthenware coffee-pots, they brought for the prisoner they had hardly known, his first snack. For I had arrived home just at coffee-time. In a moment five cups of coffee steamed on the table and the heavenly fragrance of coffee, bread and butter and pastry hovered above the old furniture transforming the room into an oriental paradise.

One of my companions who had walked out of the prison gate with me was luckier than I, for arriving home he was met by his entire family. The other found his wife, and they set out immediately towards the school, to pick up their little girl. As the children streamed out of the building and dispersed noisily, the returned prisoner felt suddenly confused. Zsuzsi had been a little over two years old when her father had been taken away. More than five years had gone by since he had last seen her. The released prisoner glanced irresolutely at the crowd of children, then turned to his wife:

'Which is mine?'

10

The Funeral of an Era

MY taxi-drive home from the prison, my friend's involuntary question, 'Which is mine?', inspired one of the best Hungarian short stories of the last decade, Tibor Déry's 'Love'. Our experiences not only aroused writers and artists, old friends, and vaguely familiar neighbours who received the returning prisoners with deep emotion, but the entire country. There were but few Hungarian families that did not greet in their own homes or in that of their next-door neighbour's, a pale, emaciated denizen of prison or concentration camp, with broken teeth or prematurely bald head. Even in the gloomy offices where we had to pick up our military service papers, work permits or other documents, the hard faces of officialdom relaxed the moment they saw where we had come from. They immediately tried their best to make things easy for us, or at least speed up the often complicated processes of bureaucracy. Friends and strangers alike competed with each other in their solicitude and surrounded the returned prisoners with tender warmth and sympathy.

First, those accused in the Rajk trial were sent to the Kútvölgyi Street sanatorium of the Communist Party for a general check-up. Here, I came across victims of other trials, and in the waiting room of the X-ray department, one day, János Kádár sat down beside me. Of course, I did not know then about the tape-recording of the conversation Kádár, then Minister of the Interior, had had with Rajk, in which he persuaded him to help the Party by accepting false charges. All I knew was that the ravaged man sitting next to me had spent four years in prison.

Kádár did not wait for me to ask questions, he began to talk. Already at the time of the Rajk trial, he said, he was surrounded by a ring of *agents provocateurs* at the Ministry of the Interior. He was keenly aware of this, but could not talk about it, even to his wife; nor did he mention it in the Central Committee, although he realized that the party leaders must have some knowledge he himself did not possess. Thus, up to the moment of his arrest, he had lived through several months of extreme tension. After his arrest, he had been tortured by Gábor Péter's henchmen and then, after being

216

sentenced, he had been sent to the Conti Street prison. This is where, along with others, Cardinal Mindszenty was held captive. The prisoners were not badly treated, they received decent though insufficient food, but most of them, including Kádár himself, spent their time in solitude. It had not taken him long to read and re-read all the books in the modest prison library.

During his captivity, the former Minister of the Interior had written letters, memoranda, petitions, to Rákosi–or, as Kádár said, 'Comrade Rákosi'–in which he tried to clear himself of the charges brought against him. But the ÁVH gaoler had naturally omitted to forward his prisoner's letters. Finally, when Gábor Péter and his accomplices were arrested, one of Kádár's epistles reached Rákosi's desk. At this point, Kádár spoke of the First Secretary of the party with deep gratitude, for it was to Rákosi he owed his release. Upon receiving the letter, Rákosi had immediately taken the necessary steps and had even granted the released prisoner an interview.

'Why didn't you write to me before this, Comrade Kádár?' asked Rákosi, for he, of course, knew nothing of the suppressed memoranda and letters. Then, on learning what had happened, he went off into paroxysms of indignation.

Rákosi questioned his guest about his state of health, recalled his own prison experiences under Horthy, then steered the conversation to the present:

'And what would you like to do now, Comrade Kádár?' he asked.

In his reply, the released prisoner explained that he had only two professions to choose from, for he was competent in nothing else: he could either return to his original trade and become a manual worker, or he could do Party work. Rákosi hastened to reassure him, saying that there could be no question of a man of Kádár's abilities returning to manual work; the party needed him.

This story, told by the ex-prisoner huddled in his hospital gown beside me, was not only surprising; it also furnished food for thought. Was János Kádár the only man in Hungary ignorant of the fact that 'Comrade Stalin's best Hungarian disciple' had been the Budapest director, the puppet-master, of not only the Rajk affair but of all the important show-trials? After all, Rákosi had even boasted of this at the very time when Kádár was Minister of the Interior. Why was Kádár play-acting for my sake? After all, he knew that I too had had an opportunity to look behind the scenes. Why was he trying to make me believe that he attributed responsibility for the innumerable political murders, the inhumanity and torture, to the newly-imprisoned ÁVH officers, Gábor Péter and his men, thus exonerating the still free and active General Secretary of the Party? Whatever the complicity that bound him to Rákosi, I thought, there was absolutely no point in his stressing his loyalty in front of people excluded from the inner party circles, even if he were hoping against hope that one or another of his declarations of love would reach Rákosi's ears by way of gossip or through the network of spies.

An explanation of this dissimulation was not only to be found in fear, but also in Kádár's plans. Though it appeared astounding to me that after what had happened to him he should still wish to get back into the Party organization and eventually into its inner circles, this was just what he was resolved to achieve at any price. For the time being, he was paving his way harmlessly, one might say, making a show of naïve ignorance, unsparing in his efforts to declare loyalty far and wide. After the Hungarian uprising of 1956 *no* price was too high for him to pay to further his career, neither moral depravation, nor mass human sacrifice.

Several victims of the Rajk affair followed Kádár's example, though while still in prison they could find not one redeeming feature for the actions of the Soviet Union or those committed in the People's Democracies. When I asked one of them bluntly why he had accepted a political appointment, he spread his arms wide:

'What can I do? I have neither trade nor profession. I am a professional revolutionary, that's all I'm good for,' he replied, looking at me as if I were upbraiding a taxi-driver for driving his motorcar in case he should knock down some innocent pedestrian.

But this professional revolutionary, at least, did not dissemble except when he was forced to and remained human until he was compelled to become inhuman. The majority of the former prisoners, however, many of whom remained in leading posts even after the revolution, forgot the past with the extreme zeal of new converts as soon as they were readmitted to the inner concentric circles, and were intolerant of any criticism, however private, however mild it might be in comparison to those they themselves had made unceasingly in prison.

The way back was open to nearly every victim of the Rajk affair; most of them were offered their former posts, and later, even higher positions. But my close friends and I refused responsible posts, we dreamt of books, of a quiet desk. We did not regard ourselves as professional revolutionaries. Thus, when the Deputy Minister of Agriculture sent for me and asked me dutifully whether I would again act as head of the press and information department or become editor of a central agricultural journal, I replied with a decisive 'no'. He seemed relieved. The highranking officials were afraid that the very presence of the ex-prisoners might be enough to cause trouble. But I was received with open arms at the publishing house where I undertook the task of editing works translated from the Spanish.

I was not, however, to start work for the time being; the doctors of the Kútvölgyi Street party-hospital sent me first to a sanatorium to have my bone-tuberculosis treated.

The specialist who examined me shook his head doubtfully and wanted to know whether I had been involved in an accident because, in his opinion, the injuries on my ribs were due to fracture, not to tuberculosis. For several weeks I was X-rayed and examined repeatedly, then the specialists assembled for consultation. It was almost flattering to be considered such a curious medical case. I was sent from one hospital to another, until finally I was told not to take any more antibiotics, as there was no need for them. The lesions on my ribs were undoubtedly not caused by tuberculosis but were of a traumatic origin. At some time, haematorrheas had formed around them and these must have caused the painful inflammations, swellings and high temperature; lack of food, faulty diagnosis, inefficient and insufficient medical care, had not, of course, contributed to any improvement in my condition.

The X-ray plates showed the misshapen scars of two rib fractures in my chest and three in my back. One created a particular sensation because, probably as the result of a well-aimed kick, a piece of bone approximately an inch and a half long had been chipped off the rib and from this, in the course of time, had grown a pair of props that joined the two fractured ends, bridging them in viaduct fashion. My doctors were constantly pumping me for details: how had I survived nine days and nights of standing without sleep, food or water? Then, bearing in mind particularly the lack of water, they told me that it was most unseemly that I should have survived at all.

As soon as I left the sanatorium I went to work at the publishing house. It seemed as though I would be allowed to live undisturbed, for not only was I promised a flat and material compensation, but I was also entrusted with the revision of the Reverend Györy's translation of Cervantes, an excellent piece of work when it was published a hundred years ago, but now somewhat antiquated. Thus, while waiting for our re-trial and rehabilitation, I could spend my time, if not in the Hungarian, at least in the Spanish past and with my favourite figure, the ingenuous and noble Don Quijote de la Mancha.

My work and the medical verdict made me happier than the foreseeable outcome of what would probably be merely a formal *in camera* trial.

On the sunny spring morning that it took place, the boredom of the proceedings was relieved to some extent by the testimony of the witnesses. For the court had summoned the former ÁVH officers, Ervin Faludi and Tibor Szamosi, who were now no longer members of the secret police but who had participated in the preparation of the Rajk trial.

Faludi stood arrogantly before the judge's platform. Yes, it had been his job to interrogate one of my fellow-accused and he still did not consider the charges unfounded. Questioned by the presiding judge, József Domokos, Faludi reluctantly admitted that he was basing his statement merely on guesswork, on impressions, and was unable to produce any sort of proof. The former ÁVH officer insisted proudly that he did not feel sorry for what he had done; he had acted as he did to serve the Party, in obedience to the orders of his superiors. More modest and somewhat confused, Szamosi also asserted his party-loyalty and went on to say that when he took over the interrogation of György Heltai, he had believed that certain events proved the guilt of the arrested man. Now, however, he saw how mistaken he had been and expressed his regret.

'How did you prepare Heltai's deposition?' one of the lay judges of the People's Court, Árpád Házi, asked Szamosi.

'I made the prisoner write reports,' Szamosi replied.

'And did you compile the deposition made from them without alteration?'

For a moment, Szamosi did not reply; then he took the plunge.

'Directed by my superiors, I made the prisoner's notes a little more pointed,' he answered.

'What do you mean by "pointed?" Give us an example.'

'For instance,' Szamosi stammered, 'for instance, I recall that Heltai wrote: "I was in contact with the Yugoslav Ambassador Mrazovich and, on the Minister's orders, I told Mrazovich..."' The former ÁVH major fell silent, and only on Árpád Házi's not too amicable prompting did he continue, pausing after each word: 'I left out... "on the Minister's orders..." and put in something else instead.'

'I see. And how did the sentence go after you had put in something else?'

Szamosi's reply came unwillingly, hesitantly:

'I was in espionage contact with the Yugoslav Ambassador and handed him the following information . . .'

'So this is what you call "making the deposition a little more pointed?"'

'That was the term we used, sir.'

Had they asked us, we prisoners could have testified that Szamosi was telling the truth.

When the ÁVH investigators were trying to extract some damning statement from a prisoner of long standing or getting him to implicate someone as yet at liberty, they would always demand a *somewhat pointed*, or *politically slanted* deposition. *Pointed* and *politically slanted* belonged to the most frequently used terms in the ÁVH vocabulary, like *contact*, *essentially* and *realization*. However, Árpád Házi was not interested in investigating Szamosi's veracity.

'I have no more questions,' he said. 'Thank you,' and he made a slight movement, as if he were suddenly brushing something off the sleeve of his jacket.

Although the guard posted at the entrance to the court-room was the sole audience at the *in camera* trial, Szamosi's questioning was followed by a brief period of absolute silence and then a hardly audible commotion, as if the one-time prisoners were making ready to change places–and not merely symbolically–with their ex-gaolers, the ÁVH officers, who were on the defensive like cornered criminals. This situation seemed more amazing, more significant to us than the verdict of 'Not guilty' pronounced soon afterwards.

My interrogator, Colonel Farkas, had not been summoned to attend the trial, though he, too, had removed his ÁVH uniform. For he had been given a higher post than either Faludi or Szamosi: he was organizing secretary at the party headquarters for Greater Budapest and a speaker at numerous mass meetings. I saw his name printed in giant letters on a poster on the wall of the Üllöi Street flats, near my mother's apartment. The party protected Farkas from any kind of interference–all the more easily as it met with no significant resistance in the state administration, where, at the time of our re-trial, the office of Prime Minister had already been taken over from Imre Nagy by András Hegedüs, a great admirer of Rákosi and one of his Party functionaries.

In Hungary, Imre Nagy's defeat was attributed primarily to the fact that even after the criticism voiced in Moscow, Rákosi was allowed to remain master of the party machinery and could prevent the dismissal of its bureaucrats, though everyone knew that they were consistently sabotaging Imre Nagy's programme officially approved in 1953. My one-time interrogator Farkas belonged to Rákosi's close, though perhaps not inner-most circle. So it is understandable that he should have been spared the painful ordeal of our re-trial, though his testimony would have been far more interesting than that of Faludi and Szamosi.

This tactfulness was just as characteristic of the ambivalence in the Hungarian situation as the scornful gesture with which the communist, Árpád Házi, abjured any suggestion of complicity with the one-time ÁVH witness.

Ambivalence did not mean that anyone else, apart from the communists, was in a position to voice an opinion. The ambivalence was within the Communist Party itself where its members were divided. Those released from prison were not intimidated by the Prosecutor's threat of ten years' imprisonment should they talk; with very few exceptions, they talked. And, confronted with the talk by the survivors and the even more eloquent silence of the dead, of the executed, as well as those who perished in prison or were driven to suicide, a large number of hitherto believing and even privileged communists found themselves at the crossroads.

This is how Tamás Aczél and Tibor Méray, two pampered, but now disillusioned writers of the Party, reported on their own reactions as well as those of many of their fellow writers:

> They were ashamed of their stupidity, and of having believed, and of having become the propagators of the most revolting lies. Now they took from their book-shelves the *Blue Book* about the Rajk trial, and they re-read the accusations and the confessions. How transparent and crude it all was!... They were ashamed and they felt that unless they wanted to be sucked in the mire of their lost consciences, they had to do something. (Tamás Aczél and Tibor Méray: *The Revolt of the Mind*; Frederick Praeger Publishers, New York, 1959)

The reactions, the rebellion and the conversion of those communists shaken in their convictions were watched with suspicion by many people in Hungary. To tell the truth, I myself doubted some of them; perhaps only because one is apt to trust other people's sincerity less than one's own. It seems to me natural, and only at first sight contradictory, that the disillusioned were driven into opposition to the Stalinist Party leadership by the same spiritual factors, the same humanitarian passions, that had, once upon a time, made them join the ranks of Stalin's followers, Moscow's political soldiers. Thus, their conversion consisted merely in a return of their sentiments and emotions–after various detours–to their original starting-point.

I say 'sentiments and emotions'. For if we discount those who on the eve of the seizure of power joined the Party as a political investment, offering good prospects for a career, and confine ourselves to the genuine, convinced revolutionaries, we can safely say that the majority had been drawn into the communist camp not so much by sociological considerations or economic arguments, as by their emotions. Certainly emotion came first, and theory second. This was also true of the intellectuals. For many thousands were roused to moral indignation by the Hungary of the '20s amd '30s, by the tragi-comic backwardness of the country's institutions, their cynical injustice; and in the '40s, by the crimes committed by the Hungarian fascists in imitation of their German counterparts. This moral indignation sought and found a form, a system, in Marxist economics and Lenin and Stalin's theory of the State.

But after the release of 100,000 internment camp inmates and the unveiling of the mysteries of the show-trials, it no longer remained a secret, even for numerous communists, that Marxist theory itself had become a pretext in the hands of the Soviet-type Party leadership for revolting acts of immorality. Thus, with a sense of '*déjà vu*', a large proportion of Hungarian Communists found themselves on the same psychological terrain from which they had started; but now moral indignation, aggravated by a feeling of guilt, was directed not against Admiral Horthy's twenty-five-year rule–which compared with the present, seemed almost mildly patriarchal–nor against fascism, which by now had been rendered harmless, but against the Communist Party and communist institutions.

It was by a similar roundabout way that another humanitarian factor–active solidarity with the victims of social inequality–returned to its fountainhead.

In semi-feudal Hungary, left-wing intellectuals had especially identified themselves with the peasants whose lot was comparable with that of the mediaeval serfs, and with the Hungarian workers who, by Western standards, slaved for a miserable pittance; later, when Hungary allied herself with Hitler, many held that the way to demonstrate their concrete solidarity with those cheated of their rights, those persecuted and outlawed, was to join the illegal and persecuted Communist Party.

After 1945, when the Party first became legal and later the governing force of the country, it demanded from its followers, with the rigidity of ideologies which regard themselves as the sole repository of truth, total devotion, absolute and abstract loyalty. Therefore, it prohibited any concrete loyalty, any concrete solidarity that protected individuals, because ready sympathy or a fanatical search for truth might have resulted in a Party-member siding with an enemy of Muscovite communism. After the Rajk-trial, a disciplined communist could no longer remain loyal to his friends, his family, or even to his principles, for the party would accept or reject principles with the same facility with which it would liquidate people, once they had lost their tactical usefulness.

In the fifties, this abstract party loyalty which excluded all concrete solidarity was kept alive, not by faith and devotion alone, but by ever-recurring waves of fear. Fear must have played its part at public party meetings, where children would disown their parents and parents their children, and fear must have taught communists not to maintain contact with the families of arrested persons. They would pretend not to recognize them in the tram and if, by chance, they ran into them in the street, they would quickly cross over to the other side. A woman doctor who had apparently been a good friend of mine for fifteen years, refused to treat my mother, who had always been under her care, when she went to her consulting-room as a patient. She punished my family for my crimes by depriving my mother of medical treatment. During those years of dehumanization such cases were the rule and the honourable exceptions were few.

When the inmates of the internment camps were released and the rehabilitation of those sentenced in the show-trials began, it was the Party itself that allowed free rein to the hitherto prohibited sympathy and solidarity with those who had been undeservedly victimized. Thus, that passion for solidarity which once upon a time had sprung from humane instincts, but had turned inhuman in the mesh of a Party discipline demanding blind faith and abstract loyalty, had once again come into its own. Side by side with the faithful friends came those who had wavered, but who now greeted the released prisoners, and the improvised homes of the men who a short while ago had been branded as spies and traitors became places of pilgrimage.

The monolithic nature of communist ideology and Party indoctrination was chiefly responsible for the fact that the inner struggle of the individual Party members could neither remain passive, nor be restricted to the condemnation of individuals or organizations. For, because of the rigorous logic of the dogmatic thinking process imposed upon them, the disgruntled and the doubting were compelled to question the entire system of Moscow-type Party dictatorship. Thus, responsibility for the waves of doubt that rose higher and higher, rests not merely with communist practice as applied in Hungary, but also with Lenin's blundering attempt to achieve total mastery over men's minds.

After the 1917 seizure of power, Lenin could have rested content with the fact that success had pragmatically justified his Party-theory, for the communist vanguard that captured by storm not only the Winter Palace but also other fortresses of Czarist autocracy had indeed been a well-organized minority. But as new power systems are wont to seek moral justification for their existence and actions, and as Lenin had a deep respect for tradition and was rather conservative in his tastes, he conformed to the historical convention that prescribes self-justification and linked his party-theory which, in fact, canonized purely technical and organizational principles, closely to his moral theories.

Hungarian Party members could read in numerous books and pamphlets referring to Lenin, the bluntly simplified formula: 'Everything that is beneficial to the working-class is moral.' It is, of course, the vanguard of the working-class, the Party, that is called upon to decide what is, or is not beneficial to the working class. Consequently, everything judged useful by the Party is, *ipso facto*, moral.

This dangerous simplification presupposes the absolute and abstract loyalty of the faithful. But when Party members begin to wonder whether or not they can trust the Party leadership, this doubt, according to Lenin's own logic, is not abstractly moral but also practical and political. If Party members feel that their Party transgresses moral law, they must ask the question whether the Party's policies are truly beneficial to the working-class? And conversely: if they do not consider the Party's actions beneficial they must necessarily doubt the Party's moral justification.

When László Rajk and his companions were sentenced, wavering communists could still seek and find comfort in Lenin's moral theory. For, if they did not believe that the Communist Minister had once been a police spy and afterwards the agent of foreign powers, they could calm their consciences by quoting Lenin. I have met people who, at the time of our arrest, reassured themselves by saying that it must obviously be beneficial to the Hungarian and international working-class if Rajk and his group were liquidated, and, as what is beneficial is also moral, it was a matter of indifference whether it was on a basis of true or fictitious charges that this former militant communist was removed, not only from public life, but from life itself.

Following Lenin's thought, therefore, what became fateful for the Party was not, in fact, that it had to admit the innocence of those sentenced in the show-trials, and therefore the immorality of their execution and the assassination of their characters, it had also to confess that the show-trials had injured the cause of the international working-class. This closed the magic circle. The Party had irrevocably condemned itself, it had shaken belief in its infallibility and proclaimed the bankruptcy of Party-theory–of Marxist ideology according to its Soviet interpretation. What was originally purely moral doubt became practical; for anything that once seemed beneficial to the Moscow inner-circles or its Budapest subsidiary might in the future prove harmful in its consequences and therefore, if only therefore, immoral. In the shadow of such possibilities it became problematic for purely selfish reasons, almost out of self-defence, whether it was not dangerous to pledge abstract loyalty to the Party, and share in the responsibility for actions, the *genuine* motives and aims of which are known only to the few initiated, while the ordinary Party members are fed clichés instead of facts. Would not the devoted communist be called to account one day for that very same blind discipline with which he obeyed the orders of the Party leaders? Carefully weighing the personal risks it seemed less dangerous to join the opposition than to follow the Party leaders of the moment through fire and flood.

Thus, the pragmatism which had hitherto served so well, defeated its own ends. Where it had once offered comfort it now bred uneasy tension; its very simplicity which had once offered security to the individual now threatened him with sinister involvement. Suddenly, everything was topsy-turvy. Lenin's theory of the state became for the first time within the Hungarian Communist Party the source of an 'anti-state' trend, and eventually, that same doctrine which had been for decades the mortar that held the bricks of the Soviet empire together was between 1954 and 1956 transformed in Budapest by the chemical effect of events, into an explosive.

In Hungary, as well as abroad, outsiders noted with some malice but at the same time with sceptical indifference the pangs of conscience and the inner struggles engendered by the Rajk-affair in certain Hungarian communist circles. To them, Rákosi, Imre Nagy, and the disillusioned intellectuals were simply communists, birds of the same feather. They did not realize that the simultaneous admission of the immorality and harmfulness of the show-trials was not only arousing abstract moral doubt but, as things were in Hungary, was bound by the very logic inherent in the doctrine to have practical consequences, too. They did not take into account that once confidence in the party and in the party leaders was shaken and the theory began to act in reverse, part of the former revolutionary force that had for long formed the conservative and monolithic Stalinist organization, again became destructive, revolutionary, but this time the rebellion was within the party, and directed against the Party, whose cohesion on the national and international scale alike had significantly decreased since Stalin's death.

Had the Hungarian Communist Party remained united, the dictatorship could have only been overthrown by foreign armies, never by the unarmed, anti-communist forces within the country. All the more so, as these considered themselves politically unarmed, for before 1956, no-one had a chance to engage in any public or political activity, even in the most mildly euphemistic sense of the word, except communists, and even they only within the Communist Party.

Hence the far-reaching consequence that in a Hungary inert with fear, it was precisely the communists, disappointed in their expectations and cheated in their blind faith, who formed the most militant opposition to Mátyás Rákosi and his followers. At more and more Party meetings, and ever more openly, the question was asked; what did Rákosi do in those 'sleepless nights', when, as he rhetorically explained, he was busy unmasking Imperialist spies?

In the eyes of the Party opposition the concept of Stalinism was identified with 'Comrade Stalin's best Hungarian disciple' and exemplified most strikingly and unequivocally by László Rajk's show-trial. More fuel for the fire was provided by the fact that though the survivors of the show-trial had been released and the charges against them declared false, Rákosi still showed himself unwilling to rehabilitate the principal accused: Rajk. Only in November, 1955, at Moscow's bidding, was he compelled to retract the slanderous accusations against the Yugoslavs that he had for years reiterated and, following this withdrawal, the allegation that

Rajk had been Tito's agent. To justify Rajk's execution, Rákosi still maintained that he had been a spy of the Horthy police. Though Rákosi was merely fanning the flames with these prevarications, it was neither the general mood of disgust, nor the opinions voiced in the Party organizations, but once again Moscow's warning that forced him to yield to the opposition's wishes and rehabilitate Rajk.

It was not even in Budapest but in a small provincial town, Eger, that he finally declared in off-hand fashion, though in a very carefully thought out speech, that:

> After the unmasking of the Imperialist agent Beria, as well as Gábor Péter and his gang in Hungary we have, on the initiative of our party's leaders, re-examined the Rajk case. It has been established that the Rajk-trial was based on provocation. Therefore, on the basis of a resolution passed by the Central Committee, Comrade László Rajk as well as other comrades has been rehabilitated. (*Szabad Nép*, March 29th, 1956)

Thus Rákosi spoke of Rajk as 'Comrade Rajk' and shifted the entire responsibility for the show-trial on the dead Beria and the imprisoned Gábor Péter. But these tactics failed to achieve their aim. So much so that when, after his Eger speech, the First Secretary put in an appearance at a Party rally in Angyalföld, one of Budapest's most populous proletarian districts, a young secondary-school teacher stepped up on the platform and told Rákosi to his face that the people had lost confidence in him and that he should therefore retire from public life. Although the Party's Central Committee did not voice such a demand, several members of the Committee were of the opinion that Rákosi should make a public confession of his mistakes.

The First Secretary's almost pitiful cowering roused no sympathy. On the contrary, public opposition to him was becoming increasingly evident. Theatre and cinema-goers reacted to every work referring to violence or political murder as if it alluded to Rákosi; to them Rákosi was Richard III, and Rajk Lord Hastings, Rákosi was Macbeth and Rajk the murdered Duncan. Night after night, the audience in the National Theatre would interrupt the performance whenever any lines could be interpreted as an allusion to the contemporary political situation with loud cheers and stormy applause.

It was in such an atmosphere that Imre Nagy's adherents celebrated the 60th birthday of the ex-Prime Minister who had been expelled from the Communist Party on June 19th, and who was becoming increasingly popular throughout the country. On June 27th, some 6,000 persons attended the press and literary debate arranged by the Petöfi Circle. A large part of the audience, unable to get into the crowded hall, listened to the speeches relayed over loudspeakers. The meeting loudly and openly acclaimed Imre Nagy and demanded his return to political life.

Next day the Poznan revolt broke out in Poland. Rákosi promptly used this as a pretext for counter-attack. He denounced the debates of the Petöfi Circle as an anti-party movement, prohibited their continuation, expelled from the Party several of the speakers in the Petöfi debate and prepared to throw the ÁVH once more into the battle. It became general knowledge in Budapest that Rákosi had a list of the 400 most dangerous members of the opposition, so that they could be arrested. But this time, intending to proceed more cautiously than in the Rajk affair, in order to gain approval for his plan, he summoned the Central Committee for July 18th. This meeting of the Hungarian Party leaders was honoured by an unexpected guest, Anastas Mikoyan, who not only rejected Rákosi's plan but conveyed the Kremlin's emphatic advice that 'Comrade Stalin's best Hungarian disciple' should resign from his office as First Secretary of the Party.

Although Moscow's political line had again stiffened after the melting smiles at Geneva, the XX Congress, and Khrushchev's denunciation of Stalin and Stalinism, the Soviet leaders had learned a lesson from the Poznan events, and they had no wish to provoke similar occurrences in Budapest. Therefore they thought it more expedient to remove the bone of contention: Rákosi. They replaced him by Ernö Gerö, another of their trusted men, a former International instructor and an NKVD agent in the Spanish civil war.

But when Moscow placed Gerö at the centre of the Hungarian concentric circles, the centrifugal movement had increased in volume and speed to such an extent that it not only endangered but disrupted the entire system of magnetic cohesion. This break-up affected not only the outer and middle party circles but also the state organization and the ÁVH itself.

Within the Party there had developed a strange multi-party system. The monolithic organization of the Hungarian Workers' Party had split into three principal groups. Though the dividing line between them was initially somewhat blurred and their constituent elements fluctuated, the three different trends were becoming increasingly clear.

The first group, that of the Stalinists, consisted of Rákosi's devoted followers, and also those who considered Rákosi's person a handicap and would have liked to get rid of him, in the interest of the preservation of the Stalinist policies.

The numerically strongest group was made up of Imre Nagy's followers, including a great number of former political prisoners. One wing of this group strove for the realization of socialism, trying to reach back to some nostalgically remembered 'democratic Leninist tradition' which in reality had never existed. What they wanted was a democratic, or at least more democratic, socialism that from the communist view-point would be to some extent traditional. The other, larger, wing of Imre Nagy's followers insisted, equally in the interests of socialism, on the application of exclusively democratic methods. They desired what might be called a socialist democracy; a system in which a plurality of opinions could not merely be voiced but could also become a political force; that is, a system which would not try to force salvation upon the majority according to the wishes and views of a minority.

Both wings of Imre Nagy's group–the partisans of a more democratic socialism as well as the partisans of socialist democracy– wished to put an end to Hungary's colonial dependence on the Soviet Union with due regard, of course, to the proximity, the interests and the hysterical security-complex of their big neighbour.

The third principal group in the party was the 'middle-of-the-road' group. It consisted mainly of higher functionaries in the party and state administration. They were in favour of reforms, but their main consideration was the maintenance of Party Peace, of Party unity.

The leading personalities of the various groups would often confer together on concrete matters–at Party Headquarters, at the state office or organizations–in the customary manner of parliamentary parties. The leaders of the Hungarian Workers' Party not only admitted the existence of an opposition, but attempted to neutralize it, no longer by intimidation but by means of bargaining, enticement and bribes. Even minor members of the opposition were offered appointments as Ministers or Deputy-Ministers.

In practically every Communist Party there is more or less a permanent secret struggle for leadership between factions. There have been numerous splits in Communist Parties, but there is no precedent for such an open disintegration of an almost parliamentary character.

So strange a situation could never have arisen during Stalin's lifetime, when the ÁVH was at the peak of its power. For then the secret police would not only have prevented such divisions, but would have nipped in the bud any heretical utterances or other preliminaries to dissolution. Thus, if, objectively, we review events from 1954 to 1956, we must come to the conclusion that a popular uprising would hardly have been possible in Hungary in October 1956, had not the party within the party, i.e. the ÁVH, begun to totter.

The position of the ÁVH, which appeared solid as a rock, was shaken not by Gábor Péter's arrest but by Stalin's death. The reins of the Soviet Party and the Soviet secret police were no longer in the hands of a single dictator, but were instead the object of a struggle for power, splitting the innermost circle of the Kremlin, and this jammed or even cut off the Moscow transmission lines to Gábor Péter's successors.

The break-up of the ÁVH's unity and power meant, in effect, the end of the system called 'dictatorship of the proletariat', whose prerequisite in the Hungary of those days had been the dictatorship of the party within the party, i.e. the secret police, fed by direct transmissions from Moscow's sources of energy. Therefore, in 1956, both wings of Imre Nagy's followers felt justified in hoping that there were good prospects for the introduction of either a socialist democracy or a more democratic socialist government.

At the outset, only a politically well informed inner opposition, familiar with the mechanism of Party and state organization, was in any position to struggle against autocracy. But as the dictatorship of the secret police became gradually weakened, political forces, rapidly gaining in weight and scope, began to make themselves felt throughout the country. Then, as Miklós Molnár and László Nagy remarked when analysing the role of the inner-party opposition:

> In the period following Rákosi's fall and preceding the revolution it is no longer the inner-party opposition that stands at the helm of the movement but rather it is the constantly swelling revolutionary flood that carries with it the opposition and Imre Nagy himself.*

Imre Nagy, together with that wing of his group which remained faithful to Communist tradition, could easily have been by-passed

* Miklós Molnár, László Nagy: *Imre Nagy, réformateur ou revolutionnaire?* Publications de l'Institut Universitaire de Hautes Etudes Internationales, No. 33, 1959.

by the revolutionary surge. If this did not happen, it was because those of Imre Nagy's followers who desired a socialist democracy and those democratic groups outside the Communist Party were drifting together and the outlines of some sort of national united front were beginning to take shape.

Political unity—whether we consider mass movements or the lessons taught by hundreds of years of state alliances—comes into being almost invariably in the pursuit of negative aims: not for, but against something. And when this negative aim is accomplished, unity is generally shattered, as for instance when the anti-Hitler alliance was dissolved. One is justified in supposing that the same fate would also have overtaken the united front created in Hungary by the end of October 1956; but, difficult as it would be to specify its conflicting and dividing elements, its negative aims are clear and simple. For however we formulate it, there can be no doubt that it was directed against the iron-fisted policy and Soviet-type communism, and the Russian colonial rule so closely bound up with it.

Even Imre Nagy, himself, who had no wish to break with Moscow and intended to wage his battle within the Party, came out, in his essays, against the bloc-policy. What he wanted to ensure was Hungary's independence and right to self-determination in the spirit of the Bandung treaty and in addition, in case of an armed conflict between the Big Powers, his country's neutrality. His followers, and also men of various shades of political opinion in the emerging united front, conceived any change in Soviet-Hungarian relations partly along Imre Nagy's lines, partly in more radical form; and their ideas, too, were a mixture of day-dreams and realistic political considerations. But everyone, with the exception of the hardened Stalinists and those persons directly responsible for police brutality, wanted to see an end to rule by terror, the dictatorship of the secret police and the show-trials.

At first, the non-Party people, that is, the majority of the population, regarded the Rajk case as an internal affair of the Communist Party. They watched the struggle, the defeats and minor victories of the Party-opposition fighting for Rajk's rehabilitation with suspicion and indifference. But the suspicions cherished by the indifferent and by the doubters of every shade of opinion lessened considerably when it became clear that Rákosi's fall and the weakening of the ÁVH were due, in no small degree, to the Rajk trial and to the movement which, particularly in its early stages, sprang from the pangs of conscience caused by the Rajk affair.

Before long, the execution of the former Minister of Foreign

Affairs became, independently of his person and actions, a symbol; the symbol of the draconic sentences passed on innumerable Hungarians of various party affiliations, and of secret political assassinations in general. Therefore, in the eyes of the people, Rajk's rehabilitation and solemn funeral set the seal on the ÁVH's downfall. And because even those who did not cherish the memory of the former Minister of the Interior also wished to witness this momentous event, Rajk's funeral broadened into the first, mighty though unorganized, open-air demonstration of the united October front, and the silent threat that came from the hundreds of thousands who filed past prophesied the events of October 23rd, 1956, with all their lights and shadows.

On October 1st, 1956, a hunt was arranged in the Crimea in honour of an eminent guest, the Yugoslav Head of State. Moscow spared no efforts in its zeal to pacify Marshal Tito and settle the Yugoslav-Hungarian dispute for, since the slanderous statements voiced in the Rajk trial, tension between Belgrade and Budapest had not relaxed, in spite of Rákosi's fall. Therefore, the Soviet statesmen summoned Ernö Gerö to the Crimea in order to give the new First Secretary of the Hungarian Party a semi-official opportunity to break the ice.

After Gerö's return home, and presumably as one result of the Crimean conversations, it was announced that the funeral of László Rajk and of his three companions executed along with him – György Pálffy, Tibor Szönyi and András Szalai – would take place on October 6th. Until then the Hungarian Party leaders had not only repeatedly postponed the date of the funeral but had haggled like hawkers with the widows of the victims, principally Julia Rajk. After the Crimean negotiations however, they had to give in. They abandoned the idea of burying Rajk in secret. Though on the very eve of the funeral, they were still wrangling as to who should pronounce the valedictory address at the grave of the rehabilitated victims. Julia Rajk had insisted that not only party representatives should make official speeches, but that one of Rajk's fellow-accused should also be allowed to say a few words. As it happened, Julia Rajk asked me to perform this service. Not that I had been among László Rajk's close friends or collaborators; but because at the time of the trial, circumstances and – as it had turned out – my fortunate impulses had saved me from becoming the tool, the stage property of those producing the play, and so from appearing publicly as a witness against Rajk.

The day before the funeral, late in the afternoon, Károly Kiss summoned me to Party Headquarters, obligingly sending his car to fetch me. Kiss belonged to that wing of the Stalinist faction which, though for personal and tactical reasons it had tried to rid itself of Rákosi, feared any change that might endanger its own position. He looked upon the rehabilitated prisoners with suspicion and dislike, especially in my case, for I had only recently refused the proffered post of Deputy-Minister of Public Culture, declaring that neither my principles nor my moral outlook allowed me to collaborate with the government. Thus, I was not in the least surprised when Kiss informed me with obvious hostility of the Central Committee's resolution that I was not to stand by Rajk's coffin as his fellow-accused but only as a former fellow-student, and even then, only if I previously submitted the text of my speech to the party for approval.

The functionaries arranging the funeral were evidently aware that I would not agree to censorship and made this condition as a pretext to break the agreement they had already made with Julia Rajk. I reassured Kiss that, although I saw through his game, he would not have to use force to remove me from the speaker's platform, all the more so as I did not particularly relish the company I would have to keep. Censorship was quite unacceptable to me; I was sorry about this for one reason only, it prevented me from fulfilling Julia Rajk's wishes. Whereupon I walked out of Party Headquarters without taking advantage of Kiss's repeated offer to have me driven home.

As the prospect of any sort of public appearance always gave me cold feet and as–I must admit–I didn't trust even those who perhaps deserved trust, I felt almost relieved that I would not have to breathe the same air with the official speakers. So I registered and dismissed the machinations of the Party leaders with the shrug of a man to whom no foxy trick comes as a surprise. Not so Julia Rajk.

Ever since her own release from prison, she had fought with a determination, an energy and a fortitude that would put any man to shame, to see justice done to her dead husband and her son, young László Rajk. Her actions were not inspired by political motives, nor did she wish to attract attention or fill the role of a public figure. She was driven by her passionate human sympathy for a real human being, the sympathy that had once led her, too, to the Communist Party, and from which she, too, had been long debarred by that same Communist Party. So, she refused to submit to the Party's decision that her husband's fellow-prisoners should stand mute beside the coffins. She telephoned Károly Kiss late in the evening and enlightened him as to the basic ethical principles involved in keeping one's word. Although Károly Kiss, cornered as he was, dared not take responsibility for an independent decision, Julia Rajk would not be put off and finally she got her way. Next day, a few minutes before the beginning of the ceremony, I was approached by Ferenc Mezö, a Central Committee member belonging to the pro-Imre Nagy wing of the middle-of-the-road group, who informed me amicably, but officially, that the Central Committee no longer objected to my speaking and would not insist on censoring the text.

The coffins of László Rajk, György Pálffy, Tibor Szönyi and András Szalai stood on a dais in the cemetery of Kerepes in front of the Mausoleum built for Lajos Kossuth, leader of the 1848-9 Hungarian War of Independence. The wind tore wildly at the flames of the giant candelabra standing beside the coffins and made the long, narrow pennants on their tall poles crack like whips; as, once upon a time, the leather belts of our guards used to crack on our bare backs. Low dark clouds thickened overhead; from time to time, if only for a second, the sun would shoot a slender ray through the murk, like a bright, sharp knife striking the ground. Soon, it began to drizzle; the flames of the candelabra smoked and sizzled but burned on.

It was against this almost theatrical and unreal background of light, shadow and sound, that the survivors of the show-trial stood as a guard of honour round the coffins of their executed fellow-prisoners. Many of them would have shrunk back in disgust had they known who would, after a while, take their place. For one after another, the state and Party leaders of the Stalinist era, those directly or indirectly responsible for the political murders and man-hunts, took their place beside the coffins. Only Mátyás Rákosi and Gábor Péter were missing. But even without them, the nightmarish tension and the procession of stiff-faced criminals and their henchmen, pretending to mourn their victims, suggested the sinister phantasmagoria of a Shakespearean tragedy.

While the invited guests inside the rope-barrier and military cordon were at once bound together and split asunder by such ambivalent attractions and revulsions, the uninvited mass beyond the barrier seemed all the more united. For, although in obedience to the confidential orders of Party headquarters, numerous Party secretaries and functionaries of various districts had done their best to dissuade the flocks entrusted to their care from attending the funeral, approximately a quarter of a million people filed past the coffins.

In a political situation so full of contradictions the editor did not prevent the reporter of the official party organ from describing what he had witnessed. And, this is what we read in the first-page report, published in *Szabad Nép* on October 7th:

> Workers, in blue overalls, holding in their hands their square little lunch-boxes—as they had come out of the factory. Students, boys, girls, in groups of threes and fours, with brief-cases. Soldiers, civilians, with crepe bands on their sleeves. Children, leaving their games, cling, moved, to the hands of their mothers. I am looking at a little boy—he is standing beside his father's coffin—he, too, is holding his mother's hand. László Rajk junior, eight years old, who was still an infant when his father was dragged to the scaffold and his mother to prison ... A stormy autumn wind chases the low-lying clouds, a cold, prickly rain falls unceasingly—but I see no umbrellas. They come, their heads bared ... thousands march up, their eyes glued to the coffins, without uttering a word, a sound; only the eyes are glowing, only the faces stony ... It is not only mourning that silences the people before those coffins, but also passionate hatred ...'

The reporter must presumably have noticed, though he was not allowed to say so, the innumerable plain-clothes ÁVH-men in the silent procession. But they found no employment in this dignified mass demonstration, other than to master their own fears.

At three o'clock in the afternoon, Antal Apró, member of the Political Committee, deputy chairman of the Council of Ministers, stepped on to the speaker's platform. He was followed by Ferenc Münnich, then Károly Janza, deputy Minister of Defence, then myself and finally László Orbán, head of the Party's propaganda section.

Apró promised that the perpetrators of the 'shameful illegalities' would be called to account for their deeds. 'Before the grave of our comrades,' he said, 'we swear in the name of all communists that, learning from the mistakes of the past, we shall do our utmost that outrages like those to which our dear comrades fell victim, shall never occur again.'

Yet, this same gentleman who spoke with such eloquence at the

grave of the executed Rajk, a few weeks later, after the collapse of
the revolution, demanded that Kádár should carry out even more
mass-executions by rope and firing-squad, without trial or verdict.
Nor does it emerge from his subsequent words and actions that he
considered it a 'shameful illegality' when Imre Nagy and his companions, who left the Yugoslav legation with Kádár's guarantee of
safe-conduct, were dragged secretly to the gallows in an unknown
place, by unknown persons of unknown nationality.

But while Apró was still making promises 'in the name of all
Hungarian communists' that such 'outrages' would never occur
again, he went on to say:

> Many are asking themselves: what guarantee do we have
> that illegalities, offences against the law such as these, will
> never again take place in the future?–It is a justified question.
> It is a question to which we are obliged to give our people an
> answer. The guarantee is the party. We, communists are the
> guarantee.

The other speakers also referred to the Party, the communists, as
sureties that–as Ferenc Münnich, first Minister of the Interior in
the Kádár government after the revolution, and later Prime Minister
put it:

> Leninist democracy should prevail most deeply in our party,
> so that socialist democracy be unshakably strong in our country,
> and socialist humanism, legality, and everything else pointed
> out by the XX Congress of the Communist Party of the Soviet
> Union in its epoch-making work.

In his funeral speech bidding farewell to Pálffy, Károly Janza,
Deputy-Minister of Defence, also declared that events such as these
that had taken place in the past, would never again happen, 'this is
guaranteed by the all-powerful will and ability to act of the communists'. According to Orbán, the unmasking of the 'base accusations'
of the show-trial had benefited the communists: 'It has made our
Party not weaker but stronger, for by revealing the truth, the Party
has, at the same time, removed a blemish from its reputation. And
now,' Orbán added, pointing theatrically towards the children of the
victims 'they are no longer orphans. The great family of communists
enfolds them in its embrace. In place of their fathers, the Party will
be their father.'

Side by side with such funeral orations, it was not so much what I
said in my brief speech that drew attention, as what I did not say.

For everyone understood what it meant that in my speech there was not a single word about the Communist Party or about that socialism which, in the eyes of the Hungarian people, was equivalent to Moscow-type dictatorship. Not only the ears of the Party leaders were sensitive to this omission, but also the ears of those who remained aloof from politics. Thus, the rejection of the Communist liturgy appeared a challenge, and it was because of this challenge that after the revolution, the commander of the Hungarian armed forces declared that Géza Losonczy and I had planned the outbreak of the revolution for October 6th. And yet, all I said after a few introductory words was:

> Trumped-up charges, the gallows, threw László Rajk into an unmarked grave for seven years but today his death looms like a warning symbol before the Hungarian people and the world. For when thousand upon thousand pass before these coffins, it is not only to pay the victims the last honours; it is their passionate desire, their irrevocable resolution to bury an epoch; to bury, for ever, lawlessness, tyranny, the Hungarian disciples of iron-fisted rule: the moral dead of the shameful years.

Apart from many of those absent and not a few members of the guard of honour, several of the speakers could safely take the appellation 'moral dead' as meant for them. And the anomaly of their position was further increased by the fact that they referred to the Hungarian Communist Party, not only morally but now almost physically defunct, as if it were still at the peak of its limitless power. Yet on October 6th, it was clear to the quarter of a million demonstrators attending the funeral, indeed to the entire country, that those very acts of terrorism which in the past had been intended to demonstrate the unity and *jus gladii* of the Party had, in their ultimate consequences, practically atomized this organization.

After the funeral orations, each of the four coffins was hoisted on to the shoulders of four pall-bearers. Four colonels walked before them, carrying the medals of the executed victims on four velvet cushions. Soon, the new graves disappeared under mountains of flowers. On the wreath laid by the fellow-prisoners, a streamer bearing a few short words fluttered in the wind, the same words I had in conclusion shouted into the microphone: 'We shall not forget!'

For a brief moment, the cracking of the salvoes rose above the whistling of the wind, the whipping of the flags, the sizzling of the candle flames. The ceremony was over, but a close ring of men and women still surrounded the graves. It was not only from human sympathy; it was also a political demonstration as if, by their very presence, they were casting their vote. Thus, though the executioners had carried out the death sentences pronounced at László Rajk's trial, the victims did not serve the grotesque secondary sentences pronounced on them: loss of office and loss of their political rights for ten years. On the contrary, hardly seven years later, they filled higher public office in their graves than they would have done had they never been sentenced, never been executed. They had become the promoters, the symbolic unifiers of a political movement that led to the landslide of the 1956 popular uprising. Yet, had they lived, perhaps one or other of them might have bitterly opposed such a revolution.

Thus, with a salute of guns, László Rajk's rehabilitation was completed, but that of the hundreds of thousands marching in demonstration – and of those not yet marching – had only just begun.

Postscript

WERE I richer in erudition, were I not afraid that the subject might dry up my sense of humour, I should, perhaps, by way of experiment, attempt to write the history of mankind as a succession of show-trials. I would reach back to the show-trials of Socrates of Athens and Jesus of Nazareth and then describe, over the centuries, their less exalted kin; to establish, in the end, not without some malice, that in their ultimate consequence nearly all show-trials have proved failures and have led to results sharply conflicting with the intentions of those who staged them.

László Rajk's case is no exception. As far as international relations are concerned, Stalin intended the Budapest trial to be one of his victorious battles in the crusade against Tito. Its purpose was first to blacken, then to liquidate, the Yugoslav heretics and prove that only one road leads to socialism: the Stalinist one. A few years later, the false charges brought in this and similar trials made an important contribution to the moral justification of revisionism by helping to persuade both communists and fellow-travellers that socialism can perhaps be achieved in many ways, but not the Stalinist way, not by Stalinist methods.

From the Hungarian uprising, Moscow could draw two conflicting lessons. On the one hand, that the rigid Stalinist pattern of party and state management was in urgent need of revision, and on the other, that while the immediate consequences of disruption in a satellite secret police force–a provincial Party within the Party–might mean the overthrow of the local communist dictatorship, the chain-reaction of the explosion could endanger Moscow's entire field of power.

Realizing the need for revision, Stalin's successors strive by persecuting other revisionists, to keep for themselves the monopoly of revisionism. However, without endangering the existence of socialism as interpreted by Moscow, that is, the totalitarian dictatorship of a bureaucratic caste, tactical, economic and cultural concessions cannot go beyond the point at which they would threaten the power of the political police.

Though the Moscow leaders may harbour no intention of removing undesirable persons or groups by means of show-trials, the political police must at all times be strong enough to put on a show-trial if required.

Therefore, if we do not hear of spectacular court cases or mass-arrests, and if disgraced politicians may, for the time being, collect stamps as a pastime, this does not entitle us to assume that hundreds of human lives may not be sacrificed on some political altar in the near future. For the show-trials were no more than symptoms of the hectic functioning of Stalinist leadership, and from the partial or temporary absence of these symptoms, we cannot presume a change in the essence of Moscow dictatorship, that is, in the function of the political police.

As far as the post-1956 Hungary is concerned, János Kádár's government differs in numerous, by no means unimportant, respects from Mátyás Rákosi's government. But as early as November 1956, the Russian MVD experts, sent to Hungary with the second Russian interventionist wave, built up a Hungarian secret police organization exactly similar to that functioning in Stalinist times.

On November 29th, 1956, Imre Nagy's coalition government officially the ÁVH. Thus, after the crushing of the Hungarian revolution on November 4th, 1956, the functions of the political police were taken over by the MVD itself. During the month of November, it was Russians who arrested and Russians who interrogated; the Hungarians served only as interpreters. It was for such auxiliary tasks in the service of the MVD, that several high-ranking Hungarian Muscovites, who had fled to the Soviet Union at the end of October and in early November, were sent back home. After the revolution, the MVD set to work to create a new Hungarian political police, a Party within the Party, from elements loyal to Moscow, with a view to restoring gradually the direct Moscow-Budapest transmission and chain of command that had been completely disrupted by the popular uprising. The former officers and investigators of the ÁVH emerged from their hiding-places. They again formed the backbone of the new political police, together with members of a few armed police detachments who had fled to the mountains of Buda and those communists who had joined the Russian armies as stooges and guides.

In many respects it seemed as though everything was starting all over again. All the more so, as at the conferences of the Communist Party numerous speakers demanded a revision of the revision of the Rajk case. They regarded the suspicion that the rehabilitated prisoners had been the agents of foreign powers as well-founded, for after all, 'they prepared, sparked off, and directed the counter-revolution'. Mátyás Rákosi's followers were particularly voluble on this subject, hoping through nullification of the rehabilitations, to rehabilitate Mátyás Rákosi and, along with him, Stalinism in Hungary.

Rákosi's reappearance would have been against the interests of the new First Secretary, János Kádár. At the same time, he could not do without the Hungarian Stalinist bureaucrats, who were the first to join the new Communist Party, gravely short of manpower and faced with great organizational problems. They soon occupied important Party and state positions and continued to apply their old methods. An article published in the official Party organ under the title 'Close-up of five nameless false witnesses', which reiterated and even added to the charges brought against me in the Rajk trial, was also simply another manifestation of the old Stalinist practice.

In Budapest this article was intended as a reply to the report prepared by the UNO Special Committee on the Hungarian revolution and the events following the revolution, submitted to the General Assembly on September 10th, 1957. The Party organ picked five persons whom the Budapest authorities suspected of having testified before the Special Committee. Of each of these *Népszabadság* published a police photograph, their personal details and criminal record. We were described as fascists, terrorists and foreign agents. The paper did not even attempt to refute the evidence collected by the Special Committee, for this was well-known in Hungary and hundreds of thousands of Hungarians could have testified to its truth; it only sought to disprove the report by throwing doubt on the credibility of the supposed witnesses.

'Béla Szász'–*Népszabadság* wrote of me–'has been in close contact with the British espionage organization, the Intelligence Service, and has been working for the British espionage organization from 1941 until today. Béla Szász, who returned to Hungary from the Argentine as an agent of the Intelligence Service was sentenced by the Court for espionage to ten years imprisonment as a primary punishment, and to the loss of his political rights for ten years and confiscation of all property as secondary punishments. In the course of the investigation and the trial Béla Szász pleaded guilty and confessed that as an agent of the British espionage organization he had forwarded vital information on Hungary's political, economic and military situation. (*Népszabadság*, September 15th, 1957)

Not even the Public Prosecutor's indictment had contained the accusation that I had 'forwarded vital information on Hungary's political, economic and military situation', thus I could not have admitted any such thing at the secret trial; but even had I done so, the People's Court had found the charges false and had rehabilitated me. This is what the Western press pointed out, and the *Neue Zürcher Zeitung* added that in so far as Budapest was again reaching back to slanderous accusations already retracted in the Rákosi era,

> the present wielders of power in Hungary are doing their utmost to maintain the charges voiced in the Rajk trial. Presumably because the present Prime Minister, Kádár, who was then Minister of the Interior, played an important part in the proceedings. (*Neue Zürcher Zeitung*, September 22nd, 1957)

Thereupon the Hungarian Legation in Berne wrote a long letter to the *Neue Zürcher Zeitung*, asking it to publish its statement that the 'Revolutionary Worker-Peasant Government of the Hungarian People's Republic' had already made clear its attitude concerning the illegalities committed in the Rajk affair and this attitude had not changed since. In its reply, the Swiss newspaper pointed to the clumsy propaganda-trick which Budapest had employed instead of trying to refute the facts contained in the UN report. (*Neue Zürcher Zeitung*, September 29th, 1957).

I do not believe that either János Kádár or the then Minister of the Interior, Ferenc Münnich, were behind the heavy-handed blunders in *Népszabadság*; I rather think the article sprang from some sort of Stalinist guerilla-activity, some disdainful flouting of the people's memory. But the article in the Party-bulletin, which described me as a doubtful witness, quoting in support of this the very same accusations which this same Party organ had once rejected as false, strengthened my conviction that I cannot remain silent on the way in which the totally false confessions were manufactured in the workshops of the Russian and Hungarian secret police.

Still less can I remain silent as, by recalling the deeds of the Party within the Party and the consequences of these deeds, I am not only recording past events but may forecast also the eventual future. For in Moscow's inner and outer magnetic fields – with or without show-trials, with open or hidden violence, the battle waged by autocracy through its political police against whole populations is still going on, as it has done for decades. On the other hand, apparently, the majority of the Russian leaders have come to realize that some reform in method, even at least a partial break with the past, is inevitable. It is doubtful whether they can–time and again glancing back to Stalin–stop halfway in their conservative reformism, whether they will lose their equilibrium in one or other of their veerings. These questions arise all the more sharply as any kind of relaxation of dictatorship strengthens the voices of those hitherto condemned to silence. Not only Russian intellectuals and many of the specialists are filled with a passionate desire for change but the same wish, as a political undercurrent, also drives the apparently inert masses of the Soviet empire towards political activity. They long ago realized that, historically, Stalanist socialism is more closely related to the day before yesterday than to yesterday. What it achieved was not Marx's and Engels's humanist visions, not the dream of the withering away of the state, but the ideal of Czarist autocracy and police-rule in a form more total than any Russian monarch would ever have dared contemplate. And yet, the present can become the forerunner of the day after tomorrow, if only because its children–as in Hungary in 1956– will disown it and seek a new road, perhaps a new third course between two old ones.

The outcome of such a negation is of course, doubtful. The contrary of an obvious lie is not necessarily the truth but often another lie. Change, novelty, begins in any case with negation, the disowning of the old. By the first 'No', the intellectual life of the individual cuts the umbilical cord tying it to its parent, the past.

We, in the socially and culturally backward countries of Europe, looked around us with a bad conscience and rejected the world of our fathers, so full of the sediment of the past. And when we turned towards the East, it was almost exclusively the spirit of negation that impelled us to do so. As we set sail from the comfortable harbour of mental security, we may have resembled Christopher Columbus in that we, too, had no idea where we would land. Yet, while Columbus, sailing towards the treasures of the Indies, was searching for a new course towards an ancient empire and instead set foot in the New World, we were searching for a New World and discovered, instead, only a new course leading to an ancient empire.

Still, even today, I could not agree with those Philistines who chided and warned us against leaving our fathers' harbour; for if we landed on deceptive shores, it was not because on the coast we had left, everything was as it should have been. If Columbus failed in his aim, did this vindicate the Philistines of his day, who dismissed him as a crazy adventurer for believing that we live on a sphere, on the other side of which people hang with their heads down and the rain falls upwards?